AMERICAN
ESSAY SERIALS
FROM FRANKLIN
TO IRVING

AMERICAN
ESSAY SERIALS
FROM FRANKLIN
TO IRVING

by Bruce Granger

THE UNIVERSITY OF
TENNESSEE PRESS
KNOXVILLE

COPYRIGHT © 1978

BY THE UNIVERSITY OF TENNESSEE PRESS, KNOXVILLE.

ALL RIGHTS RESERVED. MANUFACTURED IN THE UNITED STATES OF AMERICA.

FIRST EDITION.

·

Library of Congress Cataloging in Publication Data

Granger, Bruce Ingham.
  American essay serials from Franklin to Irving.
  Bibliography: p.
  Includes index.
  1. American essays—History and criticism.
  2. American periodicals—History. I. Title.
PS426.G7   814′.1′05   78-4120
ISBN 0-87049-221-7

for Rosemary

PREFACE

"THE PERIODICAL ESSAYIST has not received a suitable degree of esteem and admiration from the world, whom he has endeavoured to benefit," wrote the Boston Anthologist Arthur Maynard Walter in 1805. "If the periodical compositions of England are in general forgotten, what fate awaits the American essayist?" These prophetic words describe all too accurately the critical neglect into which the periodical essay, among important literary genres in colonial America, has fallen. In the two centuries since it flourished, there have been only two comprehensive studies of this genre: an unpublished dissertation by Ernest Claude Coleman, "The Influence of the Addisonian Essay in America Before 1810" (Urbana: University of Illinois, 1936), and Martin Christadler's *Der amerikanische Essay, 1720-1820* (Heidelberg: Carl Winter, 1968). While Christadler mentions all the essay serials examined in the present book and discusses several of them, he ranges through a broad spectrum of nonfiction prose, most of it at best peripheral to what one ordinarily thinks of as essay writing in the eighteenth century, as for example sermons, scientific and speculative reflections, and political speculations.

Since American essayists, like their English counterparts, sometimes ignored Addison's injunction to remain neutral, the periodical essay in America developed in two general directions; in Coleman's words, "the essay which purported to be 'elegant, instructive, and diverting' [and] the essay which formally dealt with immediate problems of social, economic, political, and educational importance." This book focuses on essay serials which are primarily elegant, instructive, and diverting—that is to say, literary—rather than on those of immediate purpose, like William Livingston's *Independent Reflector* (1752-53) which defended civil and religious liberty at

New York. Fifty-one literary serials, which appeared in newspapers, magazines, and pamphlets between 1722 and 1811, form the basis of this study; a checklist is given at the end. Most of the misprints in quotations from the essays have been let stand; at a few points where such errors render the text obscure, they have been silently emended.

Of the many who have given assistance to the making of this volume I owe a special debt to my colleague David P. French for his helpful criticism as the manuscript took shape; to the American Philosophical Society, the National Endowment for the Humanities, and the Arts and Sciences College of the University of Oklahoma for summer grants-in-aid; to the Faculty Research Committee of the University of Oklahoma for largely defraying travel expenses; and to the staffs of the American Antiquarian Society, Boston Public Library, Historical Society of Pennsylvania, Library of Congress, New-York Historical Society, New York Public Library, University of Oklahoma Library, Virginia State Library, and Yale University Library for their unfailing courtesy. Finally, I am grateful to the editors of *Costerus Essays in English Literature and Philology* and *Early American Literature* for permission to use material from two articles, "The Whim-Whamsical Bachelors in *Salmagundi*" (*Costerus*, 2 [Spring 1972], 63-69) and "John Trumbull, Essayist" (*EAL*, 10 [Winter 1975/6], 273-88).

BRUCE GRANGER

Norman, Oklahoma
July 1977

CONTENTS

AMERICAN
ESSAY SERIALS
FROM FRANKLIN
TO IRVING

I. INTRODUCTION

M ONTAIGNE SAYS in the Preface to his *Essais* (March 1, 1580): "I want to be seen here in my simple, natural, ordinary fashion, without pose or artifice; for it is myself that I portray. . . . I am myself the matter of my book"—thus setting the tone and suggesting the topical range of the familiar essay. Conversely Shaftesbury, responding to the intellectual climate of England at the turn of the eighteenth century which encouraged objectivity in belles-lettres, declares, "I hold it very indecent for any one to publish his meditations, occasional reflections, solitary thoughts"; such authors "appear with so much froth and scum in public."[1] This neoclassical insistence, that the writer address himself to the social rather than the individual consciousness in man, helps account for the rise of the periodical essay. Because they shared Shaftesbury's belief that familiarity is indecorous, eighteenth-century English writers who might otherwise have worked in the essay tradition launched by Montaigne and carried forward by Sir William Cornwallis, Abraham Cowley, and Sir William Temple initiated a new one instead. For all its apparent intimacy of tone, the periodical essay was less personal than the familiar essay and correspondingly more dramatic.[2] The widespread success of Richard Steele and Joseph Addison's serial publications, *The Tatler*, *The Spectator*, and *The Guardian*, at their appearance between 1709 and 1714 popularized this new genre overnight. For the next hundred years the journalistic and objective style of essay established in those publications flourished on both sides of the Atlantic. But the periodical essay was more than part of a general literary response to a change in climate; it was the most nearly representative type of prose written in the eighteenth century. Whatever else they produced, major writers worked in this genre at one time or another in their career: Defoe, Steele,

3

Addison, Pope, Swift, Fielding, Johnson, Goldsmith, Mackenzie, in England; and in America, Franklin, Trumbull, Hopkinson, Paine, Freneau, Brackenridge, Dennie, Brown, Irving.

Behind the publication of the *Tatler, Spectator,* and *Guardian,*
as Walter Graham has demonstrated, lay the learned periodical
and the periodical of amusement. Denis de Sallo's *Journal des
Savants* (1665-1750) "not only gave an impetus to the issuing of
periodicals both in Great Britain and on the Continent, but
marked the beginning of a long line of serials devoted largely to
the abstracting of books for busy readers."[3] Peter Motteux's
Gentleman's Journal (1692-94), the first important English periodical of amusement, contained "news, foreign and domestic,
history, philosophy, questions and answers, letters, poetry,
music, translations, news of the learned world, 'novels,' essays,
fables, and book notices."[4] Bridging such seventeenth-century
journals and the essay periodicals of the eighteenth was Daniel
Defoe's *Review* (1704-13), which may have directly influenced
Steele's *Tatler.*[5] There is certainly truth in the view that the
periodical essays of Steele and Addison filled a literary vacuum,
in the sense that the drama had fallen on hard times and the
novel had not yet emerged to take its place.[6]

In 1667 Thomas Sprat announced that the Royal Society of
London, decrying "this vicious abundance of *Phrase,* this trick
of *Metaphors,* this volubility of *Tongue,* which make so great a
noise in the World," would require of all its members "a close,
naked, natural way of speaking; positive expressions, clear
senses; a native easiness: bringing all things as near the
Mathematical plainness, as they can, and preferring the language of Artizans, Countrymen, and Merchants, before that, of
Wits, or Scholars."[7] By the end of the century this tension
between high and low style had relaxed and there emerged a
gentlemanly middle style.[8] Among early eighteenth-century
prose writers none exemplified better than Addison this gentlemanly style, falling as it did between the ornateness of the
scholar and the plainness of the artisan. "His prose is the model
of the middle style," writes Samuel Johnson; "on grave subjects
not formal, on light occasions not grovelling; pure without
scrupulosity, and exact without apparent elaboration; always
equable, and always easy, with glowing words or pointed sen-

tences. . . . His sentences have neither studied amplitude, nor affected brevity; his periods, though not diligently rounded, are voluble and easy."⁹ A recent critic, distinguishing five types of English prose (deliberative, expository, prophetic, tumbling, indenture), maintains that the characteristic prose of the eighteenth century, "apart from fiction, was the tactful expository prose of the periodicals."¹⁰

The English periodical essay is moral in purpose and usually social in point of view. "The main Purpose of the Work," explains Steele in the opening number of the *Guardian*, "shall be to protect the Modest, the Industrious, to celebrate the Wise, the Valiant, to encourage the Good, the Pious, to confront the Impudent, the Idle, to contemn the Vain, the Cowardly, and to disappoint the Wicked and Prophane." Addison, ambitious to have it said of him that he had "brought Philosophy out of Closets and Libraries, Schools and Colleges, to dwell in Clubs and Assemblies, at Tea-Tables and in Coffee-Houses" (*Spectator* No. 10), urged writers to observe neutrality; "I never espoused any Party with Violence," declares the Spectator in the first number, "and am resolved to observe an exact Neutrality between the Whigs and Tories, unless I shall be forc'd to declare my self by the Hostilities of either Side." On occasion, however, eighteenth-century writers chose to ignore Addison's injunction and composed essays of immediate purpose.

The matter and the manner of these essays were determined in large part by a genteel, coffeehouse audience of merchants and professional men. The matter of the *Spectator* ranges through manners and morality, philosophical reflection, character, criticism, and humor.¹¹ Many of the manners essays relate to women: fashion-conscious women (No. 15), women who wear paint (No. 41), French fopperies (No. 45), party patches (No. 81), headdress (Nos. 98, 265), hoop petticoats (No. 127), female inquisitors (No. 320), May love-fits (Nos. 365, 395), women who adopt male fashions (No. 435), coquetry (No. 492). Others relate to men: fortune-stealers (No. 311), male fashions (Nos. 319, 360), frolics (No. 358), unmarried henpecked men (No. 486), drunkenness (No. 569). Still others play one sex off against the other; thus the exercise of the fan (No. 102) and the snuff-box (Nos. 134, 138), a beau's head (No. 275) and a coquette's heart (No. 281), male and female republics (Nos. 433, 434). The essays on philosophical and religious topics, frequently appearing on Saturday and designed for weekend meditation, were the most highly valued of all Addison's contributions.[12] In these Saturday papers he moralizes about Christian belief as an incentive to virtuous action (No. 441) and faith and morality (Nos. 459, 465), and reflects philosophically on living usefully and profitably (Nos. 93, 94), immortality (No. 111), the desire for fame (Nos. 255-57), cheerfulness and mirth (Nos. 381, 387), hope (No. 471), how to approach death (No. 513), the great chain of being (No. 519), and the idea of God (No. 531). There are character sketches of the envious man (No.19), the well-bred gentleman (No. 75), jilts (Nos. 187, 401) and male jilts (No. 288), she-slanderers (No. 390), Sempronia, the unscrupulous matchmaker (No. 437), angry men (No. 438), quacks (Nos. 444, 572), Fidelia, an exemplary daughter (No. 449), an effeminate husband (No. 482), biters (No. 504), the love casuist (Nos. 591, 602, 605), and Jeremy Lovemore, an importunate lover (No. 596). The critical essays, mainly the work of Addison, were one of the most popular features of the *Spectator*.[13] Four topics are treated systematically: tragedy (Nos. 39, 40, 42, 44), true and false wit (Nos. 51, 58-63), *Paradise Lost* (between Nos. 267 and 369 eighteen papers on successive Saturdays), and the pleasures of the imagination (Nos. 411-21). A number of critical essays discuss the theater and drama (Nos. 22, 65, 338, 341, 446, 502, 592) and the opera (Nos. 5, 13, 14, 18, 22, 29, 31). Others examine such aspects of style as purifying and "fixing" the English language (Nos. 135, 165), writing unintelligibly (No. 379), fine taste (No. 409), the sublime (No. 489), mixed metaphors (No. 595), and pert and pedantic humor (Nos. 616, 617).

The formal conventions that came to be associated with the *Spectator* include the persona and the club, letters real and fictitious, dream vision, foreign visitor, and oriental tale. The creation of a persona was essential to the objectivity which periodical essayists strove to maintain. "It is much more difficult to converse with the World in a real than a personated Character," declares Steele in his farewell to the reader. "That might pass for Humour, in the *Spectator*, which would look like Arrogance in a Writer who sets his Name to his Work" (No. 555).

Heir to a small estate, Mr. Spectator distinguished himself at the University "by a most profound Silence" (No. 1). Having made the Grand Tour, he now lodges "at a house of a Widow-Woman" (No. 101) in London, "rather as a Spectator of Mankind, than as one of the Species" (No. 1). Because he is broad-faced, partly he thinks "from my opening my Mouth much seldomer than other People, and by Consequence not so much lengthning the Fibres of my Visage" (No. 17), he is admitted to the Ugly Club (No. 32). Feeling his anonymity threatened, he cuts short a visit to Sir Roger de Coverly's country house and returns to London, explaining: "It is indeed high time for me to leave the Country, since I find the whole Neighbourhood begin to grow very inquisitive after my Name and Character. . . . the Country is not a Place for a Person of my Temper who does not love Jollity, and what they call Good-Neighbourhood" (No. 131). Late in the series he reasserts the neutrality he announced at the outset, protesting that his papers are not libelous: "Our Satyr is nothing but Ribaldry, and *Billingsgate*. Scurrility passes for Wit; and he who can call Names in the greatest Variety of Phrases, is looked upon to have the shrewdest Pen" (No. 451).

In the second *Spectator* paper Steele, undoubtedly influenced by the example of Defoe's Scandalous Club (in the *Review*) and his own Trumpet Club (*Tatler* No. 132), has Mr. Spectator introduce the other members of the club. It is presided over by Sir Roger de Coverly, a bachelor "crossed in Love, by a perverse beautiful Widow," who "continues to wear a Coat and Doublet of the same Cut that were in Fashion at the Time of his Repulse"; "he is now in his Fifty sixth Year, cheerful, gay, and hearty, keeps a good House both in Town and Country." The Templar "is an excellent Critick, and the Time of the Play, is his Hour of Business; exactly at five he passes through *New-Inn*, crosses through *Russel-Court*, and takes a turn at *Will's* 'till the Play begins; he has his Shooes rubb'd and his Perriwig powder'd at the Barber's as you go into the *Rose*." Sir Andrew Freeport, an eminent merchant, "calls the Sea the *British Common*. . . . He abounds in several frugal Maxims, among which the greatest Favourite is, 'a Penny saved is a Penny got.' " Captain Sentry, "a Gentleman of great Courage, good Understanding, but invincible Modesty . . . behaved himself with great Gallantry in several Engagements and at several Sieges." Will Honeycomb "is very ready at that Sort of Discourse with which Men usually entertain Women. He has all his Life dressed very well, and remembers Habits as others do Men. ... in a Word, all his Conversation and Knowledge has been in the female World." The last member is the Clergyman who "visits us but seldom"; "he has the Misfortune to be of a very weak Constitution."

Familiar letter writing, which gained prestige during the seventeenth century, became a high art in eighteenth-century England in the hands of writers like Cowper, Gray, and Walpole.[14] The conversational tone inherent in the periodical essay is owing in part to this epistolary tradition. As John Dennis observes in his Preface to *Letters upon Several Occasions* (1696), "the Style of a Letter [is] neither to come quite up to that of Conversation, nor yet to keep at too great a distance from it."[15] It can never be known how far the letters in the *Spectator* are real, how far fictitious. Donald Bond, while convinced "from the number of unused letters which have survived that a large proportion of the correspondence was genuine," is quick to add that as a rule those used "were considerably modified if not completely rewritten before appearing in print."[16] From the eighth paper on letters appear regularly. Late in the first series (1711-12) Addison has the Spectator explain why he often chooses to cast his thoughts into a letter:

> First, out of the Policy of those who try their Jest upon another, before they own it themselves. Secondly, because I would extort a little Praise from such who will never applaud any thing whose Author is known and certain. Thirdly, because it gave me an Opportunity of introducing a great variety of Characters into my Work, which could not have been done, had I always written in the Person of the *Spectator*. Fourthly, because the Dignity Spectatorial would have suffered, had I published as from my self those several ludicrous Compositions which I have ascribed to fictitious Names and Characters. And lastly, because they often serve to bring in, more naturally, such additional Reflections as have been placed at the End of them. (No. 542)

Near the end of the second series (1714) the Spectator says that if the letters "I have not made use of, were published in a Volume, they would not be an unentertaining Collection" (No. 619); and indeed, in 1725 two volumes of unused letters which had been sent to the *Tatler* and the *Spectator* were published.[17]

Dream vision follows a clearly defined pattern: "The essayist is reading, preferably from a classical author, or thinking about an idea before going to sleep. Theoretically, this stimulus produces the vision, usually carried through with much assistance from personifications of all the virtues and vices. The scene is ordinarily a plain, a woods, or a road leading to a palace or a building of some description."[18] In the *Spectator* there are twelve clear examples of the dream vision, most of them by Addison: Public Credit (No. 3), True, False, and Mixed Wit (No. 63), Gallery of Living and Dead Painters (No. 83), Months and Seasons (No. 425), Paradise of Fools (No. 460), Golden Scales (No. 463), Journey to Parnassus (No. 514), Waters of Heavenly and Worldly Wisdom (No. 524), Mountain of Miseries (Nos. 558, 559), Hearts (No. 586), Cave of Trophonius (No. 599), and Future Events (No. 604).

The appearance of the first English version of the *Arabian Nights* (1705-1708), "a book so different in character from any oriental fiction then known in England, and so far-reaching in influence,"[19] helps explain why the foreign visitor and the oriental tale were quickly incorporated into the periodical essay. While English interest in the *Arabian Nights* and other oriental literature is most clearly manifest in such mid-century serials as George Lyttelton's *Letters from a Persian in England to his Friend at Ispahan*, Oliver Goldsmith's *Citizen of the World*, and Samuel Johnson's *Rambler* (Nos. 38, 65, 120, 190, 204, 205) and *Idler* (Nos. 75, 99, 101), the foreign visitor and the oriental tale are already present in the *Spectator*. In the fiftieth number, by Addison, a friend of the Spectator, curious about the recent visit of four Indian kings, acquires from their English landlord a bundle of papers written by one of them, King Sa Ga Yean Qua Rash Tow, and discovers, when they are translated, that they "contain abundance of very odd Observations, which I find this little Fraternity of Kings made during their Stay in the Isle of *Great Britain*": The parishioners at St. Paul's "were most of them bowing and curtisying to one another, and a considerable Number of them fast asleep." One of the men appointed to attend us and act as our guides was a Whig and the other a Tory; consequently they "engage when they meet as naturally as the

Elephant and the Rhinoceros." The men of the country dress very barbarously: "Instead of those beautiful Feathers with which we adorn our Heads, they often buy up a monstrous Bush of Hair, which covers their Heads, and falls down in a large Fleece below the Middle of their Backs; with which they walk up and down the Streets, and are as proud of it as if it was of their own Growth." "The Women look like Angels, and would be more beautiful than the Sun, were it not for little black Spots [i.e., patches] that are apt to break out in their Faces, and sometimes rise in very odd Figures." Admittedly Lyttelton's Selim and Goldsmith's Lien Chi Altangi are more successful examples of the foreign visitor because sustained through a series of letters, not just one. Nevertheless Addison was the first to employ this convention in the periodical essay. The only clear examples of the oriental tale in the *Spectator* are Addison's vision of Mirzah (No. 159) and story of Shalum and Hilpa (Nos. 584, 585), but his importance "lies not in what or how much he used but what he did with the materials. [His] influence on the oriental tale throughout the rest of the century was achieved by his casual use of oriental material as illustrations for some half-dozen of his moral discussions."[20]

Upwards of five hundred essay serials were published in London during the eighteenth century.[21] While some of these are essays of immediate purpose like Swift's *Examiner*, Gordon and Trenchard's *Independent Whig* and *Cato's Letters*, *The North Briton*, and *Letters of "Junius*," the great majority are literary serials in the *Spectator* tradition. Among the most important are Ambrose Philips' *Free-Thinker* (1718-21), *The Grub Street Journal* (1730-37), Henry Fielding and James Ralph's *Champion* (1739-43), Samuel Johnson's *Rambler* (1750-52) and *Idler* (1758-60), Fielding's *Covent-Garden Journal* (1752), John Hawkesworth's *Adventurer* (1752-54), Edward Moore's *World* (1753-56), George Colman and Bonnell Thornton's *Connoisseur* (1754-56), Oliver Goldsmith's *Citizen of the World* (1760-61), and Henry Mackenzie's *Mirror* (1779-80) and *Lounger* (1785-87). Although 60 percent of these serials appeared after 1760, so sharply did the quality fall off that Mackenzie is the only important periodical essayist during the final third of the century. Indeed, the decline began even earlier. One critic, thinking in particular of Fielding's work during the 1740s, concludes that "the *novel sucked the essay dry*, and the periodical essay, in its conservative *Spectator* pattern, in the end died of sheer inanition."[22] Also contributing to the decline was a loss of objectivity in the second half of the century. Whereas Addison keeps more "outside of himself," Johnson is more personal and lacks detachment.[23] In its subjectivity and preoccupation with self a late serial such as James Boswell's *Hypochondriack* (1777-83) looks backward to Montaigne and forward to the familiar essays of Lamb and Hazlitt.[24] The career of Charles Lamb dramatizes how rapidly the familiar essay re-emerged in the early nineteenth century, to flower as never before. Whereas the papers he contributed to *The Reflector* (1810-11) were strongly influenced by eighteenth-century models, the appearance of the Elia essays a decade later makes it clear that he had freed himself from the rule of the *Spectator*.

The tradition of the periodical essay was quick to catch hold in the American colonies. Among the seven hundred volumes Jeremiah Dummer presented to Yale College in 1714 was Steele's contribution of "all the Tatlers and Spectators being eleven Volumns."[25] The *New-England Courant* for July 2, 1722, listed among the books kept in its office for the use of writers "The Spectator, 8 volumes" and "The Guardian, 2 volumes." Not content merely to read the chief English periodical collections that could be found in libraries and newspaper offices, Americans soon began working in the tradition themselves. In August 1713, although he did not act on the impulse, Cotton Mather contemplated, "Perhaps, by sending some agreeable Things, to the Author of, *The Spectator*, and, *The Guardian*, there may be brought forward some Services to the best Interests in the Nation."[26] Between September 9 and November 1, 1721, thirteen numbers of "The Telltale," which seems to have been a student periodical, circulated in manuscript at Harvard College.[27] In the same year the colonial newspaper started printing original essays, and the first essay serial appeared the following spring; these at once became a regular feature. In the 1750s colonial magazines began to carry serials, and in the 1780s there developed the practice of collecting serials and publishing them in book form. "Every magazine, and almost every newspaper, teems with periodical essays," writes Nathan Fiske at the turn of the century. "Every newspaper of the present day, must have its literary mark of distinction, the feather, or cockade of the periodical essay. . . . every vehicle of intelligence must be enriched with a dish of essays in succession, under some expressive signature or title; some, like solid beef, affording substantial nourishment; others, like sillabubs and nicknacks, tickling the palate, or only tasting sweet in the mouth."[28]

Literary serials first appeared in the 1720s at Boston where journalistic activity was greatest and literacy high. Once established there, the tradition spread rapidly southward so that by 1740 serials had been published at Philadelphia, Annapolis, Williamsburg, and Charleston. In the second half of the century the magazine, encroaching on a right enjoyed exclusively by the newspaper before 1741, carried an increasingly higher percentage of the serials being published. As in England, the quality varied inversely with the number which proliferated after the Revolution. Washington Irving's early career dramatizes the decline and demise of the tradition in the first two decades of the nineteenth century. Commencing as a periodical essayist, he soon found himself parodying the tradition and by the time of *The Sketch Book* (1819-20) he had outgrown it altogether; all but a few of the pieces which comprise that miscellany belong to the tradition of the familiar essay.

II. EARLY BOSTON SERIALS

Ⅲ

The New-England Courant, a Boston weekly established by
Benjamin Franklin's older brother James on August 7,
1721, was the first colonial newspaper to carry original essays. It
is fortunate that the *Courant* was forced by circumstance to
assume a partisan stance because it helped young Benjamin
avoid merely imitating the manner and matter of the *Spectator*.
In view of the smallpox epidemic then raging at Boston and the
fact that the Mathers, anxious to strengthen the provincial
oligarchy, had sided with Dr. Zabdiel Boylston who favored
inoculation, James Franklin was soon forced by the belligerent
tone of certain of his contributors to show his hand, and the
Courant was quickly identified in the public mind with the
cause of anti-inoculation.

Although James Franklin promised not to publish anything
"anyways reflecting on the Clergy or Government,"[1] it was a
promise repeatedly broken. When on June 11, 1722, the *Courant*
insinuated—unjustly, as it happened—that the provincial government was slow to act against pirates operating in Massachusetts waters, the General Court ordered him jailed for the
balance of the session, charging him with having printed much
"boldly reflecting on his Majesty's Government and on the
Administration of it in this Province, the Ministry, Churches
and College."[2] Six months later James was again jailed for carrying articles offensive to church and state. On this occasion the
General Court forbade him to publish the *Courant* "except it be
first Supervised by the Secretary of this Province,"[3] whereupon
he decided "to let it be printed for the future under the Name of
Benjamin Franklin."[4] On February 11, 1723, in the first number
bearing his name, Benjamin Franklin, aware that the press at
Boston had long "groaned in bringing forth an hateful, but numerous Brood of Party Pamphlets, malicious Scribbles, and Bil-

lingsgate Ribaldry," promised "to entertain the Town with the most comical and diverting Incidents of Humane Life."[5] That fall he left Boston forever.

In old age he recollected that his brother James "had some ingenious Men among his Friends who amus'd themselves by writing little Pieces for this Paper, which gain'd it Credit, and made it more in Demand."[6] In addition to James himself, this "most generous Clan of Honest Wags, Congregated in an *uncertain Place*, where *Apollo* cannot *very well* find them,"[7] included Matthew Adams, John Checkley, Dr. William Douglass, a mysterious Mr. Gardner, and (though James was not at first aware of the fact) his own brother Benjamin.[8] The Couranteers, anxious "to reform the present declining Age, and render it more polite and vertuous,"[9] began at once to entertain their readers with a series of exchanges in prose and verse between aptronymous bachelors and maids on such conventional topics as love and marriage.

Cotton Mather's son Samuel, mindful of the scandalous clubs of London, dubbed the Couranteers "the *Hell-Fire Club of Boston*."[10] And the *Boston News Letter* described the *Courant* as "full freighted with Nonsence, Unmannerliness, Railery, Prophaneness, Immorality, Arrogancy, Calumnies, Lyes, Contradictions, and what not, all tending to Quarrels and Divisions, and to Debauch and Corrupt the Minds and Manners of New-England," and threatened the same measures that had been taken to suppress the London clubs.[11] Notwithstanding these charges, the Couranteers never constituted themselves a formal club. They did, however, speak for the tradesman class at Boston in opposition to the gentry, who frequently set forth their views in the *Boston Gazette*. So earnestly did the Couranteers take Checkley's advice: "Speak to the Hearts of Men in a very easie and familiar manner, so that the meanest Plough-man, the very meanest of God's People may understand them," that a *Gazette* critic called their style "low & phlegmatic, and insipid."[12] Even so, it is probable that "they caught the literary standards of the neo-classicists better than any of their contemporaries in Boston."[13]

I

Half a century before Hugh Blair advised those who wished to acquire "a proper Style" to possess fully the thoughts on "some page of one of Mr. Addison's Spectators," rewrite the passage from memory, and then compare the two,[14] the apprenticed Benjamin Franklin adopted this exercise in hopes of becoming "a tolerable English Writer." At age sixteen he was excited by the example of the other Couranteers

> to try my Hand among them. But being still a Boy, and suspecting that my Brother would object to printing any Thing of mine in his Paper if he knew it to be mine, I contriv'd to disguise my Hand, and writing an anonymous Paper I put it in at Night under the Door of the Printing House. It was found in the Morning and communicated to his Writing Friends when they call'd in as usual. They read it, commented on it in my Hearing, and I had the exquisite Pleasure, of finding it met with their Approbation, and that in their different Guesses at the Author none were named but Men of some Character among us for Learning and Ingenuity. . . . I wrote and convey'd in the same Way to the Press several more Papers, which were equally approv'd.[15]

Young Benjamin, who contributed fourteen essays to his brother's newspaper over the signature "Silence Dogood,"[16] learned much from the manner and matter of the aggressive Couranteers. For all his apparent good humor and urbanity he was openly critical of Harvard College, the suppression of free speech, public hypocrisy, and religious zeal; however, he wrote with more restraint than the other Couranteers, whose manner often calls to mind the angrier rhetoric of the seventeenth century. Whenever his invention ran thin, he did not hesitate to borrow from contemporary English sources.[17]

The most dramatic evidence that the *Dogood* papers are not merely imitative of the *Spectator* is to be seen in the matter of point of view. Whereas the Spectator claims never to have "espoused any Party with Violence," Silence Dogood swears mortal enmity "to arbitrary Government and unlimited Power." In the opening number she observes "that the Generality of People, now a days, are unwilling either to commend or dispraise what they read, until they are in some measure informed who or what the Author of it is, whether he be *poor* or *rich, old* or *young,* a *Schollar* or a *Leather Apron Man.*" The words *poor, young, Leather Apron Man* tell us where Silence's sympathies lie and distinguish her sharply from that university man, Mr. Spectator.

Silence relates that she was born on the day her father was washed overboard on the passage from London to New England; "thus was my disconsolate Mother at once made both a *Parent* and a *Widow*." I went to school near Boston and passed "my Infancy and Childhood in Vanity and Idleness," until apprenticed to "a Country Minister, a pious good-natur'd young Man, and a Batchelor," who "endeavour'd that I might be instructed in all that Knowledge and Learning which is necessary for our Sex . . . such as all Sorts of Needle-Work, Writing, Arithmetick, &c." and "gave me the free Use of his Library." "Before I had liv'd quite two Years with this Reverend Gentleman, my indulgent Mother departed this Life" (No. 1, April 2, 1722). In time my master "cast a Loving Eye upon Me, whom he had brought up cleverly to his Hand," and easily persuaded me to marry him. "We lived happily together in the Heighth of conjugal Love and mutual Endearments, for near Seven Years, in which Time we added Two likely Girls and a Boy to the Family of the Dogoods." Then of a sudden he died. "I have now remained in a State of Widowhood for several Years, but it is a State I never much admir'd, and I am apt to fancy that I could be easily perswaded to marry again, provided I was sure of a good-humour'd, sober, agreeable Companion: But one, even with these few good Qualities, being hard to find, I have lately relinquish'd all Thoughts of that Nature." As for my character, "I am an Enemy to Vice, and a Friend to Vertue. . . . one of an extensive Charity, and a great Forgiver of *private* Injuries: A hearty Lover of the Clergy and all good Men, and a mortal Enemy to arbitrary Government and unlimited Power. I am naturally very jealous for the Rights and Liberties of my Country; and the least appearance of an Incroachment on those invaluable Priviledges, is apt to make my Blood boil exceedingly. I have likewise a natural Inclination to observe and reprove the Faults of others, at which I have an excellent Faculty. . . . for I never intend to wrap my Talent in a Napkin. To be brief; I am courteous and affable, good humour'd (unless I am first provok'd,) and handsome, and sometimes witty" (No. 2, April 16, 1722).

Although she does not preside over a club, Silence enjoys

conversing "with my honest Neighbour Rusticus and his Family, or with the ingenious Minister of our Town, who now lodges at my House, and by whose Assistance I intend now and then to beautify my Writings with a Sentence or two in the learned Languages" (No. 2, April 16, 1722). She hopes it will prove useful to communicate her small stock of knowledge "by Peace-meal to the Publick"; well she knows that the writer who wishes to please all "must one while be merry and diverting, then more solid and serious; one while sharp and satyrical, then (to mollify that) be sober and religious; at one Time let the Subject be Politicks, then let the next Theme be Love." Nor must she "forget to invite the ingenious Part of your Readers," Mr. Printer, "particularly those of my own Sex to enter into a Correspondence with me" (No. 3, April 30, 1722). Shortly we are informed that "Mrs. Dogood has lately left her Seat in the Country, and come to Boston, where she intends to tarry for the Summer Season, in order to compleat her Observations of the present reigning Vices of the Town" (No. 5, May 28, 1722). Although Silence attacks the local aristocracy of church and state, she devotes more space to less libelous topics like pride of dress, the distressing condition of widows and spinsters, funeral elegies, drunkenness, and night-walking.

Unlike Addison's Spectator who is anxious to protect his anonymity, Silence Dogood moves uninhibitedly in town and country, eager to point out the faults in others. Whereas Mr. Spectator mingles noncommittally with professional men in London, Silence speaking for the leather-apron class is quick to criticize church and state. She is a recognizable and endearing type, the gossipy widow, earthy and vernacular in expression, well educated for her time, rank, and sex, intensely human in her forwardness and show of vanity. As Franklin's earliest persona she is a vital, indigenous character, one that in retrospect is more fully realized than his later American creations, Celia Single, Alice Addertongue, Bridget Saunders, Polly Baker.

The most fully developed of the *Dogood* essays is Silence's dream vision of Harvard College. Its full significance only breaks upon the reader when it is viewed in the larger perspective of the Couranteers' running battle with the Mather party; for as artisans and scholars parted company on the question of inoculation, so too on the importance of a classical education and training for the ministry.[18] Pondering on her boarder Clericus' advice that she send her son William to college, Silence falls asleep in her orchard and dreams that a great company of youths are going to the Temple of Learning. Riches and Poverty guard the gate, "and the latter obstinately refused to give Entrance to any who had not first gain'd the Favour of the Former"; "however, as a Spectator I gain'd Admittance, and with the rest entred directly into the Temple." Learning, "apparelled wholly in Black," is seated on a throne, busily "preparing a Paper, call'd, *The New-England Courant*. On her Right Hand sat *English*, with a pleasant smiling Countenance, and handsomely attir'd; and on her left were seated several *Antique Figures* with their Faces vail'd. . . . Latin, Greek, Hebrew, &c. [who] were very much reserv'd, and seldom or never unvail'd their Faces, here, and then to few or none, tho' most of those who have in this Place acquir'd so much Learning as to distinguish them from *English*, pretended to an intimate Acquaintance with them." Those "who entred into the Temple with me, began to climb the Throne; but the Work proving troublesome and difficult to most of them, they withdrew their Hands from the Plow, and contented themselves to sit at the Foot, with Madam *Idleness* and her Maid *Ignorance*. . . . But the Time drawing nigh in which they could no way avoid ascending, they were fain to crave the Assistance of those who had got up before them, and who, for the Reward perhaps of a *Pint of Milk*, or a *Piece of Plumb-Cake*, lent the Lubbers a helping Hand, and sat them in the Eye of the World, upon a Level with themselves." At commencement time "every Beetle-Scull seem'd well satisfy'd with his own Portion of Learning, tho' perhaps he was *e'en just as* ignorant as ever. . . . Some I perceiv'd took to Merchandizing, others to Travelling," but most beat a path to the Temple of Theology. Wondering at this, "I spy'd *Pecunia* behind a Curtain, beckoning to them with her Hand, which Sight immediately satisfy'd me for whose Sake it was, that a great Part of them (I will not say all) travel'd that Road." Wishing myself at home, "I reflected in my Mind on the extream Folly of those Parents, who, blind to their Childrens Dulness, and insensible of the Solidity of their Skulls, because they think their Purses can afford it, will needs send them to the Temple of Learning, where, for want of a suitable Genius, they learn little more than how to carry themselves handsomely, and enter a Room genteely . . . and from whence they return, after Abundance of Trouble and Charge, as great Blockheads as ever, only more proud and self-conceited." Clericus, walking by, accidentally awakens Silence and, hearing her dream, explains that *"it was a lively Representation of* HARVARD COLLEGE, *Etcetera"* (No. 4, May 14, 1722).

Although this essay resembles Addison's vision of Public Credit (*Spectator* No. 3) in that the scene is a great hall in the midst of which the allegorical figure of a woman sits on a throne, it is no mere imitation. In fact, Franklin manages certain of the conventions in a far less perfunctory manner than Addison, rendering the setting in which Silence falls asleep more fully and motivating her dream more naturally. He saves the dream allegory itself from slipping into sterile abstraction by introducing such homely details as the students rewarding their tutors with milk or plum cake. Dream vision affords Franklin the artistic distance necessary to objectify and give point to his rising anger with the Harvard community and proves as efficient a vehicle, if a modest one, for exposing the ineffectualness of collegiate education in colonial America as the Hudibrastics John Trumbull employed in *The Progress of Dulness* to attack Yale College half a century later.

A fortnight after Silence had her vision a member of the Mather party, supposing James Franklin to be the author, sneered: "Is not Couranto a fine Rhetorician and a correct writer when he says in his last but one . . . 'they withdrew their Hands from the Plow.' Friend, who ever heard of ent'ring a Temple and ascending the Magnificent Steps of a Throne with a Plough in his hand! O rare Allegory! Well done, Rustic Couranto! This may cause matter of speculation."[19] What is significant here is the implied criticism of Benjamin's plainer artisan prose. The following week one of the Couranteers, by way of rebuttal, reinforced Silence's views and concluded with a pious hope:

> Long have the weaker Sons of Harvard strove
> To move our Rev'rence and command our Love,
> By means, how sordid, 'tis not hard to say,
> When all their Merit lies in M. and A.

The knowing Sons of Harvard we revere,
And in their just defence will still appear;
But every idel Fop who there commences,
Shall never claim Dominion o'er our Senses.
We judge not of their Knowledge by their Air,
Nor think the wisest Heads have curled Hair.
   May Parents, Madam, your Reflections mind,
And be no more to Childrens Dulness Blind.
May your sharp Satyrs mend the lazy Drone,
Who by anothers Help ascends the Throne.
And not by any Merit of his own.
Then will both Church and State be truly blest
With Men whose Worth will be by both confest.[20]

Elsewhere in the series Silence dwells on the conventional topic of pride, emphasizing pride of dress. To her correspondent Ephraim Censorious who hopes that she will first attack female idleness, ignorance, folly, and especially pride, she replies, "if Women are proud, it is certainly owing to the Men still; for if they will be such *Simpletons* as to humble themselves at their Feet, and fill their credulous Ears with extravagant Praises of their Wit, Beauty, and other Accomplishments," what wonder "if they carry themselves haughtily, and live extravagantly" (No. 5, May 28, 1722). Having exhorted men and women "both to amend, where both are culpable," she confesses, "I speak it to my Shame, I my self was a Queen from the Fourteenth to the Eighteenth Year of my Age, and govern'd the World all the Time of my being govern'd by my Master." She fears that pride of dress "has begot and nourished in us a *Pride of Heart*, which portends the Ruin of Church and State." Consider the current fashion of hoop petticoats. "These monstrous topsy-turvy *Mortar-Pieces*, are neither fit for the Church, the Hall, or the Kitchen; and if a Number of them were well mounted on Noddles-Island, they would look more like Engines of War for bombarding the Town, than Ornaments of the Fair Sex." Knowing that women will not give up this fashion, "I would at least desire them to lessen the Circumference of their Hoops, and leave it with them to consider, Whether they, who pay no Rates or Taxes, ought to take up more Room in the King's High-Way, than the Men, who yearly contribute to the Support of the Government" (No. 6, June 11, 1722). While Franklin may have been remembering Addison's

20

essay on hoop petticoats (*Spectator* No. 127), he domesticates this subject and accommodates it to his immediate audience, affording us a glimpse of the Boston scene; "monstrous topsy-turvy *Mortar-Pieces*" is a military metaphor that must have delighted the men and women who read the *Courant*.

Another social topic that must have interested readers of the *Courant* is insurance for spinsters. When Margaret Aftercast petitions "for the Relief of all those penitent Mortals of the fair Sex, that are like to be punish'd with their Virginity until old Age, for the Pride and Insolence of their Youth," Silence advises her and other old maids "to relieve themselves in a Method of *Friendly Society* . . . whereby every single Woman, upon full Proof given of her continuing a Virgin for the Space of Eighteen Years, (dating her Virginity from the Age of Twelve,) should be entituled to £500 in ready Cash." It will be necessary to make exceptions:

> 1. That no Woman shall be admitted into the Society after she is Twenty Five Years old, who has made a Practice of entertaining and discarding Humble Servants, without sufficient Reason for so doing, until she has manifested her Repentance in Writing under her Hand.
> 2. No Member of the Society who has declar'd before two credible Witnesses, *That it is well known she has refus'd several good Offers since the Time of her Subscribing*, shall be entituled to the £500 when she comes of Age; that is to say, *Thirty Years*.
> 3. No Woman, who after claiming and receiving, has had the good Fortune to marry, shall entertain any Company with Encomiums on her Husband, above the Space of one Hour at a Time, upon Pain of returning one half the Money into the Office, for the first Offence; and upon the second Offence to return the Remainder. (No. 11, August 20, 1722)

Like the essay on insurance for widows which precedes it (a project in which Silence had a vested interest), this one reveals the civic-mindedness of Franklin even at this early age. These two essays, reflecting the influence of Defoe's *Essay on Projects*, are the most didactic in the series.

One of the earliest examples of literary criticism in colonial America is Franklin's satire on New England funeral elegies, in which Silence praises *An Elegy upon the much Lamented Death of Mrs. Mehitebell Kitel* for the qualities it most obviously lacks

("The Language is so soft and Easy, the Expression so moving and pathetick, but above all, the Verse and Numbers so Charming and Natural, that it is almost beyond Comparison") and quotes the following couplet to support this judgment:

> Come let us mourn, for we have lost a Wife, a Daughter and a Sister,
> Who has lately taken Flight, and greatly we have mist her.

Since this new species "cannot justly be called, either *Epic, Sapphic, Lyric,* or *Pindaric,*" Silence designates it *"Kitelic Poetry"* and offers a recipe for writing such an elegy:

> Take one of your Neighbours who has lately departed this Life; it is no great matter at what Age the Party dy'd, but it will be best if he went away suddenly, being *Kill'd, Drown'd,* or *Froze to Death.*
>
> Having chose the Person, take all his Virtues, Excellencies, &c. and if he have not enough, you may borrow some to make up a sufficient Quantity: To these add his last Words, dying Expressions, &c. if they are to be had; mix all these together, and be sure you *strain* them well. Then season all with a Handful or two of Melancholly Expressions, such as *Dreadful, Deadly, cruel cold Death, unhappy Fate, weeping Eyes,* &c. Having mixed all these Ingredients well, put them into the empty Scull of some *young Harvard* . . . there let them Ferment for the Space of a Fortnight, and . . . having prepared a sufficient Quantity of double Rhimes, such as, *Power, Flower; Quiver, Shiver; Grieve us, Leave us; tell you, excel you; Expeditions, Physicians; Fatigue him, Intrigue him;* &c. you must spread all upon Paper, and if you can procure a Scrap of Latin to put at the End, it will garnish it mightily. (No. 7, June 25, 1722)

By the 1720s the elegy had seen its heyday, although it continued popular in New England to the end of the colonial period. The decline of Puritanism undermined the sensibility which had made possible poems like Urian Oakes's *Elegy upon the Death of the Reverend Mr. Thomas Shepard* (1677). Franklin, who had tried his hand at poetry and found it was not his proper element, manages to inject perceptive criticism into this satire. He here attacks not only "the antiquated spirit of the elegy" but "rooted institutions like Harvard and ministerial pedantry."[21] Indeed, Silence's comments on Kitelic poetry inspired other satires in the *Courant* on the New England funeral elegy and Harvard learning.

The liveliest of the *Dogood* essays are those on drunkenness and night-walking. Silence devises a vivid conceit to explain the different effects of liquor: "Some shrink in the Wetting, and others swell to such an unusual Bulk in their Imaginations, that they can in an Instant understand all Arts and Sciences, by the liberal Education of a little vivifying *Punch*, or a sufficient Quantity of other exhilerating Liquor." Drunkards "have invented numberless Words and Phrases to cover their Folly, whose proper Significations are harmless, or have no Signification at all. They are seldom known to be *drunk*, tho' they are very often *boozey, cogey, tipsey, fox'd, merry, mellow, fuddl'd, groatable, Confoundedly cut, See two Moons,* are *Among the Philistines, In a very good Humour, See the Sun,* or, *The Sun has shone upon them;* they *Clip the King's English,* are *Almost froze, Feavourish, In their Altitudes, Pretty well enter'd,* &c." Silence mentions these few words and phrases "because if at any Time a Man of Sobriety and Temperance happens to *cut himself confoundedly,* or is *almost froze,* or *feavourish,* or accidentally *sees the Sun,* &c. he may escape the Imputation of being *drunk,* when his Misfortune comes to be related" (No. 12, September 10, 1722). Nowhere in the series is Franklin's plain artisan prose and range of colloquialisms so evident as in this essay. Fifteen years later he compiled a drinker's dictionary, greatly expanding this list of euphemisms.[22]

On a moonlight ramble Silence overhears a woman who pretends to know her declare *"That I was a Person of an ill Character, and kept a criminal Correspondence with a Gentleman who assisted me in Writing.* One of the Gallants clear'd me of this random Charge, by saying, *That tho' I wrote in the Character of a Woman, he knew me to be a Man; But,* continu'd he, *he has more need of endeavouring a Reformation in himself, than spending his Wit in satyrizing others."* In a rush of nautical diction Silence then describes "a Crowd of *Tarpolins* and their Doxies, link'd to each other by the Arms, who ran (by their own Account) after the Rate of *Six Knots an Hour,* and bent their Course towards the Common. Their eager and amorous Emotions of Body, occasion'd by taking their Mistresses *in Tow,* they call'd *wild Steerage:* And as a Pair of them happen'd to trip and come to the Ground, the Company were call'd upon to *bring to,* for that Jack and Betty were *founder'd.*" Encountering a company of females, she concludes that they "came out with no other Design than to revive the Spirit of Love in Disappointed Batchelors, and expose themselves to Sale to the first Bidder." Shoemakers in particular are obliged to night-walkers; one, "being ask'd by a noted Rambler, *Whether he could tell how long her Shoes would last;* very prettily answer'd, *That he knew how many Days she might wear them, but not how many Nights; because they were then put to a more violent and irregular Service than when she employ'd her self in the common Affairs of the House*" (No. 13, September 24, 1722). Once again, as in Silence's account of hoop petticoats, we glimpse the Boston scene. The story which brings this essay to a close is an early example of Franklin's lifelong predilection for anecdote.

Two months after the last of these essays appeared an anonymous correspondent asked Mrs. Dogood why she had kept silent so long: "Can you observe no Faults in others (or your self) to *reprove*? Or are you married and remov'd to some distant Clime, that we hear nothing from you? Are you (as the Prophet supposed *Baal* that sottish Deity) *asleep*, or *on a Journey*, and cannot write? Or has the Sleep of *inexorable unrelenting Death* procur'd your Silence?"[23] Silent she remained; as Franklin later explained, "My small Fund of Sense for such Performances was pretty well exhausted."[24] For all his English borrowings and choice of conventional subjects, Franklin succeeds in imparting to the *Dogood* essays a measure of originality and American coloration. The frugal, industrious, prosaic widow is as memorable and appealing an American character as any he ever created. While the series cannot be characterized as one of immediate purpose, its intrinsic merit derives in part from Silence's attacks on church and state authority in Massachusetts. In this his first ambitious literary venture Franklin owes less to the example of Addison and the Couranteers than to his own sense of invention, his skill in handling the traditional conventions, and the controlled prose itself. No wonder the other Couranteers supposed the author to be a man of learning and ingenuity rather than a sixteen-year-old apprentice.

"At length," wrote Benjamin Franklin late in life, "a fresh

Difference arising between my Brother and me, I took upon me to assert my Freedom"[25] and left Boston for Philadelphia. On September 30, 1723, the *Courant* carried what is surely the most famous such advertisement in American history: "James Franklin, Printer in Queen-Street, wants a likely lad for an Apprentice."

II

Benjamin Franklin and Mather Byles were immediate contemporaries and friends; Franklin, who was two months older, outlived Byles by less than two years. And both were Boston born. But whereas Franklin had only two years of formal schooling—one of them at the Latin School when Byles was there—and spoke satirically of Harvard College, Byles graduated there in 1725 and became a distinguished Congregational minister such as Josiah Franklin had dreamed his son Benjamin might be one day. According to his biographer, Byles "wrote verse and essays for the *Courant*" while a Harvard undergraduate and by the time of his graduation was considered "the best poet and essayist in a generation which was experiencing a revival of interest in literature"[26]—a claim that might well be challenged had Franklin remained in Boston. Grandson to Increase Mather and nephew to Cotton Mather, the dynasty with whom James and Benjamin Franklin and the other Couranteers long did battle, Byles perhaps because of his youth seems to have escaped involvement in the fray, although on one occasion his grandfather "found an article on inoculation in the *London Mercury*, copied it out, and sent him running to James Franklin with a request that it be printed in the *New-England Courant*."[27] In later years these contemporaries shared an interest in science, and when at Byles's suggestion Harvard awarded Franklin an honorary degree, Franklin persuaded Aberdeen to do as much for Byles.[28]

On March 20, 1726/7, Samuel Kneeland, spurred on by Byles who wished to see a literary newspaper established at Boston to take the place of the *Courant* which had recently been discontinued, founded *The New-England Weekly Journal*. Byles and Judge Samuel Danforth appear to have been the principal editors. Kneeland at once announced that "a Select number of Gentlemen, who have had the happiness of a liberal Education, and some of them considerably improv'd by their Travels into distant Countries; are now concerting some regular Schemes for the Entertainment of the ingenious Reader, and the Encouragement of Wit & Politeness; and may in a very short time, open upon the Publick in a variety of pleasing and profitable Speculations." Three weeks later Byles, an admirer of Addison and Steele, launched *Proteus Echo*, a serial consisting of essays and poems which appeared weekly for the next year; he was joined in the venture by the former Couranteer, Matthew Adams, and his nephew John Adams.[29] More didactic and less diverting than the *Dogood* papers, this serial is more nearly Addisonian, despite the claim that Byles disdained "the manuscript imitations of the *Spectator* and *Tatler* which other students produced" at Harvard.[30] Thus the first two numbers, wherein Proteus Echo gives an account of himself and introduces the other members of the club, follow closely the plan of the *Spectator*.

At the outset Proteus informs the reader of speculations as to his identity: "Many have supposed me to be a certain Young Gentleman, who has given the Town several beautiful Pieces of Poetry: Though others say I am lately arrived from *England*, accomplished in Mathematical Learning. I have been frequently reported to wear a Band, and as often represented as a Merchant, wrapt up in a Callaminco Night-Gown, and seated very conveniently in a Compting-House. Sometimes I have been dispatch'd to *Cambridge* under Form of a Scholar, while some have not scrupled to divest me of all these my Dignities, and clap me into the Habit of an old Almanack-Maker." The fact of the matter is that "I was born in the Year 1666, in a small Cottage at *Salem*, which is the principal Reason, as I have been apt to imagine, that People have sometimes suspected me for a Conjurer. . . . When I was Three Years old, I was sent to School to a Mistress, where I learned to read with great Expedition & Dispatch; for which Reason, in my fifth Year, I was taken away and put to a Writing-Master. In my seventh Year, I could flourish a tolerable Hand, and began my Grammar. By that time I was Fourteen, I was a considerable Proficient in the Latin & Greek Languages and was admitted into *Harvard* College." During my travels to

"*China, Japan, & Bantam*" I noted down "all those things that I met with, and thought worthy Remark. From which Origin my Paper derives its Title . . . *The* WEEKLY JOURNAL." He is "a very rich Old Fellow, hale and fresh, in the Sixtieth Spring of my Life," who has carried the art of mimicry to such perfection that "I am able not only to take any sound that I hear, but I have a Faculty of looking like any Body I think fit. . . . I remember, when I was a School-Boy, my Master once gave me an unlucky Rap on my Pate, for a Fault committed by *Giles Horror*, whose Visage I had at that time unfortunately put on. . . . I am the more large on this part of my Character, because it is in a great measure, the Ground-work of these Lucubrations, inasmuch as I intend frequently to write in Quality of an Imitator. My way of bantering a Folly shall be to represent it as in a Glass, and I shall make it Ridiculous by exposing it just as it is" (No. 1, April 10, 1727).

Proteus soon experiences the disappointments that accompany authorship: "About a Week ago, the Compliments my Speculations received from a beautifull Ring of Young Ladies, shot into my Heart such a Flash of Joy, that Old as I am, I left the Company with a Resolution to write an *Epic Poem*. Fir'd with this Design, I hasted to my Lodgings, when, unluckily for the World and me, my Heroick Flame was quite put out, by seeing a Pipe lighted with one of my Composures. The Truth of it is, I have been a professed Enemy to Tobacco ever since I first wrote a JOURNAL: and I am afraid of nothing so much, as being haunted by the Ghost of my own Works, in the Shapes of Squibs, Rockets, and Flying Dragons." "I have been Credibly informed of a Young Scholar who has given himself the Trouble, in all Companies, to demonstrate by Plain undeniable Arguments, that some Papers in the *Spectater, Tatler* or *Guardian* are rather better than many of my JOURNALS." Ralph Bubble the punster "advises me to alter a single Letter in the Title of my Speculations, and call it, WEAKLY JOURNAL; which, he tells me, if I also prefix the Word *Sickly*, and couple it to the former with the Particle *and*, will be a full and true Account of my Paper." Proteus has often thought of publishing "a *Weekly Anti-Journal*, full of Cavil and Invective, not doubting but that the Satyr and Scandal with which I should bespatter me would contribute to the mutual Advantage of both my Papers" (No. 14, July 10, 1727).

"When I am at a Loss for a Subject to entertain my Readers with," writes Proteus late in the series,

> I generally pull off my Spectacles, rise from my elbow Chair, put on my Gloves, cock up my Hat, and walk abroad in Pursuit of Materials for my Paper. I have several Times this Week made Use of this Expedient, but without any the least Success. I have to no Purpose roved from Street to Street, frequented my Barber's Shop, or stepp'd into a Coffee-House to pick up Hints for a Journal. It is not easy to reckon up what a Variety of Methods I have taken to set my Mind at Ease in this Particular; How many Tea-Tables I have visited, or Companies I have been in. Nay, a Day or Two ago, after having spent the Morning in fruitless Labour of this Kind, I came Home at Noon, went into my Chamber, double locked my Door, and built a Pyramid of Chairs, Tables and Jointstools against it, and then undressed and very slily slipt into Bed, in order to fall into a Vision that might entertain my self and my Readers. These and innumerable other Contrivances I put in Execution, but all without any Effect, so that I was not without Thoughts of Writing a Speculation upon Nothing, since I could not find any thing else to write upon. (No. 48, March 4, 1727/8)

Proteus Echo is an early American example of the old bachelor, a type popularized in the *Tatler*, *Spectator*, and *Guardian*. Like Mr. Spectator he is a widely traveled scholar who has settled down comfortably and now at age sixty decides to set down his observations of town and country, though without close attention to scenic detail; indeed, in the passage just quoted it sounds as though Proteus is moving about the streets of London, not Boston. His faculty of mimicry looks toward the eccentricities that characterize bachelors after the time of Sterne.

In the second number Proteus introduces the other members of the club. Like Sir Roger de Coverly, Charles Gravely, Esq. "has the Honour of the Chair, and is every way qualified to Adorn it." An eminent merchant, he "could never be perswaded to venture his Merchandise abroad, upon any other Bottom than that of *Good Sense*. ... there is no resisting his Aspect nor Eloquence." To his right "sits Mr. *Timothy Blunt*, who lives at some distance from the Town of *Boston*. ... He is a Person of great plainness of Aspect, Speech, and Behaviour, and has such an Aversion to Bombastick-writing, that he will not allow of any thing that is Gay or Fantastical in his House or Apparel. . . . he rides to Town once every Week, and very often brings his Wallet ballanced with two Bottles of Milk, to defray his necessary Expences. His Periwigg has been out of the Curl, ever since the Revolution [of 1688], and his Dagger and Doublet are supposed to be the rarest Pieces of Antiquity in the Country." Christopher Careless "has, of all Men living, the most passionate Thirst after agreeable Society, and Conversation. . . . he is always ready with an Answer to every Question which he did not hear. . . . let him be kept from strong Liquors, and there is not a more sober temperate Person in the whole Neighbourhood." Will. Bitterly, an astrologer and fortune-teller, "has taken up a Resolution against Matrimony, by reason of several threatning Lines and Crosses in the Palms of his Hands, which he supposes portend domestick Jangles and Disasters. . . . he has very lately ventured to Prophesy something that relates to this Paper, viz. That some of the finest, most elegant and sublime Pieces that may shine out in the Course of these Lucubrations, will certainly meet with very cold and indifferent Reception, and that all the low and groveling Performances (if there should be any) will consequently meet with universal Applause." Mr. Honeysuckle is "the Blossom of our Society, and the beautiful Ornament of Litterature," a person "who lives perpetually upon Tropes and Similes. In his common Conversation, he stalks in Metaphor and Hyperbole, and his very Gesture is Allegorical." He has mastered painting as well as poetry; "having obliged our Club-room, with the Draught of a Beau, a clown and a Coquet," he "is now taking the Phisiognomy of what we call a Critick." Finally there are two Clergymen who sometimes do "us the Honour to set with us half an Hour. . . . Their Lives are regular and Exemplary; their Learning Solid and Profound" (No. 2, April 17, 1727). The members of Proteus Echo's club are not as sharply differentiated professionally as those of the Spectator. While both clubs include a country gentleman, merchant, dilettante, and clergyman, the Templar and Captain Sentry have been replaced by an astrologer and a Bostonian of unspecified profession. The club convention is here Americanized but in a manner that seems arbitrary. Proteus' club, unlike the Spectator's, is stillborn; Mr. Honeysuckle is the only member who appears later, and then merely to help launch Proteus into a dream vision.

In addition to the persona and the club, the *Proteus Echo* essays exhibit other familiar conventions, notably the fictitious letter, oriental tale, and dream vision. Some of Proteus' correspondents praise his writings and others condemn them. "With what Rapture could I dwell upon the Delicacy of your Sentiments, and the Flow of your Periods; the Propriety of your Language, and Copiousness of your Intention!" exclaims John Wonder. "How smooth and easy is the Run of your Prose? How numerous and musical the gliding Strains of your Poesy! . . . Every Time I peruse any of your Sheets . . . I quit Mortality, tread on Clouds, and inhabit Paradise." "Prithee, d'ee think People have nothing to do but to mind thy dull Morallity," cries Nic. Hobnail. "Keep your musty Maxims to your self, unless you have nothing to do but to furnish the Town with waste Paper" (No. 44, February 5, 1727/8). Another correspondent, John Crotchet, delights in telling Proteus about a confusing letter he sent:

> Once I wrote to a Friend in a Style so very perplexed and unintelligible, that I am apt to question whither he has found out the Meaning of it to this Day. . . . I found I had not one Thought in my Mind, which was in any Measure suitable for my Design, to supply which Defect, I got me an *English* Dictionary, from which I selected as many elegant well-sounding Words, as I thought would go to fill up a Letter of some tollerable Length. Being thus prepared, my next Care was to procure as many *And*'s, & *The*'s, & *Of*'s, and *Wherefore*'s, and such other little Particles as would serve to connect them into Sentences. . . . I spread them upon Paper with such Art and Dexterity that I may be bold to say few men could have gone beyond me. . . . Never was a *Delphian* Oracle more intricate and mysterious; when at the same Time the Language was rich and sounding, the Style flowing and easy, and the Period full, musical and round. (No. 48, March 4, 1727/8)

The first instance of an oriental tale in an American serial occurs in *Proteus Echo*. As he was "meditating on that new Face of things which awakens to the Eyes of a Spirit newly departed from the Body," Proteus says that he found among his papers "a small *Arabian* Manuscript which I lit upon in my Travels thro' *Persia*." Among the rest it contained a tract entitled "the Meditations of *Cassim* the Son of *Ahmed*. This being adapted to my present Design, I shall communicate it to the Publick, in a Translation as literal as the Idiom of the two Languages will admit": "I was a few Nights ago, walking over the Hills in the Western and unfrequented Paths of the City *Lima*, which looks towards the Desert of *Elcatif*, in order to refresh my self after the Studies of the Day," writes Cassim. "As I grew tired with walking, I seated my self on the Head of one of the highest among that verdant Range of Mountains, and gave my self into a profound Contemplation on the Works of the great Creator, which then presented themselves to my View, in the most charming Prospects imaginable. . . . As I melted away in these Delights, I could not help imagining that the same Employment I was then pleasing my self with, bore some analogy to those which regale the departed Spirits of Good Men." In the midst of my soliloquy on this subject, "a Philosophical Thought started to me, which I did not find easy to answer."

> "How, *said I to my self*, can the Spirits in Paradise, stript of the humane Body, taste the Delights of those lost and indulgent Climates? How will the naked Soul be able to behold the Wonders of creating Art which is so profusely poured out upon those Regions of Bliss and Immortality? Can they *see* the Verdure of the Hills, and the Flourish of the Fields, when they have left their mortal Eyes behind them? Or can they, without the *Ears* of the Body, be ravish'd with the Consort of warbling Birds, rilling Streams, and bubbling Fountains? Surely in vain will the Blossoms throw their Odours, and the Groves of Spices will perfume the Air in vain, if the power of *Smelling* be utterly extinguished in the seperate Spirits of good Men: And to what purpose will the Fruits blush, or the Breezes cool, if the *Taste* be entirely gone, and the Nerves can *feel* no more?"

At this moment a man "seated on the Head of a Mountain at some Distance" called out to me in a majestic voice: "Cease thy Curiosity, and calm thy Mind. Would you know what we do here, and be acquainted with our Enjoyments, love your Maker, converse with your own Heart, and delight in doing Good. . . . Thus Oh! *Cassim* shall the Bodies of Good Men be raised; thus shall they shine, and thus fly away. Cease then thy Enquiries; learn to live, and long to die" (No. 24, September 18, 1727).[31] It is perhaps difficult to appreciate the eighteenth-century taste for oriental literature and attempts to emulate it. Partly it was the appeal of the exotic, partly of the sublime. Byles, like Addison before him, makes the oriental tale a vehicle for moral and philosophical discussion, inventing an Arabian tract in order to discourse on man's need to curb his curiosity.

In the first of two dream visions Proteus, rising at dawn, observes his woodpile lying "under some considerable Discomposure and Bereavement." A large log "that had for some time done the duty of a Centinel" offers "the following Historical Complaint":

> I had my Birth and Education, says he, on the Edge of a great Swamp in the Town of *Scituate*. And having the start of some of my Contemporaries, and the advantage of a Superiour Bulk and Circumference, I seem'd to bid the fairest for the Supreamacy, and was accordingly, for many Years, the absolute Monarch of the whole shady Empire. I reigned long enough to bury all my Children, to see my Subjects diminished by Degrees, and at last my nearest Neighbours, riffled and captivated, and my Self left alone, and exposed to the Shocks of every Storm and Encounter. . . . Thus I continued for many Years, till a brawny Yeoman . . . fell a labouring . . . with such a Fury, as soon brought down my hoary Honours with Shatterings to the Ground. He lop't off my aged Arms, prun'd every Branch and Twig, trim'd me several Inches shorter than the Market-length, and then shipped me for *Boston*.

Having "received nothing but Kindness and Civility at your Hands" in the two years he has been in Proteus' service, the log almost lost his life tonight when "a forlorn Creature entered the Yard" and carried off "all the stripling Sticks that he could readily Command." He would have carried me off too, but being either "startled at the Footsteps of the Watch" or "gauled at the Shoulder, or Conscience," he dropped me with such violence that it "bruised several of my Ribs, and reduced me to my present Illness and Disfigurement." Proteus, "touched with a kind of Sympathy and Concern" by "this melancholy Relation," rushes to his gate but cannot find the assailant. Awakened suddenly by drunken revelers who are breaking windows, "I stood till they had fired a Broad-side upon my House, and bellowed the whole Neighbourhood to their Windows, and then silently returned to my Pillow and spent the remaining part of the Night, in reflecting upon the Variety, Strangeness, and Regularity of my Dream, and cannot to this Minute be perswaded;

that the Substance of it, is not a sad Reality" (No. 4, May 1, 1727). This dream vision departs from the familiar pattern in that the setting is more homely and realistic than the conventional plain, woods, or road leading to a public building; moreover, there are no allegorical characters. It is less didactic than diverting, even though Proteus on returning from a fruitless search for the log's assailant observes his neighbor Ichabod Thrift stealing his hay and places his reliance on God's "ever-watchful Eye" to find such thieves out.

The other dream vision follows the familiar pattern. Proteus writes that as he and Mr. Honeysuckle were out walking the other day, they "were particularly bewailing the Universal Narrowness of Spirit, and Avarice, which infects our Species. I was so affected with this last Consideration, that upon leaving my Friend, I quickly fell into a Slumber, when there suddenly arose in my Imagination the following Vision." He saw people dancing after the Goddess Wealth, "an airy Phantom, which seemed to dart a wonderful Dazzle upon their Eyes. . . . Her Ears were almost deafen'd with the Clamour of the innumerable Petitions which were address'd to her, mixt with the Murmurs and Revilings of a thousand miserable Creatures, whom she had ruin'd." Honor stood at her right hand and Pleasure at her left. Among her attendants were Honesty, Poverty, and Contentment. "If I was pleased with *Honesty*, I was as much displeased with the two other Phantoms. One of them, whose Name was *Fraud*, had a pair of false Ballances in one Hand, and many Counterfeit Bonds and Papers in the other. . . . She walked through many winding and perplexed Mazes, and was followed by infinite Multitudes, many of whom she made Rich, more she disappointed, and all made Miserable." The other phantom was Theft. "She had a brazen Front, and sly Air, and seem'd very much to affect the Night, at which Time, as my Guide inform'd me, she would break open those Coffers I saw at the feet of Wealth." Justice pursued these three phantoms. I then saw some of those who had been following Wealth "Gasping and Dying before me. Their Eyes seemed to roll with a direful Horror, every Limb of them fell a Trembling. The Phantom they had been dancing after vanished from before their Eyes, Darkness and Clouds hung over their imagination, and every now and then they would fetch the most dismal Shreik, which would pierce to my very Soul." Guilt appeared, around whom "stood many Creatures with ghastly Looks, and Whips in their Hands, with which they continually tortur'd themselves, as soon as ever they had look'd upon the Scrole. While I was employing my self in the most serious Contemplation upon such a Subject, methought the Intelligence flew away from me, at which Time I suddenly awoke very much surpriz'd & pleas'd with my Vision" (No. 38, December 25, 1727). Here the setting is conventional ("the most extended Landskips, composed of Groves, Flowers, Fruit-Trees, Mountains, Plains and Rivers"), and personified vices and virtues parade the scene. In its stylized treatment this dream is less vivid and memorable than the other about the log in the woodpile.

A clear measure of the didactic nature of *Proteus Echo* is the absence of purely humorous essays and an emphasis on morality and philosophical reflection. There are moral essays on such deadly sins as avarice,[32] idleness,[33] envy,[34] and pride[35] and on religion—its compatibility with gentility,[36] its advantages,[37] and hypocrisy.[38] Elsewhere Proteus philosophizes on the ardor for knowledge,[39] how love blinds man's reason,[40] the awe-inspiring "Works of Creation,"[41] immortality,[42] mutability,[43] those who claim to be infallible,[44] and love of country.[45] Of greater interest to the modern reader, however, are the essays on manners, character, and criticism. There are manners essays on avoiding too great familiarity,[46] politeness,[47] the art of conversation,[48] the pleasures of solitude,[49] flattery,[50] taciturnity,[51] good manners,[52] and—which deserve a close look—the Laughing Club and the vapors. "The *Spectator*, *Tatler*, and *Guardian*," writes Jack Sneer, "have been very particular in the secret History of Clubs. . . . But among all these whimsical Societies, I do not remember to have seen the Name of that to which I have the Honour of being a merry, but unworthy Member," namely the Laughing Club.

> The President of our Society is Mr. *Gorgon Grin*, a Frenchman by Birth, whose Countenance has been pucker'd up into one entire Grimace, from Time immemorial. Those who have seen a large black Monkey upon the Chatter, may form some faint Idea of his comical Phisiognomy. . . .
> The next Person in Dignity and Merriment to Mr. *Grin*, and

who bids fairest to succeed him in the Elbow-Chair, is little *Titus Titter*. *Titus* has acquired the Faculty of showing his Teeth without any Occasion at all; and the highest Applause he can bestow upon any thing, is to laugh at it. Grief, Terror, and Joy, all come alike to him, and operate the same way. . . .

As we apprehend our selves to be something under the Dominion of the Moon, we chuse to meet every *Monday* Night: Though we have a more general Meeting annually, on the First Day of *April*, when we feast our selves with great Satisfaction upon a *Rice Fool*. . . .

The ordinary manner of our Entertaining our selves, is only by hearing our selves speak, and then laughing at what we say. We generally all open together; so that a Stranger would imagine by the Confusion of Tongues, that we were laying the Plan of a new *Babel*. And as we talk in *Chorus*, so we also laugh in *Consort*. We have been taken by the Neighbourhood, who have heard our unnatural Noises, for an anti-musick Meeting; or at least they have determined us to be some disaffected Persons who have a Design to revive the old way of Singing. (No. 28, October 16, 1727)

Addison and Steele extended the club convention in the *Spectator* to include accounts of such whimsical societies as the Ugly Club (No. 17), the Everlasting Club (No. 72), the Club of She-Romps (No. 217), and the Rattling Club (No. 630), each treated in the space of a single essay. To this number can be added Jack Sneer's entertaining account of the Laughing Club.

There are several moral causes for the vapors, says Proteus. "In the first Place, a Loose and Immoral Life, which stores up a plentiful Heap of Guilt in the Mind, lays it open to the Lashes of an avenging Conscience, and stirs up a Tumult in the Passions." Another cause is idleness: "When I see *Jack Indolent* hang over a Stationers Shop for some Hours together, get acquainted with all the wild Sparks in Town, waste away his Time and Substance in some Publick House, until one or two in the Morning, I am not surprized that all his sensual Spirits have taken their Leave of him, and he is swallowed up in a Flood of unnatural and ungovernable Thoughts." Excessive solitude is a third cause. "Another Thing which breeds the Spleen, is, a perpetual Rattle and Volubility of Tongue. . . . These insufferable Talkers run on in Discourse till they drein themselves quite empty, and then . . .[are thrown] into a Fit of Melancholly, which eats up the Satisfaction of the former Loquatiousness." Lastly, "immoderate and excessive Laughter and Mirth, gives the Rise very often to the Vapours." To cure "this monstrous Distemper" Proteus proposes three rules. "First, We should endeavour to acquire and preserve a good Conscience, and have a regard in all our Actions to our Creator." "We should in the next place take care to be exercised in something which will tend to the Benefit of our fellow Creatures, the ennobling and aggrandizing our Minds, and not suffer one Day to slide over us without being able at Night to reflect we have been useful, and compose ourselves to Rest in a kind of Triumph, that we have not spent the Hours in vain." "And to Conclude this Advice, when we find a Habit of Melancholly beginning to grow upon us, we should allow our selves in some innocent and amusing Diversion, and scatter our Clouds in the Air of the World, or divert them by some Bodily Exercise, always observing to keep a strict guard upon our Actions, least while we avoid Melancholly, we contract Guilt, and increase that Distemper we endeavour to Cure" (No. 46, February 19, 1727/8). The vapors or the spleen, a depressed or hysterical nervous condition that affected both sexes, had long interested English writers, including Pope and Swift; perhaps the most notable poem on the subject was Matthew Green's *The Spleen* (1737). Here, in a wholly serious essay, John Adams describes the condition and prescribes a cure.

Of several character sketches the description of Will. Formly in an essay on taciturnity is the most memorable: "He is the most exact in his Apparel of any Man breathing; has learn'd to Dance exquisitely well; can adjust his Body to the best Rules of good Manners; and always affects to be seen with the most fashionable Gentlemen of the most polite Sense: But I scarce ever knew him to say any thing, except, *Ladies, it is very fine Weather! Gentlemen, can you tell what a Clock it is? Madam, will you please to take some of my Brazil?*" "I have sometimes been of Opinion," declares Proteus, "that *Will.* was a Man of deep Thought and Penetration, but upon a nearer view have found him in a Posture of Stupidity rather than Attention, and eating the Head of a Cane, instead of improving his own. . . . It seems he has laid it down for a Maxim never to offend; and the best way to accomplish this End he imagines, is not to say any thing. . . . I have very often, for a Trial of his Judgment seem'd to give mine upon fifty Subjects quite foreign to what in reality it was; who very submissively and honestly, was on my side were it right or wrong: And upon upbraiding him with this his servile and tame Assent to whatsoever was asserted, he returned with a great deal of concern, *I hope Sir I have given no Offence*. In short, *Will.* is one whose Brains are fuller of Snuff than Sense; The Laughing-Stock of the Ladies, the Tool of the Men of Wit, and the Admiration of Ideots" (No. 43, January 29, 1727/8). The character sketch embedded in the periodical essay is an outgrowth of seventeenth-century character writing. As Jack Indolent in the previous essay dramatized one cause of the vapors, here Will. Formly personifies taciturnity.

As Benjamin Franklin satirized New England funeral elegies, so Mather Byles and his associates ridicule *"The Art of writing Incorrectly."* By way of introducing the topic, Proteus declares in the first number, "I find I can with much more Ease & Facility, tread in the Steps of a *grub street*, or a *bombastick* Writer, than of one whose Compositions are finished with Purity and Eloquence." In the third number Proteus, desiring "to entertain the Publick, with a regular Criticism upon Nonsense," focuses on those "Admirers of Bombast and Fustian" who "blow up every Subject they take in Hand beyond its natural Dimensions; and nothing will please them that is not big and boisterous, wild and irregular." Consider Mr. George Brimstone: "He is, moderately speaking, Nine Foot high, and Four in Diameter. His Voice is not unlike the Roar and Rapidity of a Torrent foaming down a Mountain, and reverberated amongst the neighbouring Rocks." In a love poem to his mistress "I my self counted in Fifty Six Lines of it, three *Celestials*, eight *Immortals*, eleven *Unboundeds*, six *Everlastings*, four *Eternities*, and thirteen *Infinites*; Besides *Bellowings, Ravings, Yellings, Horrors, Terribles, Rackets, Hubbubs*, and *Clutterings*, without Number" (No. 3, April 24, 1727).[53]

The grubstreet style, declares Proteus in this same essay, "is easily attained, provided a Man can but keep himself from thinking, and yet so contrive Matters, as to let his Pen run along unmolested over a Sheet of White Paper, and drop a convenient Quantity of Words, at proper Intervals, on it." Dick Grubstreet "is a Fellow of a very low Descent, and compounded of the Dregs of Mortality," says Proteus in another essay. "His Ancestors, from all Generations, were Enemies to every thing that is great and noble; and always sordid and mean in their Apparel, Discourse, and the whole tenour of their Actions. . . . his Dress, and Manners, are both alike rough and unpolished. He is a mortal and professed Foe to good Sense, and the true Sublime in Writing, and whensoever he reads either, (which is only by chance,) he rejects them with an ignorant Disdain. . . . He runs on in a perpetual strain of Nonsense; or if his Discourse sometimes just creeps upon the Ground, it never flies above it." In spite of "all these odd strokes in his Character, *Dick* is universally admired by the Vulgar; and is, perhaps, one of the most considerable Authors of his Age."

> He is the Author of all the Farces we have in our Tragedies; or many Epistles Dedicatory; and most of the Panegyricks that flatter Writers in the beginning of their Performances. He is an endless Writer of Songs, Lampoons, with Pieces of Bawdry and Ribaldry; and has lent the Comedians most of the Smut, which blackens some of their brightest Productions. His Plays have very frequently been clapt upon the Stage, and as often, to his great Mortification, hissed off: not to mention the many political Essays he has given the World, and his amusing it in the Form of News-Papers, Gazettes, Mercuries, Flying-Posts, Examiners, Observators, &c. which have, by a benumming kind of magick, lull'd the Publick asleep, and made the whole Nation a sort of reading Drones.

"I have often seen him in the Streets, swinging his Cane, and rolling his thoughtless eyes in the form of a Beaux, making up to certain Ladies that glitter'd in his Eyes; while the charming Creatures, by all their subtilty and wit, have not been able to evade his Impertinence, or his Snuff." Although the vulgar admire Dick, young gentlemen "have precipitated him from the Pulpit, and entirely banished him from their Conversation: so that some believe he will quickly be forc'd to retire to the Country, or at least, lurk obscurely in the Town. . . . by sad Experience, he has found the Reputation of his Works wither, and dye away before him. He has beheld them with astonishment blaze up into Rockets; they have been offered him to light his Pipe at Taverns; and he has eat them with a great deal of gust & satisfaction at the bottom of Pies." Unable to persuade me that I needed his assistance "to give my Papers a general Acceptance . . . he had the Impudence to tell me that in short I had stole a great many strokes of low Humour from his Works, and he expected, in return, to be enrolled a Member of our honourable Society. I was defending my self from this his imputation by the Name and Authority of Mr. *Addison*, when at once he was struck into Silence, and retired with great fury and precipitance." A few hours later, though, he informed me in a letter: "This is to tell you I despise you and your Club for a parcel of ignorant and conceited blockheads and Fools. . . . I warrant you one must go to Coleg and take [3?] Degrees to read your Scollarlike Trade." A great many critics and scholars "no no more of your hi flone words than when they first went to Cambritch, and love my Works derely, and are always reading of um. And be as fine and finikal as you will, *George Brimstone* says you an't worthy to hold a Candle to him. . . . you'l let that dunce-pated Feller *Timothy Blunt* be of your Company, but you won't me, its very well. For my part, I'm as stout as you are proud, I scorn to ax any thing of you agin, I don't care a Fig for you, and you may go whisle for all me" (No. 10, June 12, 1727).

This castigation of the bombastic and grubstreet styles—and elsewhere of writing that is "Luscious," "Puerile and Boyish," "Pedantick," "Stiff and Affected," "Obscure and Perplexed," and "loose and diffused" (No. 29, October 23, 1727)—is evidence that Boston in the 1720s, feeling the impact of English neoclassicism, had begun to realize "that greater attention must be paid to elegance, grace, and ease."[54] The point was made in the previous chapter that Addison, working an amalgam of seventeenth-century high and low styles, cultivated a gentlemanly middle style. "All the Qualifications of a good Style," declares John Hughes characterizing this middle style, "I think may be reduced under these four Heads, *Propriety, Perspicuity, Elegance*, and *Cadence*."[55] Byles and his two associates, like Benjamin Franklin, admired such ideals and attacked bombastic and grubstreet writing as a violation of them.

On April 1, 1728, Mather Byles wrote the final number of *Proteus Echo*, declaring, "The Year is this Day compleated, which has rolled round from the Week which first gave the Town a Speculation in it; and the Authors never intended to exceed these Limits." The fact that both Byles and John Adams were determined to enter the ministry goes far toward explaining why the series came to an end when it did. Ten days later, on April 11, Adams became pastor of a Congregational church in Newport, Rhode Island. The subject of Byles's essay for the master's degree later that year ("polite literature is an ornament to a theologian") makes it clear that literature was never more than an avocation with him. "He was too much of a Mather to believe that it was the First End of Man. First and last he was always a minister of God."[56]

Franklin's *Dogood* papers initiated the essay serial in America, and *Proteus Echo* carried the tradition forward. Between them these two series range through the traditional subject matter and employ the familiar conventions. On balance Franklin's serial is the more successful of the two. While the reader is aware of his presence throughout, Proteus Echo lacks the earthy vitality and dramatic energy of Silence Dogood. Silence's dream vision of Harvard College is managed with greater skill than those Proteus has about the log in his woodpile and the Goddess Wealth. And whereas the reader of the *Dogood* papers hears New England speech and glimpses the Boston scene, a sense of native idiom and environment is almost wholly absent from *Proteus Echo*, even from the thirty-first essay in which the Boston earthquake of October 29, 1727, is mentioned. Nevertheless, by 1728 the tradition was firmly established at Boston and about to appear in Philadelphia, Annapolis, Williamsburg, and Charleston.

III. EARLY PHILADELPHIA SERIALS

RANCIS DANIEL PASTORIUS' OBSERVATION, "Never have
metaphysics and Aristotelian logic ... earned a loaf of
bread,"[1] aptly characterizes the prevailing climate at Philadelphia in the early eighteenth century. Here was an environment
highly congenial to a pragmatist like young Benjamin Franklin
who, having battled the New England saints and scholars, shook
the dust of Boston from his feet and journeyed southward in
1723. Six years later he launched a new essay serial. Andrew
Bradford's *American Weekly Mercury* had been in existence a
decade when Franklin and Joseph Breintnall,[2] fellow members
of the recently organized Junto, undertook *The Busy-Body*[3] as
the first sustained literary venture in what was "primarily a
news journal."[4] Franklin was incensed that his former employer
Samuel Keimer should have started a newspaper, pretentiously
entitled *The Universal Instructor in all Arts and Sciences: and
Pennsylvania Gazette*, to forestall the publication of one that he
intended to establish, and now sought with Breintnall to
enliven the pages of the *Mercury* and make it a serious competitor to Keimer's paper.

In an advertisement of October 1, 1728, announcing the
appearance shortly of the *Universal Instructor*, Keimer had
remarked that "the late *Mercury* has been so wretchedly
perform'd, that it has been not only a Reproach to the Province,
but such a Scandal to the very Name of Printing, that it may, for
its unparallel'd Blunders and Incorrectness, be truly stiled *Nonsence in Folio*, instead of a Serviceable News-Paper." He began at
once to reprint Ephraim Chambers' *Cyclopaedia* in his paper.
Having reached "ABO," he carried an article on abortion,
whereupon Martha Careful threatened that if he published anything more of this kind, "my Sister Molly and my Self, with
some others, are Resolved to run the Hazard of taking him by

the Beard, at the next Place we meet him, and make an Example of him for his Immodesty"; Caelia Shortface added, "If thou proceed any further in that Scandalous manner, we intend very soon to have thy right Ear for it."[5] The following week, on February 4, 1728/9, the first number of *The Busy-Body* appeared.

I

Franklin's Busy-Body is a more nearly Addisonian character than Silence Dogood, never so earthy and vernacular. I have continually observed, declares the Busy-Body, that *"what is every Body's Business is no Body's Business"*; I think fit therefore *"to take no Body's Business* wholly into my own Hands; and, out of Zeal for the Publick Good, design to erect my Self into a Kind of *Censor Morum.* . . . let the Fair Sex be assur'd, that I shall always treat them and their Affairs with the utmost *Decency* and *Respect.* . . . Sometimes, I propose to deliver Lectures of Morality or Philosophy, and . . . perhaps I may sometimes talk Politics" (No. 1, February 4, 1728/9). I assure you I am *"no Partyman, but a general Meddler"* (No. 3, February 18, 1728/9). It is my purpose "to inculcate the noble Principles of Virtue, and depreciate Vice of every kind" (No. 4, February 25, 1728/9); "neither Affection, Aversion or Interest, have byass'd me to use any Partiality towards any Man, or Sett of Men; but whatsoever I find nonsensically ridiculous, or immorally dishonest, I have, and shall continue openly to attack with the Freedom of an honest Man, and a Lover of my Country" (No. 8, March 27, 1729).

The feud between Franklin and Keimer carried over into the early part of the series. "O Cretico! Thou sowre Philosopher! Thou cunning States-man! Thou art crafty, but far from being Wise," inveighs the Busy-Body. "Be advised by thy Friend: Neglect those musty Authors; let them be cover'd with Dust, and moulder on their proper Shelves; and do thou apply thy self to a Study much more profitable" (No. 3, February 18, 1728/9). Keimer, choosing to recognize this as a characterization of himself, counters:

That we have Party amongst us, is too obvious; and 'tis difficult for a Man to be perfectly disengag'd. If he has no sordid or tumultuous Views, Reason and good Judgement will engage him on one Side; if *Passion* or *Prejudice* prevail, these will compell him on the other; yet it is plain that a Beauty and Merit attends the moderate and least violent. The *Busy-Body* seems to be sensible of this, when he pretends to be no Party-Man. But let him examine his own Heart, whether that be not inserted as an Attempt to screen himself from the Imputation of Malice or Prejudice. . . .

It requires a great Genius and much good Nature, to manage with Decency and Humanity the Way of Writing which the *Busy-Body* would seem to imitate; feigned and imaginary Characters may excite Vertue and discourage Vice; but to figure out and apply them by gross Description, has the ill Effect which I take this Trouble to persuade the *Busy-Body* to avoid.[6]

The worst thing I said of Cretico, replies the Busy-Body, "is that he is a *sower Philosopher, crafty, but not wise*. . . . Why should a good Man be offended with me for drawing good Characters? And if I draw Ill Ones, can they fit any but those that deserve them?" (No. 5, March 4, 1728/9). Keimer retorts:

> What a confounded Noise and Racket,
> There is about your Weekly *Pacquet?*
> Some Parts good, and some Parts bad,
> Shew it has different Authors had.
> The author of the *Good*'s unknown,
> But all the *bad ones* are your own;
> And thus your own Stuff does infest,
> And basterdizes all the rest.[7]

A fortnight after Franklin withdrew from the series Keimer chortled: "The sudden Decease of the *Busy Body* has prov'd less shocking, because he was from his Birth a very weakly Child, and born with an incurable peccant Humour which continued to float over his whole Body, till at length it settled in one of his Legs with a Violent Tumour, upon which the most skilful Doctors advis'd him to an Amputation, but his Original Stock of Life being so very low and languid, 'tis said he expir'd under the Operation, and is to be interr'd this Evening in the most private Manner."[8]

Breintnall's Busy-Body, evolving out of Franklin's, is more censorious. Not interested in raking "into the Dunghill Lives of vicious Men" who have lived in Pennsylvania heretofore, he declares, "I hereby graciously pass an Act of general Oblivion" for all misdemeanors committed between 1681 and "the Date of my First Paper; and promise only to concern my self with such as have been since and shall hereafter be committed" (No. 5, March 4, 1728/9). He urges his readers to adopt a conciliatory manner: "A rash and precipitant Manner of Reasoning, with a Mixture of Satyr and Reflection, is now become fashionable; Humour and Cavil take Place of Argument, and a noisy Buffoon is esteemed a Patron of his Country. . . . But a truly honest Man, a Lover of his Country, would detest such Practices, and employ his utmost Endeavours to effect a Reconciliation . . . having no Regard to any separate Views, his Behaviour would more resemble that of a Moderator than a Partisan" (No. 6, March 13, 1728/9). A female correspondent asks the Busy-Body how he could assume so unfit a title when everyone knows that "one of our Sex would out do a Dozen of Yours at meddling with no Body's Business, as you call it, and in Censuring of the whole Town?" But since you are acting this part, she continues, I would have you protect the reputation of my sex; if you don't, "here are Five or Six of us at the Tea-Table, who have more Sense than any of you, that will take your *Busy-Body* into our own Hands, and make every Mothers Son of you smart for it" (No. 14, May 22, 1729). The Busy-Body proposes that he and the Doctor cooperate to help readers interpret his writings correctly: "I shall move it to the Doctor, to take a large Number of my Readers under his Care, in the first Place, that by proper Physick and Diet, they may be reduced to a Capacity of applying themselves to the Meaning and Design of what they read—And then, on my Part, I shall in my Writings convey to them such Medicines and Instructions, for the Regiment of their Minds, as that for the Future they shall seldom need to have Recourse to the Doctor" (No. 17, June 12, 1729). Late in the series the Busy-Body confesses, "I never was so doubtful of my own Abilities as at the present Time," and cautions his readers "to scrutinize my Papers, and if they find any of them to contain a greater Tendency to Vice than to Virtue, let such be hung at the End of a String for Public Examples, and to be polluted by Flies" (No. 25, August 7, 1729). Except for his defense of religious orthodoxy, the Busy-Body observes the neutrality enjoined by Addison and eschews controversy. Conceived by Franklin, who found him a convenient mouthpiece in his feud with Keimer, the Busy-Body was developed by Breintnall; it was Franklin's Busy-Body, not Breintnall's, whose death Keimer reported. Fancying himself a Censor Morum, he finds it an increasingly difficult role to play, becomes concerned that readers interpret what he says correctly, and, growing doubtful of his abilities, eventually agrees that if his papers seem to promote vice more than virtue they be publicly exposed so that they can "be polluted by Flies."

In addition to the character of the Busy-Body the series employs other conventions, such as the club, fictitious letters, and mock-advertisement. Although no club develops around the person of the Busy-Body, a group of "Twelve a-Clock Punch-Drinkers" form the Meridional Club. The Busy-Body, having at the outset invited "all ingenious Gentlemen and others" to assist him, proceeds to print letters from aptronymous correspondents like Patience, Titan Pleiades, J. Hope, Philomusus, Amy Prudent, Amicus Curiae, and Lucy Widowless. And near the end of the series there appears the following announcement: "After this Time, until the End of this Year at least, Wigs and Swords are not to be the distinguishing Marks of a Gentleman; a Cane is not to denote that the Bearer of it is lame; a soure or Conceited Countenance to be no Sign of a Man of Parts, or that such a One would make a good Schoolmaster; a round brim'd Hat, and a Coat formally plain, to be no certain Tokens of an honest Man; nor is a shabby Suite to signifie that the Wearer has met with unavoidable Misfortune" (No. 29, September 4, 1729).[9]

The *Busy-Body* papers range through all the conventional subjects except criticism: manners, morality, philosophical reflection, character, humor. Especially manners. There are essays on visitors who wear their welcome out,[10] the illiteracy of young country people,[11] and how to educate them properly;[12] but the liveliest focus on the battle of the sexes. Matilda informs the Busy-Body that she learned from her friend Flavia of Florio's inconstancy: "How was I surprized with Shame and Indignation, when she discovered to me, that my *Florio* loved her; when I heard all those Vows, Oaths and Protestations directed to her that had been before breath'd at my Feet"; whereupon the Busy-Body, who had promised at the outset to champion the fair sex, threatens, "thou discourteous Knight, thou shame to the Honour of thy Profession, thou that hast basely falsified thy Word, make immediate Reparation, or my Sword shall seek thee" (No. 14, May 22, 1729). Florio, hoping the Busy-Body "will have an impartial Regard to, and Redress the Sufferings of the Male as well as the Female World," defends himself against Matilda's charge: "I have lov'd that Charming Cruel Maid these two long Tedious Years, without One moments Respite to my burning Pangs. . . . when I found that Prayers, nor Tears, nor Oaths, nor Sighs Avail'd . . . and that *Flavia* scarce less Beautiful than She seem'd by her Looks a Partner of my Anguish, I thought my self in Gratitude Oblig'd to force my Heart from that Dear Tyrant of its Liberty, and Cast it at *Flavia*'s Feet: But still—*I love her—greatly love her*, and will since she Relents, Return, and bind myself for Life, but alas! how shall I leave the lovely Constant *Flavia*? 'Tis to relieve my tortur'd Mind in this I claim your Aid" (No. 16, June 5, 1729). Undoubtedly Breintnall hoped to increase the circulation of the *Mercury* by engaging in this war of words. The Busy-Body makes good his promise to protect the reputation of the fair sex by coming to Matilda's defense. Although Florio defends himself against her charges, the Busy-Body fails to offer the aid he claims and the affair is left unresolved. The reader might well ask why so good a friend as Flavia was the one who told Matilda in the first place about Florio's inconstancy.

Amy Prudent complains to the Busy-Body about punch-drinking husbands: "we are Wives to a certain Set of Men, that Stile themselves the *Meridional Club*, which they think Intitules them to leave their Business in the midst . . . so that they Twenty or more of them can but get together over a flowing Bowle of fresh Limes, which makes them of more fluency of Speech by far than we are over a Dish of Tea . . . when our Rooms are set in a decent order to Dine in, we are immediately discommoded with a numerous Body of Twelve a-Clock Punch-Drinkers; which beloved Liquor they pretend is to whet their Appetites" (No. 20, July 3, 1729). The Busy-Body proposes that when the men meet at noon, each wife shall "present her Husband with a Dish of Tea, to drink with his Punch, allay the Fumes of it, and sweeten his Breath. . . . The Men, having compleated the Business of their Meeting, should all return Home to their agreeable Wives, with every one his Tea Cup refill'd with Punch, for the Ladies respectively to drink with their Tea, to correct the Washiness of it, and exhilarate their Hearts." Having pointed out "the Unwholesomeness of Rum, Limejuice and Nutmeg," he adds, "I think it would have been no Imprudent Management of the Gentlemen, who have address'd me for an impartial Distribution of Justice, if they had left a Barrel of that retaining Liquor at Mr. *Bradfords*, for my own special Drinking—But I would not have the Ladies think I am so un-generous, and ill-manner'd as to expect they should, with their next Appeal, order me at the same Place Ten Pounds, at least, of the best Green Tea; neither shall I so much as mention a Loaf or two of Double refined Sugar." Amicus Curiae, a member of the Meridional Club, assures the Busy-Body:

> . . . tho' the ill natur'd *PRUDENT*, ascribes such a property to the prolifick Juice, that is not found in washy *TEA*, What wonder is it, if the generous Cordial Inspire's it's nature, and diffuses a Glad-ness in our Hearts, When on the other hand the noxious streams of that Paralytick Herb, create Disorders in the Brain and Nerves; from whence proceed the many direful Effects issuing from the Circle of the *Tea. Table*, where this Mischievous Combination was hatch'd. . . . We have all Consulted our Wives about the general Charge, and find the good natur'd Creatures, take no Part with the disturbers of our Tranquillity. . . . Thus, Sir, are we privately abus'd by these Viragoes, in Fomenting domestick Broils, and that Method not prevailing, they have openly traduc'd our Characters to your Honour; Like the Whore, *That Crie's out Whore first*, well knowing that the first Blow is half the battle; But yet as we doubt not of an impartial distribution of Justice. As the case is here fairly stated between us, and put in it's true Light, so we doubt not but they will Incur your severe Censure and Repri-mand. (No. 22, July 17, 1729)

Breintnall depicts the domestic scene realistically. Interposing on behalf of Amy Prudent and other distressed wives whose husbands are said to disorder their houses and their own minds by noonday punch-drinking, the Busy-Body gives the appear-ance of impartiality when in fact he prefers liquor to tea.

Breintnall pursued the battle of the sexes, picturing men and women alike as hardhearted. "O, the Difference between a Wife, and a Virgin courted," complains Lucy Widowless. Before marriage my husband called me "a Beauty and an Angel"; now "he tells me I am a homely Dowdy." "It is notorious that this Colony swarms with ill Husbands," declares the Busy-Body sympathetically; "what Numbers are pursuing, more earnestly than they would a Livelyhood, Gaming, Drinking and lew'd Women? These, in my Opinion, are the common Temptations, which principally lead Men out, bewilder their Understandings, and vitiate their Sight, that they cannot possibly see the Beauty, apparent to Others, in their own disregarded Wives" (No. 28, August 28, 1729). Conversely, ungenteel young Philadelphia tradesmen, anxious to marry, are perplexed because "the gay and splendid appearance which the young Ladies about our own Station, universally affect, makes it very difficult to distinguish them from People of the best Estates in Town," and therefore entreat the Busy-Body to lay his "Censorial Injunctions on the fair Ones of our Rank, that in Compassion to their Admirers, they condescend to distinguish Themselves from 'People of Condition,' in order to prevent Mistakes; For at present your Petitioners can but worship them at a Distance, without having Courage to approach them, thus guarded with an Air of Quality, and entrench'd behind double Rows of China-Ware" (No. 15, May 29, 1729).

The Busy-Body moralizes on virtue,[13] hypocrites,[14] how viciously those of high rank treat their inferiors,[15] self-interest,[16] and the fact that industry is the way to wealth. When his correspondent Titan Pleiades, seduced by astrology into believing "that there are large Sums of Money hidden under Ground in divers Places about this Town," asserts it as a fact that "the Time will come when the Busy-Body, his *Second-sighted Correspondent*, and *your very humble Servant*, will be Three of the richest Men in the Province," the Busy-Body replies that "great Numbers of honest Artificers and labouring People . . . fed with a vain Hope of growing suddenly rich, neglect their Business . . . and voluntarily endure abundance of Fatigue in a fruitless Search after Imaginary hidden Treasure. . . . the rational and almost certain Methods of acquiring Riches by Industry and Frugality are neglected or forgotten. . . . A Sea Captain of my Acquaintance [said,] I esteem the Banks of Newfoundland to be a more valuable Possession than the Mountains of Potosi."

Consider the farmer's advice to his son: "*I give thee now a Valuable Parcel of Land; I assure thee I have found a considerable Quantity of Gold by Digging there; Thee mayst do the same. But thee must carefully observe this. Never to dig more than Plowdeep*" (No. 8, March 27, 1729). The emphasis on industry in this essay of Franklin's anticipates the morality of Poor Richard. Like Silence Dogood's essay on night-walking, this one is brought to a close with an effective anecdote.

There are philosophical reflections on the Rich Man and the Poor Man,[17] vain hopes,[18] the importance of cultivating one's particular talent,[19] and the proper relationship between age and youth.[20] The Busy-Body leaves his neutral corner to defend religious orthodoxy, asserting that "The Christian Religion is a reasonable thing, and tho' it Imposeth some things as the Objects of our Faith, which are above the Stretch of human Reason (as the Hypostatical Union, &c) yet they are not Contrary to it" (No. 21, July 10, 1729). Conversely he castigates infidels: "Can any thing be a more clear Demonstration of a weak Understanding, than their Endeavours to destroy the innate Notions of Mankind; to pull down what has been built by the universal Suffrage, and Consent of the World; and in it's room erect nothing; but leave the World without any shadow of Religion. . . . Strip them once of their borrowed Wit, their *mimical Humour and Grimace*, and they will appear in their own Colours, the most awkard and despicable of their Species" (No. 28, August 28, 1729). Franklin would certainly have supported this attack of Breintnall's on free-thinking; by 1729 he had retreated from the radical views set forth in *A Dissertation on Liberty and Necessity* (1725) to a moderate deism, affirming his belief in the existence of God and the immortality of the soul.

On occasion the Busy-Body draws characters. There are contrasting portraits of Ridentius ("the Height of his low Ambition is to put some One of the Company to the Blush") and Eugenius ("who never spoke yet but with a Design to divert and please") (No. 2, February 11, 1728/9). The virtuous Cato "appear'd in the plainest Country Garb; his Great Coat was coarse and looked old and thread-bare; his Linnen was homespun; his Beard perhaps of Seven Days Growth, his Shoes thick and heavy, and every Part of his Dress corresponding" (No. 3, February 18,

1728/9). Philopseus the liar is "esteem'd as dangerous a Person among Men, as a Wolf is a Beast among Sheep. . . . private Designs were formed against him, to rid the Country of an Inhabitant as Mischievous; but he was Wealthy, and his Gold prov'd a ready Friend to succour him." His attempts to reform miscarrying, he died, "out of Credit, and out of Doors," and "the Government order'd his Effigies to be cast in Brass, with open Mouth and no Tongue in it" (No. 27, August 21, 1729).

Rarely the Busy-Body engages in humor for its own sake, as for example the "delirious Tales" which W.T., "an idle young Fellow," is given to telling:

> I was (says he) eating a Bit at my Cousin *Timothy's* when the great Storm happen'd, that blew the River *Delaware* dry by the *Falls*, Bless me! It shook the old Chairs to Pieces, That I could hardly sit my Horse. O G—d how the Trees ript up by the Roots! Cousin *Tim's* Mare was newly broke, and she flew thro' the Woods like a Vengeance—I halloo'd after him that the Woods eccoh'd again, and an old Panther answer'd me; and gad we had rare Fun of it as ever your Eyes beheld; My old brindled Dog snapt him by the Right Ear, and 'twass well for me, for he was just going to spring full at me. Cousin *Timothy* as bold as a Lyon, catch'd up a Pitch-Fork, and design'd to have poked him to the Flank, while he was worrying poor old Jowler, but *Jemmy Tomson*, came running with his Rifle Gun, which he had loaded with a Brace of Balls on purpose; and took such clear Sight at the very Heart of him. Faith I'll lay Ten to one that *Jemmy Tomson* shoots into an Augre hole twice in three Shoots at 70 Yards—He won the Saddle at *Whitemarsh*, and made but one Shoot, and a fine Saddle it was, but vastly heavy—he flung it over his back, and when he was carrying it off—You know he is but a little Man—*John*, what the Plague d'ye call him, call'd out to him to stay for Help to carry it; Whereupon *Tim.* being affronted told him, and swore to it, that he would for a Wager of 2 Quarts of Rum, and 2 Gal. of Cyder, walk on all Fours with the Saddle on his Back, and he a stride on the Top of it. Bless me, you would have burst your Selves with Laughing at the Devil of a Tortle—But *Will Rash* affirm'd, he had seen Tortle at Sea as big as a Coach, and strong enough to carry as many men as could sit on their Shells, &c. (No. 16, June 5, 1729)

Such rambling nonsense is inherently comic if not overdone; here, fortunately, it is not. Moreover, we are afforded glimpses of the environs of Philadelphia.

The final number in the series appeared September 25, 1729, a week before the provincial election, wherein the Busy-Body advises his readers, "deliberate well upon your own legal Capacity to vote at an Election of Assembly-Men, and be certain that you know their Qualifications, and Duty to their Country." "Men of Capacity, Virtue and Stability are not very plenty"; choose only such as are "fully fit and Capable." The following week, on October 2, Franklin took over Keimer's failing newspaper "for a Trifle,"[21] shortened the title to the *Pennsylvania Gazette*, and became the new editor.

Breintnall had a greater literary stake in *The Busy-Body* than Franklin, who withdrew after the eighth number and let him carry on the series alone to a total of thirty-two. Breintnall was responsible for the liveliest as well as the dullest essays: on the one hand, those on the age-old battle of the sexes; on the other, the bulk of the moral and philosophical pieces. His invention sometimes deserting him early in the series, he made good the Busy-Body's promise in the opening number to entertain readers "with some well-chosen Extracts from a good Author" and excerpted *Cato's Letters*.[22] One feels that from the first Franklin's heart was not in this enterprise, as it had so clearly been in the *Dogood* papers. His *Busy-Body* essays imitate the manner and matter of Addison more nearly than anything he ever wrote; it was perhaps his awareness of this fact that led him to abandon his part in the undertaking as quickly as he did. Although he never launched another serial, he published in the *Pennsylvania Gazette* "little Pieces" of his own "which had been first compos'd for Reading in our Junto,"[23] the most memorable being his character sketches of Anthony Afterwit, Celia Single, and Alice Addertongue.[24]

II

Circumstance and enterprise enabled Philadelphia to outdistance Boston in the second half of the eighteenth century and become, in Franklin's phrase, "the Seat of the American Muses."[25] In this cultural flowering Franklin was only one virtuoso among many, including James Logan, John Bartram, Thomas Godfrey, Thomas Hopkinson, and William Smith— men who among them established the first subscription library, one of the first magazines, and the first scientific society in the colonies and founded the College of Philadelphia. Culture in the Quaker city rested on a broader base than at Boston. "The poorest labourer upon the shore of *Delaware*," wrote Jacob Duché in Revolutionary times, "thinks himself intitled to deliver his sentiments in matters of religion or politics with as much freedom as the gentleman or the scholar. . . . such is the prevailing taste for books of every kind, that almost every man is a reader; and by pronouncing sentence, right or wrong, upon the various publications that come in his way, puts himself upon a level, in point of knowledge, with their several authors."[26] While the vital literature of Philadelphia was predominantly utilitarian, "it formed a foundation upon which later imaginative writing in America could be built."[27] The chief outlet for this writing in the two decades before the Revolution was the magazine rather than the newspaper, and it was here that the two most notable literary serials appeared.

The first of these serials, *The Prattler*, was published in *The American Magazine and Monthly Chronicle for the British Colonies* (1757-58), edited by the Reverend William Smith, provost of the College of Philadelphia, who "was eager to fit Philadelphia into the London mold, making it the literary and artistic center of the colonies, with [himself] as a sort of Pennsylvania Dr. Johnson presiding over all."[28] The Preface to the *American Magazine* stated that part of each issue would be "set aside for MONTHLY ESSAYS, in prose and verse," which, "we hope, will not be the least valuable part of our work. . . . we shall think ourselves under particular obligation for every *essay* that may be communicated to us by others, so far as they tend to promote *peace and good government, industry* and *public spirit, a love of* LIBERTY *and our excellent constitution,* and above all a veneration of our holy undefiled CHRISTIANITY."[29] Smith himself sought to make good this promise by writing *The Hermit*, an eight-part serial consisting chiefly of sermons bearing such titles as "On the Perfection and Efficacy of the Christian Religion" and "A Solemn Meditation on the Late Fast."[30] The magazine also carried two serials of immediate purpose, *The Antigallican* and *The Planter*.[31]

The Prattler, most of it written by one who signed himself

"Timothy Timbertoe," began to appear in the second issue.[32] The fact that several of the numbers are signed by combinations of initials is possible evidence that it was the work of several hands; "the contents and moods suggest that they may have been local college students."[33] Timothy Timbertoe, encouraged by the editors' invitation to submit contributions instructive and entertaining, decides to become a correspondent. While others are sending you military and political intelligence, foreign and domestic, he declares, "I shall employ my pen on less ambitious topics; such as tattle from the tea tables, characters from the coffee-house or adventures in private life. In short, gentlemen, I aim at no higher office in your work than to be permitted to hold the *Glass to folly*, wherein she may contemplate her own visage, and perceive what it would otherwise be difficult to persuade her of." His childhood friend Dick Dimple has consented to give his history. Timbertoe "was born in a town situate at a little distance from the city of *Philadelphia*," writes Dick in a less than flattering account, "of parents whose care and anxiety for him merited a much better reward than they have received." Although "educated by the parson of the parish . . . he turned out little better than a fool. About four years ago he assumed, or rather usurped, the character of a *poet*, but never rose higher than an *Acrostic* or *Aenigma*." Even though his manner made him insufferable, "no body durst offend him; for, if they did, he was sure to make a ridicule of them in all companies, and to expose them wherever he went." Two years ago "his parents mov'd up to *Philadelphia* on account of their health," where "I have heard that he does nothing but saunters about the coffee-house, strolls along the wharfs, or drinks tea with the ladies." He is such a scandalmonger that he has even been known to "peep thro' a key-hole, or listen at a window, or steal gently into a closet, or behind a bed, all with the same spightful design, to hear and carry away what was said, and laugh at it when he had done so. Indeed he is wonderfully well adapted for things of this kind, as he can walk or stand for an hour together on his toes, and tread as lightly as a cat" (No. 1, November 1757). In short, Timbertoe is a dilettante in the mold of Will Honeycomb, most at home gossiping over teatables or in coffeehouses and silently gathering scandal. Although the set-

ting is ostensibly Philadelphia, he resembles a London maca-
roni.

Timbertoe, "tickled with the thoughts of having commenced
author" but hearing "that many people could not find the *Wit* of
my last piece," finds "a sort of malicious joy" in sending the
editors a paper on scanty female dress, wherein Adam Project
maintains that since frugality is a virtue, we cannot commend
the ladies too much.

> So far have they carried this virtue, that, rather than put their
> husbands or fathers to the *Expence* of buying cambricks or mus-
> lins, they expose their *tender* heads to the *inclemencies* of this
> severe season, wearing no caps and not much of either for hand-
> kerchiefs, their bosoms finding little more favor than their heads.
> . . . Their gowns, petticoats &c. have undergone the same curtail-
> ing. Nay even their *Shoes* have decreased in proportion to their
> *Head-Dress*; so that if a *Modern* fine lady's whole garb (except her
> *Hoop*) should be shewn an hundred years hence, posterity would
> believe their great grand-mothers were all dwarfs.

"As this seems a fair challenge to the *other* sex, I expect every
day to see the *Gentlemen* begin to *strip*; and doubt not but the
spirit of emulation will at last bring us to the primitive happy
state of innocence, and a *Fig-leaf*." In another paper Hymenaeus
Phyz, convinced that "WEDLOCK is the true sublunary SUMMUM
BONUM," marries "a lady equally admired for her sense and
beauty," only to discover that they are "not *fitted* for each
other." Hearing it affirmed that matrimonial happiness depends
on a "secret *Sympathy* of soul," I decided, says Hymenaeus, "to
enquire, whether there were not certain outward corporeal in-
dications, lines of the face and hands, moles and other marks of
body, whereby this *mutual Sympathy of Hearts*, was discover-
able." He became "so compleat an adept in the art, as to pronounce, at first sight, whether a husband and wife, are *fitly
match'd*," and now offers his "advice in all *matrimonial Delib-
erations*, to any gentleman or lady, who shall please to visit me
on that account, at my lodgings at the ADAM and EVE, in BRIDE
ALLEY beyond BRIDGE, at any hours of the day, between *Eight*
and *Six*, GRATIS; and they may depend upon the strictest
secrecy."

> N.B. I have tables of calculation, shewing to a second, how long, in
> any assigned case, LOVE will last after *Fruition*; how many *Grains*

of Gold are sufficient to turn the *Balance* for or against a *Match*. I can also shew any lady or gentleman, the face of her lover, or his mistress, in a *concave Mirror* very curiously contriv'd. I can furnish them with a most excellent set of instructions for the observance of mid-summer eve. I have a great variety of *Posies* for rings, and divers kinds of *Amulets* to procure love, cause constancy, help sterility &c. &c. &c. all made at the most favourable *Crises* of *Conjunction*; with other mysteries too tedious to enumerate.

"And now, gentlemen," Timbertoe tells the editors, "I think I have retrieved my character as a wit. But it will be said that the aforesaid papers are none of mine. What then? They are of my *Communicating*; and if I was not a *Wit* myself, I could neither have fellowship nor communication with *Wits*" (No. 2, December 1757).

Timbertoe confesses that since becoming "an author, and consequently a man of importance, I cannot help shewing it in my outward behaviour. I assume a peculiar gravity of countenance, a sober deportment, and great taciturnity; nay—I even imagine that I have grown two inches in height within this three months; and accordingly *over-look* many people whom I used to think my superiors." Returning from a ramble through the city, he finds two letters on his table. The first is from Aminadab Broadbrim, who approves of the paper "on the flagrant indecency of the females dress," but dislikes that on matrimony: "The *Doctrine of Fitnesses*, I look upon as frivolous and impertinent. . . . It is my opinion, that if I am worth a thousand pounds, it is *fit* that I should marry one who is worth as much more. Or if I can give my daughter a thousand pounds, I think it very *unfit*, that she should throw it away upon one, who cannot produce a third part of that sum." The second letter is from an indignant Barbara Shallow, who cries: "Blest and sweets! that such a little upstart as you should take upon you to censure the behaviour of people of fashion, and dictate to them the particular modes of dress! . . . Dear hearts! cannot we ladies talk as we please, and do every thing else as we please, without being called to account in such a ludicrous manner by such a scurrilous fellow as you?" Speaking for "an honourable convention of ladies in this city, representing the free-women of this province," I warn you, Mr. Timbertoe, "and all your brethren of the *prattling* race, that, in

55

case one single word shall appear in any of your future papers, tending to censure our dress or behaviour, or any of our proceedings whatever, you, together with all your aiders and abettors, shall be prosecuted" by being "kept in close custody, during our pleasure, in a cold, narrow, smoaky room, at the house of a formal, old-fashioned gentlewoman, who professes herself a strict member of the KIRKE"; she "shall have strict orders to watch you narrowly, and to let you have no intercourse with any body, not even your dearest friends, either by letter or conversation, but what she must see and hear." When you are returned to your own house, she "shall always attend you; you shall constantly be subject to her authority and in the strictest and most literal sense be under a *Petticoat-Government*." Timbertoe replies that "if this honourable convention have thought proper to assume to themselves a right to call persons to account for speaking the truth, and holding the glass to folly, I must beg leave to question their jurisdiction, and to assure them, that, *in these respects, I also am perfectly* FREE, *and accountable to no body for my proceedings*" (No. 3, January 1758).

Two months later "A. Blockhead" tells the editors of the catastrophe that has befallen his cousin Timbertoe. "Soon after the receipt of that angry letter from *Barbara Shallow*, he came down to our house, and seemed much dejected and out of spirits. On my rallying him about it, he told me, that was not what most affected him, (tho' he owned it had somewhat shocked him) but, Crys he, 'here is what gives me my chief concern,' stripping down his stocking and shewing me his leg, which was become of the same appearance with his toe—'can you, cries he, now blame me?' adding, with a sigh, 'it will certainly spoil my dancing.' " He disappeared for a month and when he returned, "how changed from what he was! pale and emaciated. . . . All we could get out of him was, that he was *unwell* and desired to retire. . . . He then curst your delusive invitations, bewailed his unfortunate inclination to *Wit*." When he bid me feel his limbs,

> I found all his lower parts absolutely hardened. I proposed sending for assistance; but he refused it, saying that he knew he was beyond the power of medicine, strenuously asserting, that he was under the influence of *Witchcraft*, and gave many broad hints, that he was convinced *Barbara Shallow* was the principal cause of this, as well as of all his other misfortunes. . . . his *Metamorphosis*

56

visibly encreasing, about four in the morning he was entirely *transmuted,* and *ceased to live.* . . . this of *Poor* TIM'S is, I believe the first instance of *Lignifaction* to be met with. . . . I should be glad that some of your *Magazine-Men* would come down to BOOBY-HALL, and see this modern miracle, as you might then be better able to transmit an account of it to the royal society.

The editors offer a reward to whoever can work a cure: "If any gentlemen of the faculty, can *dissolve* this *Charm,* and raise up our late *friend,* so as that he may live, move, walk and *write* again, they shall be entitled . . . to one *Shekel-weight* of hair, taken from one of the *Perewigs* of old GALEN, and sent us from beyond seas; besides an *annual Present* of our magazine neatly bound and gilt, so long as the effects of their said cure shall continue. If they should not succeed, we will nevertheless pay the expence of *Horse-hire*" ("An Account of the dismal Catastrophe of the learned, and ever-to-be lamented Timothy Timbertoe, Esq.," March 1758).

Hymenaeus Phyz, learning of Timbertoe's metamorphosis, resolves to restore "him to his pristine state of flesh and blood." Assuring the editors that he is "no mercenary *Quack* or *Empirick,*" Hymenaeus relates how he set out for Booby Hall with an "*Anti-hebetic Unguent*" he had discovered. He asked to be left alone with the patient, applied the unction, and returned to the family. "In about an hour's time, I went to see what effect my operation produced, and found, (so potent and so speedy is this divine specific,) the body *carnify* and *reanimate* apace. In less than two hours after, the revivification was compleated, and both the sensual and intellectual powers gradually recovered." At present Timbertoe "talks and acts a little wildly, speaks of certain strange scenes he hath been eye-witness of, during his *Transmutation,* and affirms strongly that he enjoyed the full exercise of all his mental faculties, notwithstanding the change his body underwent. As I doubt not, his discomposure will wear off by degrees, he will be able to renew his correspondence with you, the next month, and then you may expect his own account of these wonderful scenes" ("Further Account of Timothy Timbertoe, Esq.," April 1758). The Ovidian convention of metamorphosis, appropriated by the periodical essay after the time of Steele and Addison, is here handled with imagination and whimsy. What more natural than that one named Timothy Timbertoe, distressed by Barbara Shallow's angry letter, should experience lignifaction or that his correspondent Hymenaeus Phyz should be the one to discover and administer the antidote that revives him.

"After four months tedious silence," declares Timbertoe, "I once more take up my pen to write to you." In spite of his determination to hold the glass to folly, "*Folly* has still continued a *Fool*, *Ignorance* a *Knave*, and *Women Vanity*. And, from the powers of these, united together, I have been doomed to suffer what never befel a poor christian before in a civilized country." Last February, when "two tall, wan, old, fury-looking women" appeared in his apartment, he realized "that Mrs. *Shallow* had determined to execute her threats, and that I was sent for by the honourable convention of ladies mentioned in her letter to me."

> Being conducted thro' many unfrequented lanes and paths, I found myself on the approach of night, in view of a large heavy-headed building, with many carvings, breakings and ginger-bread figures, on its walls; whose form and structure put me in mind of an enormous GOOSE-PYE, which I had once seen my mother make, in sheep-shearing time. . . . I was soon carried into a large *Room* or *Hall*, in which I beheld a semi-circular table, surrounded entirely by women; whose grotesque and strange appearance, was so far from commanding respect, that I should certainly have treated them with ridicule, could I have met them single and apart. (No. 4, June 1758)

"At the upper end of the table, raised a few steps above the rest, a matron was seated; toothless, wan and meagre, to whom, contrary to the common rule, age had not given even the appearance of wisdom." On her left hand was "a sour-faced, thick-lip'd young wench" serving as clerk. "On her right sat a pert-looking hussey who seemed conscious of her superior rank and qualities. Her face was well nigh eclipsed by a huge deep *Frizet*, or kind of wig, that covered her head; and she seemed to be a very leading person in the *Convention*. I soon guessed that she was my identical friend Mrs. *Shallow*." The other members were a motley group: "Some wore aprons, and some carried baskets, and some greasy bags, the ensigns of their various callings; for some of all callings made a part of this august body—*Orange Maids, Poulterers, Pastry-Women, Leather-dressers*, and God knows how many more." Silence being commanded, the matron charged me with being "the writer and promoter of many *infamous Lampoons*" against her sex. She then gave the clerk a poem called *Hoop-Faction* to read. The convention hearing the lines,

> Tis an old maxim—give a woman way
> And all shall prosper—if the men obey!
> From *Adam's* time, our sex have had their will
> And 'tis but fit that we should have it still,

so fastened their eyes upon him that he thought he "should have been that moment condemned without further ceremony if the old matron . . . had not fixed on her spectacles" and asked why sentence should not immediately be pronounced against him. "With the most solemn protestation I denied that ever I had writ or dictated [the] least word or sentence of what was read. This put the whole body into a still greater rage, and the witnesses were that moment ordered to be brought in. What sort of evidence they gave against me, how just a trial I obtained, and what remarkable speeches were made by some of the *Ladies* present, will appear in my following papers" (No. 5, July 1758).[34]

In spite of the promise of further numbers the series broke off at this point, even though the *American Magazine* ran for three more issues. Clearly the author's (or authors') powers of invention had run out. However, *The Prattler* does fulfill Timbertoe's promise to retail "tattle from the tea tables, characters from the coffee-house or adventures in private life." Adam Project's paper on scanty female dress and Hymenaeus Phyz's paper on matrimonial happiness are social topics well calculated to engage the interest of contemporary readers. These papers provoke predictable responses: the Quaker Aminadab Broadbrim approves of the first but not the second; Barbara Shallow cries out angrily against the first and threatens to have Timbertoe confined if he engages in further censure of female dress or behavior. A firm narrative line built on incidents from Timbertoe's encounters with Miss Shallow pulls the series in the direction of fiction. He is convinced that she is the cause of his lignifaction and the one responsible for his being hauled before the convention and charged with writing lampoons against women. Indeed, *The Prattler* reads like a novel in embryo.

III

A more ambitious and successful serial still, *The Old Bachelor*, appeared in *The Pennsylvania Magazine; or, American Monthly Museum* (1775-76), published by Robert Aitken who employed Thomas Paine as contributing editor. Aitken announced that in the plan of the work a number of pages "will be set apart for original American productions, and the greatest attention given that none be admitted but such as are of real merit"; he promised to "endeavour to furnish the public with an amusing and instructive Miscellany."[35] A correspondent (probably Paine) declared in the first issue: "It has always been the opinion of the learned and curious that a magazine, when properly conducted, is the nursery of genius; and by constantly accumulating new matter, becomes a kind of market for wit and utility. . . . The British magazines, at their commencement, were the repositories of ingenuity: they are now the retailers of tale and nonsense. From elegance they sunk to simplicity, from simplicity to folly, and from folly to voluptuousness. . . . America yet inherits a large portion of her first-imported virtue. . . . A magazine can never want matter in America, if the inhabitants will do justice to their own abilities."[36] On March 4, 1775, Paine wrote Franklin with his characteristic lack of modesty that Aitken "has lately attempted a magazine, but having little or no turn that way himself, has applied to me for assistance. He had not above 600 subscribers when I first assisted him. We have now upwards of 1500 and daily increasing."[37] However, Paine and Aitken, "both prickly characters, got along badly. . . . The outbreak of war, coupled with the strain of working for Aitken . . . hastened Paine's departure from the magazine."[38]

The principal authors of *The Old Bachelor*, which began to appear in the third issue and ran to twelve numbers, were Paine and Francis Hopkinson.[39] Paine, who gave up his editorship in the summer of 1775, seems not to have had a hand in the later numbers. Hopkinson, on the other hand, continued active throughout, informing Aitken late in the series: "I am a great admirer of the Spectators, Tatlers, and Guardians. I never read them but with pleasure and improvement. The *utile* and *dulce* are so happily blended in these elegant compositions, that I think they must be held in high esteem, so long as the English language is known and understood."[40] Judging by the narrative and dramatic nature of *The Old Bachelor*, to say nothing of other of his works like *A Pretty Story*, it is clear that Hopkinson had the makings of a novelist.[41]

"I have just met with something that has put me exceedingly out of temper, and fitted me to write, I believe, *elegantly*," the Old Bachelor (George Sanby) informs Mr. Aitken. "It has warmed up my passions to such a pitch, that I think I can quarrel as *sublimely*, as my brother bachelor, Dr. Johnson." He has just seen "a man and his wife the happiest people I ever saw in my life. . . . I hate such sights—I had rather see a good battle between them, and the cat and the dog keeping up the quarrel—I'd have them always at it." Asked why he doesn't get married, the Old Bachelor replies: "A fine affair I should make of it at sixty-five! . . . I ought to be *hanged* for not being married *before*; but I ought to be *hung* in *chains* if I get married *now*. If the law will leave me out of the question, and I don't much care whether they do or not, I'd give my vote to make it felony for any man to remain a bachelor after forty." Being reformed these two years, he repents the consequences of his fornications: "To beget them was a *natural crime*, to disown them a *proud* one, and to neglect them a *cruel* one" (No. 1, March 1775).

Having promised to give Mr. Aitken the rest of his story "the next time you make a visit to bachelors hall," the Old Bachelor offers the following lines in the second number:

> Fair Venus so often was miss'd from the skies,
> And Bacchus as frequently absent likewise,
> That the synod began to enquire out the reason,
> Suspecting the culprits were plotting of treason.
> At length it was found they had open'd a ball,
> At a place by the MORTALS call'd Bachelor's Hall;
> Where Venus disclos'd ev'ry fun she could think of,
> And Bacchus made nectar for mortals to drink of.
> Jove highly displeased at such riotous doings,
> Sent TIME to reduce the whole building to ruins.
> But time was so slack with his traces and dashes
> That Jove in a passion consumed it to ashes.

"As many of my papers are burnt, and the rest thrown about in confusion," he explains in a postscript, "you must wait a month or two longer to hear the conclusion" (No. 2, April 1775).[42]

Freely he admits that keeping bachelor's hall has its inconveniences. "When our Hall was burnt I got cold at the fire, and have been laid up with the gout ever since. . . . I can hear singing, and fiddling, and dancing, going forward below stairs, as if nothing was the matter above—my illness seems to promote mirth in the house." His servants are always ready with an excuse:

> A few nights ago, I heard one of my maids creeping softly up stairs several hours after [I thought] every one was gone to sleep; and, being determined to detect her in her intrigue, I called to enquire the meaning of such doings, when the girl, with her hair about her ears, and three quarters undrest, opened the door with, *Law Sir! I am so glad, it isn't so, for I dreamed that how you was dead, and so I slipt on a few things, and came up to listen whether I could hear you.* I knew it was all a lie, yet I was fairly silenced by it.

"I know as little of what goes on in the house, as if I was a lodger. . . . Last year one of my maids was ill upwards of two months; I really believe she laid in in my house, and as far as I know the bantling is there now. I have a strong suspicion that my gardener and housekeeper are married, and only stay with me till they can crib things enow to furnish a house with. . . . If a bachelor had as many eyes as Argus he would be cheated." Wryly he concludes: "Now if I had married in proper time, all these evils had been prevented. I should have had somebody to have cared for, and been cared for by" (No. 3, May 1775). The domestic milieu of bachelor's hall is vividly rendered. The gout-ridden master is at the mercy of his fun-loving, philandering servants who take advantage of his illness to run riot downstairs and are always ready with an alibi.

"As badly off as I am," declares the Old Bachelor, "I had rather be a solitary bachelor, than a *miserable* married man. No wife is better than a bad one, and the same of a husband." Consider the causes of unhappy marriages. There are "the rash and amorous, whose hearts are ever glowing with desire," and who marry to appease this desire. Then there are those who "hunt out a wife as they go to *Smithfield* for a horse; and inter-marry fortunes, not minds, or even bodies"; whereas "the rash who marry inconsiderately, perish in the storms raised by their own passions, these slumber away their days in a sluggish calm, and rather dream they live, than experience it by a series of actual sensible enjoyments." "As matrimonial happiness then is neither the result of insipidity, or illgrounded passion, surely those, who make their court to age, ugliness, and all that's detestable both in mind and body, cannot hope to find it, tho' qualified with all the riches that avarice covets, or *Plutus* could bestow." Let us emulate the American Indian who believes there should be "mutual affection" in marriage, convinced that "God made us all in pairs; each has his mate somewhere or other; and 'tis our duty to find each other out, since no creature was ever intended to be miserable" (No. 4, June 1775).

The Old Bachelor can console himself if he will with a Philadelphia tradesman's account of the expense and trouble he was at in taking his wife to visit Mrs. Snip in New York. "As our daughter *Jenny*, could by no means be left at home, many and great were the preparations to equip Miss, and her mother, for this important journey . . . my purse sweat at every pore." When we were ready, "the old negroe wench was called in, and the charge of the house delivered to her care—the two apprentices and the hired maid received many wholesome instructions and cautions for their conduct during our absence—all which they most liberally promised to observe." Many were the difficulties we encountered on the way. The chaise overturned and "we were all tumbled hickledy-pickledy into the dirt. Miss *Jenny*'s face all bloody—the woods echo with her cries; my wife in a fainting fit, and I in great misery, secretly and devoutly wishing cousin *Snip* at the d——l." At New York "we tarried a tedious week. My wife spent me a great deal of money in purchasing a hundred useless articles, which *we could not possibly do without.* . . . On the seventh day, however, my wife and her cousin *Snip* had a very warm debate, respecting the comparative elegancies and advantages of the cities of *New York* and *Philadelphia.* . . . The next morning my wife declared that my business absolutely required my attendance at home." After "many distressing disasters, after much vexation and trouble, we at length arrived at our own door," only to learn "that one of the apprentices had gone off with the hired maid, no body knew where,—the old negroe wench had got drunk, fallen into the fire, and burned out one of her eyes,—and my wife's best china bowl was broke to pieces. My wife's usual ingenuity contrived to throw the blame of all these misfortunes upon me." "This is only a miniature picture in the decorations of the married state," the tradesman informs Mr. Aitken, "which I hold up to the view of your Old Bachelor, in hopes it may tend to abate his choler, and reconcile him in some degree to a single life" ("Consolation for the Old Bachelor," June 1775). The Old Bachelor replies that the tradesman is hen-pecked, "and hens never triumph over any other than a dunghill cock; the want of dignity in the one begets insult in the other. . . . A governing woman is never truly happy, nor a submitting husband perfectly reconciled. . . . when a woman acts the man, the man acts the fool. . . . Were I young and had a wife you should see other doings" (No. 5, July 1775). The tradesman's journey to New York is filled with realistic details: the impudent carters who obstruct the way, his panicky wife and tearful daughter troubled on board the ferry by flies and their kicking horse, the accident on Rocky Hill caused by the wife's seizing the wrong rein. Such details suggest that Hopkinson might have succeeded as a picaresque novelist.

"Oh! that I had been made an oyster!" frets the Old Bachelor. "I should have propagated my species in a numerous offspring, without the help, without the plagues, without the expence of a female assistant. . . . Tis true I should forfeit what are called the enjoyments of life; that is, I should not eat turtlesoup and venison, 'till I nauseated both, nor drink Madeira and claret 'til my head aked—true—neither should I be tormented with the treachery of servants, the hypocrisy of relations and nominal friends, or the insults and sarcasms of my fellow oysters." Languishing in bed with a cold, neglected by his servants who "rioted and plundered below,"

> I supposed myself dead—I saw my own funeral—Not a single tear to embalm my memory. A few straggling neighbours attend the scanty procession, conversing on politics as they follow me to the grave.——The following day some person in the next street asks one of my near neighbours, 'How does the old bachelor, I hear he is sick.'—'He was sick, but he is well enough now; he was buried yesterday.'—'Dear me! I never heard it: how has the old Curmudgeon left his estate?'—'To the Pennsylvania hospital.'—No more is said about me—they pass on to other chat. After three days I am no more remembered than if I had never

existed—except by the managers of the Pennsylvania hospital.—No widow to be visited and comforted for the loss of me: No children to keep my name and memory alive in the world, and to talk of their father some ten or a dozen years after my decease.

Officious relatives pestered him with questions about his will, and his doctor "denied me every thing I desired, and forced upon me every thing I loathed and abhored." At last he persuaded an old negro servant to bring him cool water. "It threw me into a profuse sweat, and a deep sleep.—It saved my life.—I began to recover from that time." Whenever he wishes he had married as a young man, he has only to "look round amongst my acquaintances, and see an insulting tyrannical wife, a reprobate spendthrift son, and a daughter running off with the first vagabond that offers"; then he blesses his stars that he is single. "Upon the whole, I *find* so many reasons to wish I was a married man, and see so many reasons to rejoice that I am not, that I am like the pendulum of a clock, hanging in suspence, and perpetually vibrating between two opinions" (No. 6, October 1775). This number illustrates the conversational tone of the series as a whole. Embedded in the narrative is question-and-answer dialogue, further evidence of Hopkinson's novelistic ability.

Prompted by the Old Bachelor's last number, a correspondent "L.D." sends a copy of "a curious *Bachelor's* will" to Mr. Aitken, "intending it as a model for your old gentleman in case he should take it in his head to leave the fretful state of celibacy":

I W.N. of D. in the county of S. bachelor, being sound both in body and mind, but apprehensive I shall shortly quit this vain and forlorn state of celibacy; which I hope to exchange for a more comfortable and happy one, through the aid and indulgence of a kind and virtuous help-meet; do make and ordain this my last will and testament, in a manner and form following:

IMPRIMIS. I give and bequeath, to my good friend, Mr. W.M. all my manor of *Long-Delay*: consisting and being made up of the several farms and messuages, called, or known, by the names of *Doubts, Fears, Bashfulness, Irresolution, Uncertainty, Ficklness, Obstinacy,* &c. &c. &c. . . .

ITEM. I give and bequeath unto my good friend, Mr. J.A. my dwelling-house and courtlage; called by the name of *Vain-Hopes.* . . .

W.N. desires his executor Mr. J.A. to write "an epithalamium on this happy occasion; in order that this my departure, into the blessed regions of matrimony may be decently celebrated." He further desires that his legatees may by these bequests "be the better fitted, and disposed, to follow me, into that happy state into which I am now about to enter." W.N.'s will, executed "this 20th day of March, A.D. 1765," is witnessed by Marmaduke Matrimony, William Wedlock, and Fanny Forwardly (No. 7, November 1775).

The Old Bachelor goes to the aid of a young lady who fainted when the chair in which she and her mother were riding overturned. Holding her in his arms trying to revive her, "I felt an anxiety I never felt before. Love, though I knew it not, stole into my heart, in the disguise of compassion." Secretly wishing himself twenty years younger so that he might with propriety seek her hand, he was preparing to visit her when accidentally he caught sight of the words on the first leaf of the family Bible, *"George, the son of Thomas and Alice* Sanby was born in the *city* of *London*, on the 10th of October, *anno domini* * * * *," which "lowered the top-sails of my vanity in a moment, and dispersed all the gay ideas I had assembled before me." Nevertheless "I spent the afternoon and a good part of the evening most agreeably" in her company and "returned home in high spirits, much enamoured with the young lady's person, deportment, and amiable disposition, as far as I could discover it on so short an acquaintance. I thought no more on the accident of the family Bible; but indulged myself the remainder of the evening in a thousand golden dreams." In a postscript he informs Mr. Aitken, "Pray let Mr. L.D. know that it is not impossible but I may yet marry, whatever he may think of it; and, if I do (upon a supposition that he is a bachelor) shall not fail to draw a Will according to the plan he offers, and will make him my sole heir and executor, in reward for the pains he hath taken" (No. 8, December 1775).

Aspasia advises the Old Bachelor not to court the young lady, assuring him she has no ulterior motive. "I am no discreet virgin, that has schemes upon your sweet person; nor am I a widow that has just dried up her tears for her last poor dear: Neither have I daughter, sister, or kinswoman, for whom I have formed prudent plans for future settling. I am myself a married woman, and most sincerely hope I shall never be flung into a situation, that can admit of my committing matrimony again." Young ladies who marry older gentlemen are apt to keep different hours:

> I make no doubt but very damp cold nights you have felt these ten years past; you have imagined that if you were married, your night-gown would be folded on a chair, and laid by your bed-side; and that your linen-cap would be regularly shifted every Wednesday and Saturday, and put inside your cotton one, and placed on your pillow; and the cloaths tight tucked in round you; and the servants in their apartments, and the house quiet by the time the watchman called ten o'clock; with many other little subordinate comforts of a like nature. But instead of all this, depend upon it, your wife will have her young friends about her, long after that hour, giggling and tittering at a thousand little freaks and vagaries, that you cannot see into the humour of. In vain may you pull out your watch, or yawn, or complain that you did not sleep well the preceding night: The best you can expect in that case is, that Mrs. Sanby will say, 'Pray, my dear, let me be no restraint on your hours; there's the candle, please to go to bed.' . . . So you take up the candle, and retire to your own chamber; perhaps the lady follows reluctantly, or perhaps she sits up a couple of hours longer, which will appear four to you; for every time the door opens, or a foot is on the stairs you are on the listen, with all the organs of hearing on the full stretch.

"I own I have many pardons to beg of the young lady that you have honoured with so tender a regard, [Mr. Sanby]. But I must confess it is your happiness I have ultimately in view, more than hers." She begs him "to read with attention the Reflections of Marriage, so judiciously and candidly given us by that accurate and discerning writer Epaminondas[43]. . . . Recollect also the humourous and picturesque description of the unfortunate trip to New-York, sent for your consolation" ("To the Bachelor," January 1776). Aspasia pictures the consequences of a January and May marriage. Once again the domestic scene is made to come alive.

Testily the Old Bachelor tells Aspasia "that a bachelor of some standing is not often greatly delighted with the advice or remarks of married ladies when they are too particular." Then, criticizing her mistakes in phraseology, he comments on the expression, "For every time the door opens or a foot is on the stairs you are on the *listen*": "Now, Madam, be pleased to know that *listen* is what we call a *verb*, and not a *substantive noun*, as you have made it in that sentence. . . . my most dear lady, if ever you and I should happen to meet at a friend's house, or if you will condescend to pay my wife a visit the week after my marriage, the moment that you are upon the *speak* I will be upon the *listen*." He wonders what induced her to choose the pseudonym Aspasia: "She was, I admit, a person of some note, a celebrated courtezan in Athens. I also confess that, if we believe some authors of considerable name, she actually became an *unworthy member* of the married state, having by her arts induced Pericles, one of the most eminent orators and statesmen of that city, to marry her. It is not, however, easy to conceive that either of these circumstances recommended her name to you, and therefore I suppose it was her fame for eloquence, in which she is said to have been so eminent, that Pericles was often upon the *listen* in her discourse, and that he was formed by her to the art of speaking" (No. 9, April 1776).

An old maid of forty, encouraged by the tenderness he showed the young lady, addresses the Old Bachelor in a very different fashion from Aspasia:

> If your personal accomplishments are equal to your mental, you cannot but be the favourite of our sex, and your continuing single so long, must have proceeded from your own free choice. Indeed your mental endowments alone, are sufficient to recommend you to any discreet and sensible virgin. . . . I never relished much the pleasure of sense. . . . Knowledge and virtue only I admire. . . . Until I knew the literary merit of you, Mr. Bachelor, my heart was never pierced by Cupid's arrows, and I felt none of the uneasy sensations of love. Your first paper gave me the first wound, your last completed the business, and left me bleeding at your feet.

She finds much merit in St. Paul's injunction, "Be not unequally yoked," since it implies that "an Old Bachelor should marry AN OLD MAID" ("To the Old Bachelor," June 1776).

Conventionally the old bachelor, a character long associated with the periodical essay in England, was good natured, old fashioned, a member of the gentry in easy circumstances, and, especially from the time of Sterne, eccentric. Hopkinson's George Sanby—for the character is largely his creation—stands near the head of a succession of American bachelors, which include Freneau's Hezekiah Salem, Dennie's Lay Preacher, Wirt's Dr. Robert Cecil, Irving's Jonathan Oldstyle, and the whim-whamsical bachelors in *Salmagundi*. Sanby is as memorable a bachelor as any in this gallery, an erstwhile fornicator now experiencing the inconveniences of keeping bachelor's hall, but too chauvinistic to take the plunge into matrimony. Hopkinson demonstrates a novelistic ability to paint a scene, draw a character, and create an incident; witness the vivid milieu of bachelor's hall, characters like Aspasia, and the tradesman's journey to New York. In addition to his admiration for Addison and Steele, Hopkinson was influenced by Laurence Sterne, a Philadelphia edition of whose works appeared in 1774; this influence is most apparent in *Old Bachelor* No. 6, wherein an ailing, self-pitying Sanby imagines how quickly he will be forgotten after his death and, when restored to full health, is perfectly ambivalent toward the married state. Although the series ended abruptly with the demise of the *Pennsylvania Magazine*, what more fitting conclusion than to have an old maid confront an old bachelor with a proposal of marriage.

IV. EARLY SOUTHERN SERIALS

ALTHOUGH there was much belletristic writing in colonial America, letters as a profession did not enjoy the prestige granted law, medicine, and divinity. This was especially true in the South. Willard Thorp observes that if a young southerner "indulged himself in verse-making or essay-writing, he must do so strictly as an amateur. Writing was not a profession."[1] "It requires no small Degree of Resolution to be an *Author*, in a Country where Gentlemen, with little Judgment, are so facetious and satyrical as in this," remarks an anonymous Maryland writer; "he becomes a Mark of publick Censure, and sometimes a standing Object of Raillery and Ridicule."[2] Nevertheless, while southerners built their reputation in one of the respected professions or politics or agriculture, many of them instinctively chose letters as an avocation. "From at least the time of William Byrd II," writes Richard Beale Davis, "the Virginia gentleman had not been averse to employing his pen in brief prose pieces." Many "could and did write their comments on economics, agriculture, politics, literature, and manners to the Williamsburg, Virginia, *Gazette*"; these comments "were in form and purpose, especially those on literature and manners, more like the periodical prose of the *Spectator, Rambler*, and *Citizen of the World*, semi-formal familiar essays."[3] Among Byrd's letters and literary exercises, for example, are sketches of his friends, his enemies, and himself, cast in the form of the eighteenth-century character essay.[4]

I

Newspaper history in the South—and as an important department in it the periodical essay—has its beginning with English-born William Parks, who was appointed public printer of Maryland in 1727 and of Virginia in 1732 and continued active until his death in 1750. In this capacity he established the first southern newspaper at Annapolis in 1727 and another at Williamsburg nine years later. Unlike many early colonial printers, he consistently "made definite and successful effort to encourage local men of letters by the publication of works of purely literary intention," notably the poems of Richard Lewis and Ebenezer Cook in Maryland.[5]

The Maryland Gazette was established in September 1727.[6] Although the paper carried much belletristic writing, original and borrowed, during the six years that Parks edited it, only one literary serial, *The Plain-Dealer*, appeared in its pages, and of its ten numbers only the first two were original.[7] At the outset the Plain-Dealer, arguing the merits of excerpting "from a good Choice of *English* Authors," informs the editor: "All that I propose . . . is, to give the Public a more elegant and useful Entertainment than your Paper has generally afforded them. . . . If you approve my Proposal, and at present want Leisure to proceed therein, I can undertake to supply you with Materials for at least one Month."[8] Perhaps realizing that all the following numbers would be extracted from Ambrose Philips' *Free-Thinker*, the Plain-Dealer confesses: "I do not arrogate to my self the Credit of Inventing *all* those *Speculations*, which by me may be exhibited to the Publick. . . . wheresoever in my Reading, I meet with any Thing which may conduce to the Bettering the Lives, or improving the Conversations of my Country-men, I shall make no Scruple to translate or transcribe it, and retail it." "For my Part," he promises, "I shall spare for no Pains, to make the Thoughts I publish, agreeable and useful, that those who read them, may at once receive Instruction, and Diversion." He concludes, "As to the fairer Part of the Creation, I promise my self a Kind Reception at their Hands, since I propose in the Progress of these Lectures, to point out all those Imperfections that are the Blemishes, as well as those Virtues which are the Embellishment of the Sex; to furnish their Breasts with Knowledge, without fatiguing their tender Spirits in the Attainment of it; so as in the End to set them upon the Level with the Men in their boasted Superiority of Reason, by diverting their Minds from useless Trifles, to give some finishing Touches to those who are already the most beautiful Pieces in human Nature."[9] The Plain-Dealer does indeed offer his readers of both sexes heady fare, discoursing on philosophical doubting (Nos. 3 and 5), poetry and painting (No. 6), superstition (No. 7), virtue and vice (No. 8), and freedom of thought and of government (Nos. 9 and 10). The series as a whole, but especially the fairy tale about Florella whose mother chose to have her grow up witty, beautiful, and unhappy rather than ordinary, ugly, and happy (No. 4), tends to support the view of one scholar that in the decade following the *Tatler* and the *Spectator* fable, allegory, legend, and fairy tale began to appear frequently in English periodical writing.[10]

The Virginia Gazette was established August 6, 1736. In the first issue Parks called for original contributions: "if any ingenious, public-spirited Gentlemen, who have Time to spare, will employ their leisure Hours in the Service of the Publick, by Writing any Speculative Letters, Poems, Essays, Translations, &c. which may tend to the Improvement of Mankind in general or the innocent Diversion or Entertainment of either Sex, without Offence to any in particular, they may depend on a Place in this Paper; and their names concealed if desir'd."[11] In the same issue there appeared the first number of *The Monitor*, a literary serial that will be examined shortly. Three years later, on August 10, 1739, Parks declared that, having originally "propos'd to entertain my Customers, now and then occasionally, or when there was a Scarcity of News, with Pieces Instructive and Diverting," but being disappointed in my expectation of "the Assistance of the Gentlemen of this Country," he has sometimes reprinted "such Pieces, as may answer the Ends propos'd. . . . The Guardians, Spectators, Tatlers, Magazines, &c. are inexhaustible Treasures, out of which may be extracted everything that is necessary for the Support of Virtue, the Suppression of Vice, the Promotion of Learning, Wit, Ingenuity, &c." Even so, more than half of the essays which appeared in the *Gazette* between 1736 and 1766 are, like *The Monitor*, apparently original.[12]

Before examining *The Monitor*, notice should be taken of the only other important literary serial in the *Virginia Gazette*. In January 1752 there was published *Miscellaneous Poems*, a collection of religious poetry by the Presbyterian minister Samuel Davies. Two months later, on March 20, the *Gazette* carried the first part of an eight-installment attack upon Davies' book under the title "REMARKS on the Virginia PINDAR" by "Walter Dymocke Anonymous," who has been identified as the Anglican clergyman John Robertson.[13] The attack continued for four months and in time attracted defenders and counterattackers. Walter Dymocke opens his attack by announcing that "a very ingenious Writer has lately published two whole Books of Divine Poems, judiciously selected from a much larger Number, which laid by him in Manuscript, with a learned Preface before them. . . . I intend a short Criticism upon his Performance, in order to justify that Character which He Himself . . . has given of it to the Public." In subsequent essays Dymocke quotes lines from Davies in order to ridicule them, a method which makes treatment of this serial difficult short of familiarizing the reader with the poems themselves.[14]

Although the first five issues of the *Virginia Gazette* are not extant, the fact that the sixth issue, on September 10, 1736, carried *Monitor* No. 6 makes it all but certain that the first five numbers of the series appeared in the first five issues of the newspaper. Seventeen numbers of *The Monitor* survive.[15] The fact that *Monitor* Nos. 6, 7, and 9 are signed "X," "S," and "I" suggests multiple authorship. It seems likely, the more so since it was apparently the officers at the College of William and Mary who petitioned the Assembly to let Parks come to Williamsburg, that a group connected with the College collaborated to write these essays.[16] In all probability the first number of *The Monitor* reiterated Parks' request in his first editorial for essays "which may tend to the Improvement of Mankind in general or the innocent Diversion or Entertainment of either Sex"; indeed, in the eleventh number a correspondent reminds the Monitor of "the Design you have undertaken of adding to the Instruction of your Readers, while you entertain them, and of mixing their Improvement with their Diversion" (October 29, 1736).

The Monitor bears out the observation: "Literary London was far nearer Williamsburg than Boston,"[17] in that it conforms closely in manner and matter to the English periodical essay. There is less in this serial relating it to a local milieu than in northern serials of the same period like the *Dogood* and *Busy-Body* papers or even in *The Meddlers Club* of Charleston. Nevertheless, *The Monitor* manages the conventions and ranges through the traditional subjects in a way that is lively and engaging. At the moment we meet the Monitor, who must surely have been introduced in the earlier missing numbers, he is surprised as he lolls in his elbow-chair by the appearance of a creature who demands an interview. She introduces herself as "a Woman of Fashion . . . born and bred in *France*," who has six daughters capable of serving the Monitor:

> There's my Eldest Daughter Miss *Leer*, is as good a Girl at Attraction as any in the Country. . . . Then my Second, Miss *Sly* . . . she's as Secret as Death. . . . My Third Daughter, Miss *Fidget*; She's here and there and every where; she never misses a Tea-Table, if there be Ten within the Compass of her Visits in a Day. There she hears Slander, Back biting, and Scandal; which may turn out to some Use. . . . As to my Fourth Daughter, *Amoret* . . . She's for ever moist'ning her Lips with her Tongue, that gives them a pouting Ripeness that tempts all the young Fellows in the Town; then she's a Girl of a very inquisitive Temper. . . . My Fifth Daughter, *Phillis*; She's an unaccountable Girl. The first Week of every Moon, she's dying for Love of some *Adonis*, or other. She's for ever receiving or answering of *Billet-deux*, and Scraps of Poetry; which may not be amiss. . . . As to my youngest Daughter, *Euphemia*; She's courted by Sir *Politick Wou'd-be*.

The Monitor agrees to employ them, but first administers the Free Masons' oath behind locked doors (No. 6, September 10, 1736). Even as the Monitor, "having settled the different Emploiments of my Female Assistants, according to their several Capacities, [orders] them, at the End of every Week, at farthest, to make a Return of all their Remarks, Letters, Poems, Billet-deux, &c. to the Club," Miss Fidget reports on fashion mongering (No. 7, September 17, 1736). Her "Diligence and Assiduity to be the First" in the Monitor's favor causes so great a dispute among the other assistants that he settles matters at once by appointing Miss Leer "Sister, in the Service of the Club; Miss *Sly*, for Observation; Miss *Fidget*, for Scandal; Miss *Amoret*, for Discoveries; Miss *Phillis*, for Love Affairs; and Miss *Euphemia*, for Politics" (No. 8, October 1, 1736). Here, then, we meet the Monitor's club of female assistants.[18] The distribution of duties among the six makes clear the predominantly social nature of the series. But, as in the case of *Proteus Echo*, there is little attempt hereafter to develop the club; four of the assistants communicate only once and Phillis and Euphemia not at all.

The character of the Monitor, however, is developed. Miss Fidget reports that his name was brought up at the card table: "O, Lud! says Mr. *Bergamot*, don't name the stupid Toad,——I think him every Day worse and worse. Truly, says Mr. *Timothy Qual*, I think we People of Fashion, ought to suppress him, and put a Stop to such a Heap of Nonsense; but I suppose (with a wise Leer,) the poor Devil has a Share with the Printer" (No. 15, November 26, 1736). Out riding one day, the Monitor hears "the Cry of Hounds, and my Horse (for want of Exercise) grew Headstrong, and carried me in the midst of them. . . . After I had taken a thorough View of them, I went away: I had not gone a Quarter of a Mile, but the Gentleman, that was Master of the Hounds, overtook me, and press'd me to go to his House and dine with him. I accepted of his Offer; and met with an elegant Entertainment, and a round Company." But when they begin losing their tempers, the Monitor begs to be excused in spite of his host's entreaties that he spend the night (No. 16, December 10, 1736). In an essay that reflects the then current interest in *Arabian Nights* literature, the Monitor gives the history of his metamorphosis, from human being to dog to ape to bear and back to his human form again. As an ape he "was turn'd over to the Bishop of *Toulon*, as Train-bearer at the Office of *high Mass*," and as a bear he was about to be killed by dogs at Hockley in the Hole when Doctor Faustus waved his wand "and I instantly re-assum'd my first Body, to the great Surprise of the Spectators. . . . These Transformations and Transmigrations, may seem strange to some incredulous People; therefore, to prove the Veracity, and make it incontestable, I refer you to *Plato's* Book of his Republic," which proves that they "are as liable to this Part of the World as any other." "I regard no Hours," concludes the Monitor; "by Day or by Night every Man is welcome. My House stands in the midst of a Wood; and for the Ease of Travellers [who?] are disposed to visit me, my Man *Dominic* has been employ'd for this Month past, to set up Hands in all cross Roads, to prevent Gentlemen losing their Way." Able to unfold such mysteries as the interpretation of dreams, "I am no *Empirick*, as to *Divinity; Physic;* and *Law*: As I propose to deal honourably by Mankind, I leave each Profession to each Professor" (No. 17, December 31, 1736). The character of the Monitor is not as sharply defined nor as memorable as that, say, of Silence Dogood or the Old Bachelor (George Sanby).

Toward the end of the series, however, his character comes into sharper focus when he and Zoilus charge each other with being dunces and writing nonsense. Zoilus, determined "to clear the World of that worst Kind of Vermin, Scribblers," touches off this debate by admonishing,

> This *Monitor* pretends to preach
>   In sacred Wisdom's Schools;
> But I'll a useful Lesson teach,
>   Worth all his silly Rules;
> By which he'll mend, what's gone before;
> And this is, *Never to write more.* (January 21, 1736/7)

"My worthy Friend *Zoilus*, intimates, he was in a perfect good Humour when he wrote his Song," replies the Monitor. "*I believe him sincerely*: And, in Answer, I can assure him nothing can make me ill-natur'd, at this Juncture, but the want of Wood and a chearful Glass." Thereupon the Monitor retorts,

> Since injur'd Wit is thus reliev'd,
>   By such an able Pen,
> *Zoilus* the First!——the First receiv'd,
>   We hope will write again;
> Whose Works, no doubt, will stand the Test!
> Believe me, Sirs,——they're void of Jest. (No. 19,
>   January 28, 1736/7)

"There is no Tribe of *Mortals* so incorrigible, as your *Mortal-Writers*," Zoilus informs Parks. "The Person with whom I am at present engaged, is not only to be reckoned among these, but has long since been absolutely dead; and his Corps only, for these Five or Six Months past, has stalked about to the great Nuisance of the Publick." Zoilus concludes his rebuttal by announcing:

> To all Gentlemen and Ladies, who delight in the Noble and Princely Diversion of Hunting: This is to give Notice, That a Dunce will be hunted every other Friday, in the Gazette, 'til he is fairly run down. He is an Animal of a most peculiar and singular

Nature; being very long-winded and pertinacious; and is known to afford excellent Sport, having tired more People, than all the Foxes that ever Yorkshire produced. He is intirely void of defensive Arms; but if he be left at full Liberty, he has a certain offensive Weapon, something like a Gray-Goose Quill, through which is distilled an atramentous, poisonous Juice, which has often had most dismal and calamitous Effects, and has been observed, instantly, and at first sight, to deprive several Persons of all Manner of Patience. And, that he may be hunted to some Tune, Musick shall attend the Company in the Field; and after the Chase is over, the Gentlemen and Ladies shall be diverted with a Song. So, God save the King. (February 4, 1736/7)

Criptonimus, one of the Monitor's correspondents, dreams that on a trip to Williamsburg he espied a man, "*a true Emblem of Solidity,*" carrying books with such titles as *The Pearl of Eloquence, A Help to Discourse,* and *The Spiritual Mouse-Trap*: Or, *The painful Speaking Trumpet to his Auditors*. "In about a Quarter of an Hour, a Lady appear'd; her Mien was tatter'd, *a fierte* in her Looks, and very hagged; her Garment was Patch-work, compos'd of *Verse* and *Prose*." The two embrace and go into a large brick building arm in arm. In an attempt to discover the identity of the man, replies the Monitor, "I have taken some Pains to consult the Stars; and if I am right, the first Letter of his *Character*, is the last in the *Alphabet*." The lady is no other than the Goddess of Dulness (No. 22, February 25, 1736/7). Zoilus, convinced that the Monitor "writes Nonsense," ridicules his last song: "He accuses me of Bombast, and the Lord knows what; whether justly or not, must be left to the Determination of others. My only Design was, to rid the *Press* of so empty and incorrect a *Scribbler*; which End being obtain'd, I shall leave Room for an abler Pen" (March 18, 1736/7). With these words the heated interchange between the Monitor and Zoilus comes to a close.

In addition to the persona and the club *The Monitor* makes use of other conventions associated with the periodical essay: dream vision, metamorphosis, fictitious letter, mock-advertisement. Notice has already been taken of Criptonimus' dream vision about Zoilus and the Goddess Dulness and the Monitor's history of his metamorphosis. Besides letters from members of the club there are others from the Reverend Gentleman "J," Zachary Downright, Timothy Forecast, Criptonimus, and of course Zoilus. And there is an announcement about a gentleman who admires Miss Amoret: "Whereas a *Gentleman*, who, towards the latter End of the Summer, usually wore a Blue Camlet Coat lin'd with Red, and trim'd with Silver, a Silver-lac'd Hat, and a Tupee Wig, has been often observ'd by *Miss Amoret*, to look very languishingly at her the said *Amoret*, and particularly one Night during the last Session of Assembly, at the Theatre, the said *Gentleman* ogled her in such a Manner, as shew'd him to be very far gone; the said *Miss Amoret* desires the *Gentleman* to take the first handsome Opportunity that offers, to explain himself on that Subject. N.B. She believes he has very pretty Teeth" (No. 11, October 29, 1736).

The Monitor fulfills his promise to instruct and entertain the reader by ranging through the conventional subjects, notably manners. He and his assistants discuss French fashions,[19] being in love,[20] keeping one's temper,[21] tale-bearing,[22] good nature,[23] and hoops. Happening upon a company of scandal-mongering ladies at tea, Miss Fidget tells the Monitor that one of them asked her: "did you observe Miss *Airy* in Company last *Sunday*? . . . when she enter'd the Doors, I could not tell what to take her for: Her Hoop was of such a prodigious Extent, that I wonder'd how she got in; and her Gown pinn'd up to such a monstrous Height behind, that her Head but just appear'd visible above it." "What a shameful and preposterous Thing is it," observes the Monitor, "that the most beautiful Part of the Creation, should run into such monstrous Extravagancies of Dress; which, instead of setting them off (as they pretend) make them only appear abominably ridiculous. . . . probably, in a short Time, this mountainous Heap which they now wear behind, will rise up as high as their Shoulders; and then a Hump-back will be accounted no Piece of Deformity" (No. 7, September 17, 1736). Compared with Silence Dogood's essay on hoops, this one is unimaginative and inadequately developed—just the sort of composition an undergraduate, bound by the example of the *Spectator*, might have produced.

It is indicative of the essentially lighthearted tone of *The Monitor* that morality is seldom dwelt upon. The Reverend Gentleman "J" expresses the hope "that we may see, in these our Days, Virtue and good Manners, encouraged, Vice and Folly depressed, and Mankind reformed." Speaking in his professional capacity, he observes: "should we suffer our Time and Pains to be taken up with entering upon Details of little Peccadillos, half Vice, half Folly, it were a kind of Prostitution of our Function. . . . In such Cases, therefore, the *Press* is a natural and necessary Auxiliary to the Pulpit: 'Tis our Light Horse, whilst we attack the main Body of Atheism, Profaneness, and Immorality, makes Excursions abroad, picks up little straggling Parties of inferior Enormities, and, if I may use the Expression, reaches, within Pistol-shot, what escapes the Brunt of our Canons" (No. 11, October 29, 1736). This minister, urging the Monitor to encourage virtue and decry vice, employs an effective military figure to describe the respective roles of pulpit and press. He hopes that the Monitor's female assistants "will not fail to give you all Intelligence necessary to the carrying on so good and useful a Design." Shortly one of these assistants furnishes such intelligence. Reading Helena Fidget's account of the frequenters of the card table, one of whom tells her, "the Business of my Life is Eating, Drinking, Sleeping, Dressing, and going Abroad," the Monitor maintains that Idleness "is the Seminary of Mischief, and frequently the total Ruin of those that give Way to it. . . . Ambition, Pride, and Envy, are his constant Attendants; and, when once a Stop is put to his Career, he is the most miserable of Mankind" (No. 15, November 26, 1736).

In a manner reminiscent of William Byrd's characterization of a prude,[24] the Monitor assures his assistant Arabella Sly, who was chided by Miss Tancrede for laughing at a humorous scene in *The Beaux' Stratagem* without putting her fan before her face, "There is nothing more commendable in the Fair Sex, than a free and easy Behaviour: A Woman of Sense may take all innocent Liberties, without deserving that malicious Title of a Coquet; and may observe a proper Decorum, without coming under the Censure of a Prude." He then relates the unsuccessful courtship of a prude:

> Honest *Jack Pamflino* informs me, that he observed a strict Decorum at his first Approach, and had the Humour to salute her Cheek: At his first Visit he remark'd her whole Time was emploied to keep her Feet from peeping from under her Petticoat, and examining the Pins of her Neck-Handkerchief, lest one of them should be displac'd, and expose the charms that lay under

Cover. . . . The discourse running upon the News of the Town, he unluckily, related a Fact of a certain Lady's losing her Garter in the Drawing Room: upon which she flew out of Company in a great Passion, and was above a Fortnight before she would be reconcil'd to receive another Visit from him. . . . The Day of Marriage being fix'd, honest *Jack* thought himself sure of his Mistress; but, unfortunately, happen'd to praise the Fashion of the Ladies wearing their Stays low before; which exasperated the Virtuous Dame in such a Manner, that she declared, that the Very Expression was indecent: This put her into another Phrenzy, discarded her Lover, never to see him more.

Three weeks later she married a country gentleman who died a few days after. "The Lady, so disconsolate at the Loss of her Husband, was not to be comforted; her Affliction insupportable; and, had it not been for another Lover which she accepted of in Three Days after the Funeral, she was resolv'd, like the *Ephesian* Dame, to have been interr'd with her dear Husband" (No. 9, October 15, 1736). We learn that Byrd's prude, who would "sink into the ground if anybody should see my ankle," has had a child by her uncle's coachman. Miss Tancrede's behavior is more hypocritical still. She calls to mind Petronius' discreet Ephesian widow who, being determined to die in the vault where her recently dead husband has been laid, is induced by an amorous soldier to take food and presently to accept him as her lover.

In the first of two essays which examine the qualifications for criticizing music, the Monitor asserts that "altho' the Ear is the Vehicle of the Sounds in Musick, as the Eye is of the Colours in Painting; yet the Pleasure of the One, as well as the Other does not consist in the Perception of Sounds or Colours, but in the Perception of Harmony, Beauty, or Symmetry arising from them. . . . To call Musick therefore a Pleasure of the Ear, is no less improper, than it would be to stile Reading the Pleasure of the Eye, or Writing the Pleasure of the Hand." Unless men are moved by harmony, they should not set themselves up as experts. "I warn them from intermeddling with it in any Manner whatsoever; for Fear of making that foolish Figure which is so well describ'd in the old Proverb, *Asinus ad Lyram*" (No. 10, October 22, 1736). Zachary Downright, having read these remarks, assures the Monitor that music is lost on most people.

80

When he attended the opera in London, he noted that "tho' not a Hundredth Part of the Audience either understood Musick, or Italian; yet, when a *Connoisseur* gave the Word, 'twas Tinder to the Soul. O Cara! Bravo! Bravissimo! &c. went thro' the House. . . . at last, I grew tir'd of the Expence, and asham'd at my Folly, for throwing away so much Money, and more Time, upon a Jargon of Sounds, without Sense." My father and mother "made as much Harmony between them, as I have heard at any One of these Operas; My Mother had as shrill a Pipe as ever was heard; My Father as deep a Bass; both excellent Lungs. . . . Sometimes they went off together like unto a full *Orchestra*, that made the House ring again; the first whose Breath fail'd, made a Pause for a few *Bars*, whilst the other carried it on; then joyn'd; then single; and often ended as they begun." The Monitor reiterates, "A good Ear has infinitely more Right to form a Judgment on the Matter at Hand, at an Entertainment of Musick, than a Man who has spent a Life in *Rapin, Aristotle,* or *Bossu* without it" (No. 12, November 5, 1736). Early in the *Spectator* a number of the critical papers discuss English opera with more particularity than these *Monitor* essays on harmony; however, the discussion here is amusingly domesticated by Zachary's account of how his mother and father harmonized.

On one occasion the Monitor, after the manner of Addison's "Will of a Virtuoso" (*Tatler* No. 216), engages in humor for its own sake. He informs the public that "on *Monday* the Sixth Day of *December* next, in the Evening, between the Hours of Five and Nine, will be sold, by Inch of Candle, at our *Club-Room*, a small, but curious, Collection of RARITIES, Part of the Personal Estate of my old Friend Jack *Nearsight*, deceas'd." Among the lots to be sold are "The *Timpanum*, or Drum, of a Mouse's Ear," "The *Diaphragma* of a Louse," and "The *Os Pubis* of a Wasp." The ninth and final lot consists of "A *Small Cap* made out of the false Belly of a *Possum*, neatly dress'd; With many other Curiosities of the like Kind. Also several Pieces of *Poetry*, particularly One upon a *Spider*, which was the first Production of his Brain after he became a *Virtuoso*." It reads in part:

> Insidious, restless, watchful Spider,
> Fear no officious Damsel's Broom:
> Extend thy artful Fabric wider,

And spread thy Banners round my Room. . . .
Whilst I thy wondrous Fabrick stare at,
  And think on hapless Poet's Fate;
Like thee, confin'd to lonely Garret,
  And rudely banish'd Rooms of State.
And as from out thy tortur'd Body,
  Thou draw'st thy tender Strings with Pain,
So does he labour, like a Noddy,
  To spin Materials from his Brain. . . .
Thus far 'tis plain you both agree,
  Your Deaths perhaps may better shew it,
'Tis Ten to One, but Penury,
  Ends both the Spider, and the Poet.

"There is likewise a *Satyr*, upon the *Freshes* of *James* River. And a *Panegyrick*, upon the *Oisters* of *York* River." Then this final note: "Virtuoso's are allow'd to view the Goods from the last of this Month, to the Day of Sale, *Sunday* excepted" (No. 14, November 19, 1736). In much the way that Jack Nearsight's goods are to be disposed of at auction, Addison's Nicholas Gimcrack bequeaths to his wife "One box of butterflies, one drawer of shells, a female skeleton, dried cockatrice," to his daughter Elizabeth "My receipt for preserving dead caterpillars, as also my preparations of winter May-dew, and embryo-pickle," and to his doctor "My rat's testicles and whale's pizzle."

The Monitor, while closely imitative of English periodicals, is a spirited, wholly social serial such as a group of college undergraduates might well have composed. To be sure, it is flawed. The appearance of Zoilus suggests that the author, or more likely authors, were running out of material and seeking by this device to keep the series alive. Seldom do we, as in the reference to "the *Oisters* of *York* River," glimpse the Virginia scene; the tea and card table society visited by Miss Fidget resembles London more nearly than Williamsburg. Moreover, the syntax is at times uncertain and the satire often crude. In spite of such shortcomings, *The Monitor* stands forth as a memorable performance. Even though we do not have a full portrait of the Monitor (after all, the first five numbers are missing), he emerges as an individualized character. His club, although patterned after the Fiddle-faddle Club in the *Grubstreet Journal*, is lively, especially its most active members, Helena Fidget and

Arabella Sly. The Monitor's account of his metamorphosis is handled with considerable skill. Overall the series succeeds within its modest limits.

II

The South-Carolina Gazette was established at Charleston on January 8, 1731/2, and with occasional short suspensions ran until December 1775. Until the eve of the Revolution the editors tried to avoid offending the constituted authorities.[25] Thomas Whitmarsh, the first editor, at once asked that his contributors "carefully avoid giving Offence, either publick, or private; and particularly, that they forbear all Controversies, both in Church and State," assuring his readers:

> I'm not High-Church, nor Low Church, nor Tory, nor Whig,
> No flatt'ring young Coxcomb, nor formal old Prig. . . .
> Any faults of my Friends I wou'd scorn to expose,
> And detest private Scandal, tho' cast on my Foes. . . .
> No Man's Person I hate, tho' his Conduct I blame,
> I can Censure a Vice, without stabbing a Name. . . .
> To no Party a Slave, in no Squabble I join;
> Nor damn the Opinion, that differs from mine.[26]

Later editors reiterated this policy of neutrality. On May 6, 1751, Peter Timothy, alluding to satiric verses he had published, expressed the hope that "my Publication of them will offend *no one Person*, especially, as my Chief End is to encourage the poetical Spirit that has but lately made its Appearance amongst us." In spite of such professions the *Gazette* sometimes engaged in controversy, notably when the Methodist preacher George Whitefield visited Charleston in 1740.[27]

Those who contributed to the *Gazette* "took Addison and Steele for their models, adding Johnson and Goldsmith toward the middle of the century."[28] Individual essays began appearing as early as the second number, and in 1735 *The Meddlers Club*, a serial whose name calls to mind Franklin and Breintnall's *Busy-Body*, ran for a short time. "We have forsooth set up for Reformers . . . or Meddlers of Nobody's business, or to speak plainer, of every body's," explains Bob Careless, who is delegated to introduce this "parcel of young illiterate Fellows assembled together" to erect a club. Jack-would-be-taller, "tho' he is the least person among us, yet according to the old Proverb, *of little head great Wit*, we have, and I hope not unjustly, thought that a littly Body must have most Sense. His Talent consists chiefly in contradicting others, and thinks he knows more than all the Club." Tom Snigger's "Talent lies most in telling Stories, and because no body else will, laughs at them himself." Dick Haughty "thinks merit no where but in fine Clothes, but is otherwise a very agreable person." Will Generous "is not covetous, tho' a little conceited." Ralph Hippo "was formerly Clerk to a Horse Doctor, from whom *Ralpo* has gain'd so much Experience, that he is ever boasting, that he believes himself able to wash the fairest Woman's hands clean when they are dirty, if she would let him, tho' perhaps it might cost her Life." As for myself, says Bob, "I am the most careless Fellow breathing." "You may depend upon hearing from us once a month without fail, especially if the Town receive [our performances] well. . . . we have resolved not to meddle with Church or State Affairs, but to learn Morality ourselves (which we want God knows), satyrize our Friends, and speak well of our Enemies. . . . We derived our name from a *Medlar*, as some call it, which is never ripe till rotten, and I believe we shall be the same" (August 16, 1735). Will Generous sends an account of some of the club's proceedings. The other five members having debated whether an author can be known by what he writes, Will tells them "that it was common for People to debase every thing themselves are incapable of doing, altho' it was obvious, that the Itch of Scribling was very predominant at this Time: yet there were few that could write well, and they that could, would not. . . . I believe there are many abler pens in this part of the World, than any of our six, yet if they won't take up the cause, I think no body can justly blame us for our good Intentions" (August 23).

In the third number (August 30) the members offer their opinions on "the *Vice of the Bay*":

—Says *Dick Haughty*, I can't help taking Notice of the great Concourse of People of both Sexes that assembles on the Bay almost every Evening. . . . in my Opinion, it is a Custom that will never resound to the Honour of *Carolina*, and tends to promote Vice and Irreligion in many Degrees. . . . I think there are many more fitting places to walk on than the Bay: For have we not many fine Greens near the Town much better accommodated for Air, than a Place which continually has all the nauseous Smells of Tarr, Pitch, Brimstone, &c. and what not, and where every *Jack Tarr* has the Liberty to view & remark the most celebrated Beauties of *Charles-Town*, and where besides (if any Air is) there's such a continual Dust, that I should think it were enough to deter any Lady from appearing, least her Organs of perspiration should be stopt, and she be suffocated.

'Besides, says *Ralph Hippo*, Salt-Water Air does not agree with chaste and virtuous Minds, for 'tis notorious that Sea-faring Men are more venerial than others." "I shall only add, says *Tom Snigger*, that I have heard it said, that most Women love Sea-faring Men better than Land-Men, and who knows but most that appear there do it with a design to pick up a Sea spark." Jack-would-be-taller has the final word:

> . . . should one of those illustrious Fair Ones happen to be singled out by one who was no better than a common *Jack Tarr*, but should have borrowed some finer Clothes, and should pretend to be a Gentleman, and tho' of so short an Acquaintance as two or three Evenings, after promising the Fair One Marriage, should find her pliant, desire her to walk a little further in private, and there perform what I dare not name,
>
> > *The willing Fair she soon consents,*
> > *Till marks appear, she then repents.*
>
> What a Scandal is here brought upon her Friends, if she has any! and a Disgrace to herself as long as she lives; and all this occasion'd by the Vice of the bay.

Diogenes Rusticus' letter to the printer, Lewis Timothy, ended the series abruptly: "I (who am your Subscriber and a *Carolinian*) thought I might as well for once see something from myself in your Paper, at a time when it has been lately fill'd with so unedifying and impertinent Stuff, from a Club rightly by themselves termed *Meddlers*. . . . I am sorry that they think so much of their own parts, that they would make the World believe they were *Carolinians*, when their Performance is so void of Sense, and their Design (if I may so call it) but sprung from the spurious Issue of a boosy-bottle." As for "the Vice of the Bay," "I think the Ladies are much obliged to the worthy Censors for cautioning them against *Jack Tarrs* in Gentlemens Coats; and with an Air of severity, desire they wou'd spend their evening walk on the Green, which I dare answer for them, they think much more proper for their Occasions than the Bay, the most frequented place in Town, thereby intimating their Desire to give a green Gown behind a Pine Bush, which wou'd be more pleasant than in a Cart" (September 6). This short series is built around the convention of the club, whose members profess to be readers of (and three of them subscribers to) the *South-Carolina Gazette*. Except for Ralph Hippo they lack the professional identity that helps individualize those of earlier English clubs like the Trumpet and the Spectator. Realizing that they have less wit than "a Waterman's Boy, or a Pye-corner Bard," they will nevertheless continue to meddle until "some more abler shall take up the Cudgels." The liveliest moment in the series occurs during the debate on the dangerous custom the fair sex have of walking and taking the evening air by the wharves rather than on the greens. This essay deserves to stand in company with the best of contemporary English essays, allowing us to glimpse life in colonial Charleston. It is unfortunate that after so promising a beginning *The Meddlers Club* should have proved abortive; all too soon Diogenes Rusticus takes up the cudgels and brings the series to an end.

The only full-fledged literary serial in the *South-Carolina Gazette,* appearing in the winter of 1753-54, was authored by "The Humourist."[29] Eccentricity is the hallmark of the Humourist's character. He describes himself as "a Man of a peculiar odd Way of Thinking" (November 26, 1753); "an Oddity, composed of strange Humours, full of Peculiarities; sometimes volatile, then solemn; sometimes flighty, at another Time sedate; one Minute in the Garret, and the next in the Cellar" (February 26, 1754). "The utmost Aim of my Compositions," he assures the reader, "shall be directed to please; and if I now and then chance to tour uncommon Heights, the World must understand that I am improving the Method of Writing, and that my Habitation is the Air" (November 26, 1753). "My body is small, my soul capacious, and my stature low. . . . I am possessed of an excellent perspective. . . . I term it the *Otacousticon*: By the help of this amazing machine, I can observe cuckold's horns, the philosopher's stone, and new projectors; I can discover windmills in one man's head, and hornet's nests in another" (December 10, 1753). Later in the series, on February 12, 1754, he warns modern critics:

Preserve a proper and respectable Distance, a reverential Awe to my Authority, or I will assume the Wings of *Icaromenippus*, and fly to my aerial Mansion (now ready for the Reception of its Master) and hurl Confusion on you.

If a People are to fear, it is necessary to know, whom they are to fear; the Brave are ever just. Know then, that I was born under a Planet not to die in a Lazaretto. The hot Constellation of *Cancer* presided at my Nativity. *Mars* was then predominant. Of all the Elements, *Fire* sways most in me. I have many Aspirings, many elevated Conceptions, owing, for the most Part, to the peculiar Quality of the Ground whereon I was born, which was the Top of a Hill situated South-East, so that the House must be *illustrious*, being so obvious to the Sun-Beams.

I have made a Rule, that whoever shall insinuate a Laugh, a distant Joke, or otherwise, on my Writings, and shall not own my Performance to be the best wrote Pieces in the World, the Classics only excepted, shall be look'd upon as a Coxcomb, and——; and I do hereby give any Man leave to lay him on his Center of Gravity.

Although the Humourist advertised on December 10, 1753, for "several artificers, mechanics, &c. &c. &c. *to assist the author in fitting up his aerial habitation*," no club was in fact created, only a procession of shadowy correspondents: Tom Sprightly, Ignotus, Alice Wish-For't, Calx Pot-Ash, Pine Green-Tar, Urbanicus, Proteus Maggot, Sir John Barley-Corn, Peter Hemp. The Humourist, whose eccentricities call to mind Sterne rather than Addison and Steele, made his appearance six years before *Tristram Shandy*. He is a humor character oscillating between volatility and solemnity, a writer who warns critics to keep their distance. However, his portrait, while vividly and forcefully drawn at points, remains as shadowy as those of his correspondents.

The *Humourist* essays cover the conventional range of subject matter. The first of two essays on morality considers liberty of conscience. "The worthy patriots" who composed the parliament of Paris, writes the Humourist, "oppose the vile attempts that have been made to manacle the consciences of the people. . . The design of the Pope's Bull, published in the year 1713, was to condemn a great number of propositions contained in a book, published by father Quesnell, intitled, 'the new instrument, with moral reflections upon every verse, &c. or, an abridgment of the morality of the gospel, the acts of the apostles, the epistles of St. Paul, the canonical epistles, and the revelations.'[30] . . . By the terrible roaring of this bull the Pope thought to silence the doctrines of father Quesnell, but great numbers of the French nation, have embraced them" (January 29, 1754). The other essay asserts, "we are prone to decry Reputations," and proceeds to distinguish several kinds of defamers and detractors. Some sully a man's reputation with a shrug or a sneer; others, "by a seeming Softness of Words." Still others "will condescend to collect a Catalogue of Stories, to humour a Patron and tickle a Friend. Such Men as these, do almost come up to a literal Sense of what the *Psalmist* spoke in a figurative, (*and eat up People for Bread;*) dissect Characters, and devour good Names, for the monstrous Entertainment of a servile Master." "How melan-cholly a Reflection it is," concludes the Humourist, "that *Speech*, which was given us to soften the Cares of Life, and for our Mutual Assistance, should be converted to so bad a Purpose, as the sullying the Fame of our Fellow-Creatures; and by the Success of Artifice, raising the Admiration of Mankind on the one Hand, and a dreadful Persecution on the other" (February 19, 1754).

Manners are dealt with more often than morality. In one essay the Humourist traces the New Year's custom of giving and receiving gifts ("*Tacitus* tells us, that *Tiberius* fixed the *First* of *January* as the proper Day, not only for the giving, but likewise for receiving those Tokens of Esteem") and "is sorry to say, that *modern Elegance* is endeavouring to *suppress* these *noble* Ema-nations" (January 1, 1754). In another he observes that men should suit their actions to the nature of their professions: "We are apt to start at the mere Idea of a Merry Judge, or a waggish Divine; at a facetious Statesman, or a ludicrous King. . . . It is not enough for a Man to have good Qualities, unless he knows the right Œconomy of them" (January 29, 1754). The impor-tance of using domestic rather than foreign products is the subject of two communications the Humourist receives. "I have a Fortune sufficient to purchase *Wheat-Flour*," declares Alice Wish-For't, "yet chuse to eat nothing but *Rice*, because it's of our own Growth; nor will I touch even a Piece of *Johnny-cake*, except made of *Wheat-Flour sent from the Back-Settlements*; all the Furniture of my House, &c. is of *Carolina* Make; so is my riding Chair, and most of my Cloaths. . . . I wish *every Lady* in the Province was of my Humour; what a Number of *Dollars* should we then have at Command more than at present! I hope to see *no more sent to the Northward*" (February 26, 1754). And in a petition to the "HUMOURSOME HUMOURIST, *Esq. Censor, Tatler, Spectator,* and *Guardian of* Carolina," Sir John Barley-Corn humbly shows that "the Consumption of *Home-brew'd Beer* would lessen the Import of poisonous Rum from the *Northward,* and villainous Teas from other Parts; whereby the Floridity, Beauty and Lives of many of His Majesty's Subjects would be prolonged, and the Export of Specie lessened"; "good *Beer* creates good Blood; good Blood, good Spirits; and good Spirits, good Humour" (March 12, 1754). Just as the *Meddlers Club* essay on the vice of the bay focuses on the Charleston scene, so these communications impart to *The Humourist* a South-Carolina flavor, thus saving the series from being a pale imitation of English periodicals.

Two manners essays are more fully developed, the first on self-deception. "Human Life in some Degree resembles a Masquerade," declares the Humourist, wherein "Mankind plays the Cheat." Flavio is "a Gentleman of Birth and Education" whose "chief Happiness has ever been to deceive himself. [His] greatest Ambition soars no higher than amusing himself with false and fancied Happiness, with Scenes of Rapture, and Prospects of Illusion and Deceit."

> *Tom Easy,* who is a jocose Fellow, protests, that one strong Motive for our Devotion to the softer Sex is, because they are possessed of a most incomparable Method of cheating us, and that with wonderful Dexterity. Miss *Grave-airs* cries, Lord! Mr. Sly-boots, *I am all Amazement, that a Gentleman of your good natural Endowments, should devote yourself so entirely to the Art of Teazing; there is nothing so hateful to me, as being unmercifully kiss'd, and pull'd, and haul'd.* . . . The Patriot, bellowing with Iron Lungs against Men in Power, hazards his Fame upon a mere Contingency, and forfeits his Reputation by deceiving himself into a Place: As formerly he sung of Liberty, he now makes Music of his Chains.

"By such specious Pretences, and other insidious Means," concludes the Humourist, "Mankind deceive each other; and if there happens to fall in the Way one honest Man, free from

Deceit, free from Imposition, his want of Judgment or Discernment renders him a Victim to the multiplied Attacks of fraudulent Conspiracies" (February 5, 1754). The character sketch is here pressed into service and saves the essay from slipping into sterile abstraction. Effective, too, is the snatch of dialogue from the lips of Miss Grave-airs.

In the second manners essay the Humourist discourses on prognostication:

> When I was very young, the People were superstitious, they were Conjurers, and nothing went down but Sorcery and Witchcraft. I paid a Visit one Day to a Lady of my Acquaintance, for whom methinks a Fellow of my peculiar Turn might grow young again, and as good Fortune wou'd have it, surprized her and another fair Angel at a strong Cabal over the Fumes of Coffee; presently comes in a Widow Lady, and forms the Grand Assembly of Divination: I soon discovered, that they held the Grounds of Coffee in great Esteem, and that one of these Widows was to explain the Mystery; after a short Pause, she assumed an Air of Solemnity, intimated to the Company that she was then in full Inspiration, observed the Atoms round the Cup, and gave a strict Charge to the two Maidens, by way of quickening their Attention to the Predictions of their future Fate.

"These Amusements of the Nursery create a prognosticating Spirit, and what was intended only as a Temporary Good, soon becomes a lasting Evil; thence arises weak Prejudices, Fears that form Chimeras, and make us not too frequently in direct Opposition to the Dictates of our Reason: From these idle Rehearsals, I date Degeneracy of Spirit, Doubts take Place of Resolution, and Fortitude gives way to Weakness" (March 12, 1754). For all the hours in his youth well spent among the fair sex, the Humourist remembers this incident of the coffee grounds with mortification and vows, "I should choose rather to gain upon the Minds of Youth by rational and noble Illustration, than depress them by the fallacious Workings of the Spirit."

The Humourist reflects on which profession is the most desirable. To Ignotus' query, "Of the three Professions, *Law, Physic,* and *Divinity,* which is the most desirable, not only in a *moral* but *political* Sense," he replies cynically: "*Physic:* Because the Physician knows himself both inward and outward. . . . *Adrian* the VIth speaks thus, *Were it not,* says he, *for the*

Physician, Men would live so long, and grow so thick, that one could not live for the other, and he makes the Earth cover all his Faults" (January 8, 1754). The following week an anonymous correspondent addresses the Humourist on the same subject:

> As I have always held those who practice *Physic* in great Contempt, it gave me much Pleasure to find my Opinion of that Profession confirmed, not only by the Judgment of Pope *Adrian* the VIth, but by the *Humourist* himself. . . . What [Adrian] says is literally true . . . for indeed, Mr. *Humourist*, what Man can *live long*, and *grow thick*, under a Diet of Pills, Boluses, Sage-Tea, and Water-Gruel? . . . It plainly appears then, from what *You*, Pope *Adrian*, and *Myself* have said that Physic is so far from being a desireable Profession, either in a moral or political Sense, that it is destructive, and aims at the Extirpation of the human Species.

"Law, on the other hand, is unerring in its Decisions; for, who ever found himself aggrieved by its Decrees, which the most obstinate must not acquiesce; and why should he not? sure, what it decrees must be just? It must also be granted, that *Divinity* would be of some Use to the World, if Men would but root out the Corruption of their Hearts, that they might profit by the Doctrine and Example of the Professors of it." There follows a poem which denigrates all three professions:

> *Law*, *Physic*, and *Divinity*,
> Being in dispute, could not agree,
> To settle, which, among the three,
> Should have the superiority. . . .
>   For let men live in peace and love,
> The *Lawyer's* tricks they need not prove;
> Let them avoid excess and riot,
> They need not feed on *Doctor's* diet.
>   Let them attend what God does teach,
> They need not care what *Parson's* preach.
> But if men fools, and knaves will be
> They'll be *Ass-ridden* by all *three*.

These satirical reflections undermine the three respected professions, not only medicine but law and divinity as well, suggesting that in the South at least they were not always held in high regard. Of the three, medicine was the most primitive in colonial times, a fact made apparent in these essays.

No subject engaged the Humourist's attention more often than literary criticism. In the opening number he contends that "as the Morals of People varied, so did their Species of Writing," and proceeds to illustrate:

> In the Days of monkish Ignorance, romantic Legends bore an universal Sway; and in the happy Times of good Queen *Bess*, the World was joyously entertained with Fairy Land and Tales of Chivalry. . . .
>
> In the Reign of *James* I. the People were all scared at imaginary Ghosts and headless Apparitions, with Tales of Witches suck'd by ram Cats, and Devils smoking Tobacco.
>
> The Restoration, amongst other of its happy Consequences, introduced a certain *Gaieté de Coeur*, an Ease and Familiarity, and all Things seem'd to breathe the Spirit "——Of Love and amorous Delight;" From this Moment I date the Stony-heartedness of pretty Misses to their languishing Admirers, and the glorious Opportunity for plotting Wives to bambouzle their jealous pated Husbands.

"Thus have I cursorily run over the various Tastes of Mankind in the former Ages; and therefore cannot avoid mentioning that reigning one of these Days, Novel writing without Reason, and Lies without a Meaning" (November 26, 1753). Elsewhere the Humourist maintains that an author should suit his diet to his subject. "I dare affirm, that the Song of the *Old-English Roast-Beef* was composed after a hearty Exercise of the manual Engines upon it."

> I was inclined the other Day to write a *Tragedy*, and after being for some Time lost in Thought, and panting for Expression to paint some cruel Incidents, I threw down my inky Slave, fatally calling to mind, that I had been devouring Trifle, Flummery and Whip-Syllabub; these are too tender, too soft, to raise and animate the Passions, or assist an Author in representing the Horror of a Battle, the Clashing of Arms, or the madding Wheels of brazen Chariots. . . . I ordered a large Quantity of Black-puddings to be made, in order to give a proper Lentor to the Juices, and familiarise the Soul to bloody Thoughts.

Custard is one food writers should avoid; it is "a most barbarous Thing" which "obnubilates the Understanding and hurts the Memory" (January 22, 1754).

In the first of two essays on poetry the Humourist imagines Apollo from his court on Mount Parnassus issuing a proclamation to his subjects: In order "to preserve our State from Ruin," we, "having previously taken the Advice, Opinion and Sentiments of our dearly beloved Sisters the nine Muses," do forbid "and rigorously command, all Poets, Poetasters, and Hedge-Rhymers, the Use of Verse, it being sufficient for such limited Geniuses to join in the general Acclamation (on particular Days) of *God save the King*, with the Chorus of the People: And to this Intent, we will erect and establish a Court, similar to that at *Lyons*, where, [in] Days of Yore, such Pretenders were publickly condemned to wipe off with their Tongues what they had injudiciously written" (March 19, 1754). In burlesque of criticism like Addison's essays on *Chevy-Chase* (*Spectator* Nos. 70 and 74) the Humourist comments on *The Dragon of Wantley*, a popular ballad in which More of More-Hall drinks down the dragon Sir Francis Wortley.[31] "The great Excellence of an Author is to raise Expectation, to wind up the Soul as a Body would a Clock, keeping the Springs in a continual Motion: This Rule is most incomparably observed in the Work now before us" (February 26, 1754). The following week he particularizes: "We have a charming Description of our Hero's excellent Qualities, far superior to what *Ajax* ever had Pretensions to boast, or Marshal *Saxe* to assume: He made nothing of swinging a Horse to Death and eating him: The Country People of those Days, who had with Christian Patience submitted to the Power of priestly Government, began to entertain most sanguine Expectations of our Hero's Appetite, and address'd him in one of the greatest Strokes of Oratory, that for its Singularity I cannot omit transcribing.

> These Children, as I told, being eat,
>   Men, Women, Girls and Boys,
> Sighing and sobbing, came to his Lodging,
>   And made a hideous Noise."

As Addison's Spectator had discoursed on tragedy, so now the Humourist:

> A good Tragedy is a noble Lecture, full fraught with the Precept and the Moral, as we find them so delightfully diffused through the whole System of Philosophy; the Mind is ennobled by the Sentiment, the Passions are rectified by the very Passions themselves, and calm, by their Emotions, the alternate Palpitations of the Heart. . . .
> The tragic Scene represents to us the Necessity of Tenderness on the one Hand, and that kind of Compassion which dictates a

proper Distinction of Misfortunes on the other, and teaches us to spare our Pity for those only who deserve it. . . . Who does not take a secret Pleasure in beholding *Clytemnestra* sinking into the Arms of Death, after having committed a Murder of a heinous Nature?

Then, anticipating later remarks on the Ancients and the Moderns, the Humourist concludes, "If these Efforts of the Genius were so regarded by the Ancients, and look'd upon even with an Eye of Reverence, I might justly add Adoration, we Moderns are every way justified in imbibing the same Notions, and embracing the same Sentiments" (January 15, 1754). Like Addison the author of this essay sets forth the Aristotelian view, widely held in the eighteenth century, that tragedy is "an imitation of an action that is serious, complete, and of a certain magnitude." He obviously agrees with Addison that a perfect tragedy "is the noblest Production of human Nature" (*Spectator* No. 39) and that "Our Minds should be open'd to great Conceptions, and inflamed with glorious Sentiments by what the Actor speaks, more than by what he appears" (*Spectator* No. 42).

In fact, the Humourist's attitude toward the Ancients versus the Moderns was ambivalent. Everyone, he writes, "considers himself as the Censor of the Age." Such critics "decry all Performances, not because they deserve Censure, but as soaring above their Comprehension, not as void of Matter, but as a Taste for Censure seems to indicate a more refined Judgment and extensive Knowledge than Silence or Decorum can infer." "This Accusation," the Humourist explains, "is aim'd at the modern Critics, for the Ancients were, generally speaking, a People of different Inclinations and better Dispositions." Unlike Longinus and Quintilian, "our modern Critics arrogate to themselves what does not belong them: They are Poets, Philosophers, and Divines; they are Orators, Statesmen and Prime Ministers; they are as knowing in Science as mechanic Operations: In those, a Critic is an Abstract of every Thing, and is very communicatively inclined, always giving his Opinion, as the true Standard whereby to direct the Judgment and inform the Understanding of Mankind" (February 12, 1754). In another respect, though, the Moderns are superior to the Ancients: "I have made an Observation in the Course of my Reading, that no

Part of Poetry strikes like Descriptions. . . . Amongst the numerous kinds of Descriptions, I think, none have been more generally received than those of the Morning. The Heroick Poets seem to have exercised all their Talents in varying them: They have sported with their Imaginations almost to Extravagance." Having given examples from Vergil and Shakespeare, the Humourist concludes: "I am not so attached to the Ancients, as to give them the Preference in this Part of Poetry, tho' most People are so bigotted to their Beauties, that they will allow little or no Excellence in the modern Writers: For my Part, I must confess, that I cannot find in any of the Antients, that Elegance of Sentiment, or Luxuriancy of Fancy, which many modern Writers have exemplified in their beautiful Descriptions of the Morning" (April 2, 1754). Beginning with Temple and Swift, the battle of the books raged through the first half of the eighteenth century. While the Humourist would seem finally to give the nod to the Ancients, he certainly allows the Moderns their day in court.

At a few points this essay serial is purely humorous. Among the paintings and drawings which Proteus Maggot, V.M., plans to sell at Laputa is the following lot:

Above 500 grotesque Pieces (several in the Chinese Taste) of which the *Humourist* Family are generally great Connoisseurs: Many of these are Drawings and Etchings, and give great Light into Antiquity, and a Display of the unaccountable Humours of the Ancients. In this Collection, some of the principal and most valuable are, a *Morning Auction, public Breakfastings, Humours of Change-Alley,* Exploits of a *Bottle-Conjurer,* Drawings of *Lotteries, Masquerades, Routs, Drums, Rackets, Earthquakes, Hurricanes,*—a *Toast* (with a Group of Admirers about her) qualifying herself to speak *French* e'er she can read *English,*—a *Citizen*'s Daughter just returned from Boarding-School, and a *Buck* just landed from his Travels—*Modern* Connoisseurs—Ladies kissing Monkies and Lap-Dogs, and Gentlemen Negro Wenches. (February 26, 1754)

Peter Hemp informs the Humourist, "Mr. *Green-Tar* and I, have traversed the Globe together with Harmony and in a'-Cord. I am a peaceable good Neighbour, fond of good Society, and never use any Man ill who uses me well; but, as I have a very musical Ear, I sometimes stop the Wind-pipe of those who are too fond of

Discord." "Messrs. *Indico, Pot-Ash, Green-Tar*, and *myself*," says Peter, "have offered our Services in Carolina; we can live (as in one House) with Mr. *Rice*: And as Mr. *Spectator* used to make his Lion roar, as he saw needful,[32] so I am hopeful to find you in the Humour, to speak aloud of our Utility amongst the Inhabitants" (March 19, 1754). This whimsical, punning letter, like that of Alice Wish-For't, focuses on the South Carolina scene and reminds us that the series was written in Charleston, not London.

On April 9, 1754, in what closed out the series, the Humourist declares that he "is become an Invalid, and as he loves Retirement must quit the Foolish busy World, and please his vacant Hours with the secret Satisfaction of having intentionally displeased no one. He thanks the Publick for having generously construed these Papers; but, for some private Reasons, is under a Necessity of declaring, that he will never more (either under this or any other Title, or on any Pretence, or on any Occasion whatsoever) enter the Lists of Authorism in the Province."

The Humourist is omnibus in nature in that frequently two or more subjects are dealt with in a single number, after the example of the early *Tatler* papers. Although the character of the Humourist is firmly established, he does not make his presence felt in the way that the Monitor does. There is no attempt here, as in *The Meddlers Club*, to create a social center for the series. Given the rather short life of this serial, a surprisingly wide range of subjects is discussed. The relative lack of topicality and the emphasis on literary criticism reflect the influence of Johnson's *Rambler* essays, which began to be reprinted in the *South-Carolina Gazette* at the end of 1750.[33] Unlike most other early American serials, the *Humourist* essays are wholly original except for the burlesque criticism of *The Dragon of Wantley*.

Early southern serials like *The Plain-Dealer, The Monitor, The Meddlers Club*, and *The Humourist*, modeled closely on English periodical writing, remind us that eighteenth-century Annapolis, Williamsburg, and Charleston were culturally closer to London than to Boston and Philadelphia. Essay writing seems to have come naturally and easily to the southerner whose mood is sunnier and less partisan than the northerner.

V. JOHN TRUMBULL

So HEAVILY CLASSICAL and theological was John Trumbull's formal education that only by pushing beyond its limits in defiance of authority did he win through to becoming a poet and, what is here important, an essayist. When he ventured into prose in 1769 at age nineteen, it was in the well-established tradition of the literary serial. Late in life he remembered that "The Spectator and Watts' Lyric Poems were the only works of merit in the belles-lettres" in his father's library and that when he attended Yale College in the 1760s, "English poetry and the belles-lettres were called folly, nonsense and an idle waste of time."[1] Among the literary exercises he engaged in to stimulate an interest in belles-lettres while a graduate student and a tutor at Yale were two serials, *The Meddler* and *The Correspondent*.[2] At a time when most American writers were participating in the Revolutionary debate, Trumbull "showed little disposition to employ public events as topics for his writing."[3] Where politics was concerned, he could say with Addison's Spectator, "I never espoused any Party with Violence, and am resolved to observe an exact Neutrality between the Whigs and Tories, unless I shall be forc'd to declare my self by the Hostilities of either side." But if he avoided political controversy, he did not hesitate to engage in theological and philosophical disputation. As the first part of *The Progress of Dulness* ("The Rare Adventures of Tom Brainless") prompted church and school authority in Connecticut to condemn him as "an open reviler of the Clergy, and an enemy to truth and learning,"[4] so his attacks in *The Correspondent* on metaphysical writers and incompetent or hypocritical clergymen "very much enraged some Persons of eminence."[5]

I

The Meddler, "not influenced by fame" but by "a desire to

97

make trial of his genius," at once explains that his series "will consist of essays, chiefly of the moral, critical and poetical kinds, upon miscellaneous and mostly unconnected subjects. . . . I shall carefully avoid all strokes of party spirit and personal satire, with every thing that may have the least tendency to immorality."[6] And indeed, except for the eighth number on hypocrisy in religion, he does avoid partisanship, unlike the Correspondent whose essays followed shortly. Unfortunately, the Meddler, modeled on the Spectator and other nonpartisan English personae, remains a shadowy figure.

In the first number the Meddler, following the plan of the *Spectator* and other English serials, introduces the club. A few friends, notably Mr. Thomas Freeman and John Manly, Esq., will "meet every week at the dwelling-house of the author" to assist "in compiling and correcting my writings." Freeman, a country gentleman modeled on Sir Roger de Coverly, "is a great humourist, has an odd and peculiar way of thinking, and a ready discernment of every thing ridiculous, in writings, actions or conversation: but at the same time is a great admirer of every thing that is just and beautiful. He is a friend to sincerity and plain dealing, and consequently an enemy to all kinds of affectation and hypocrisy, which he never fails to lash with satyrical indignation." Manly is very like him, though not in disposition. "Folly, ignorance and affectation, which move the mirth of *Mr. Freeman*, are regarded, by Mr. Manly, with an eye to pity and contempt only." Another member of the club is Jack Dapperwit, descended from the *Spectator*'s Tom Dapperwit. "His favourite author is Tristram Shandy, whose manner he endeavours to imitate in conversation, but so unluckily, that with very little portion of his humour, he attains only to a rambling incoherence of style and confusion of sentiment, which however among such company as he esteems polite, passes him off for a person of the greatest strength of wit and genius." Finally there is the Clergyman, "a person of great genius and merit, reverenced by all his acquaintance, and heartily welcomed by us, whenever he visits our society." Trumbull pays lip service to the club convention, whose members are pale copies of those in the *Spectator*. Little wonder that the Meddler's club is in effect stillborn; its members appear only once again, to argue in the eighth number about Freeman's recipe for making a popular preacher.

At the end of his first number the Meddler expresses the hope that he can contribute his assistance "towards instructing the unlearned, diverting and improving the learned, rectifying the taste and manners of the times, and cultivating the fine arts in this land." His essays fulfill this promise to instruct and entertain by ranging through the conventional subjects, notably manners. Several times we glimpse the coquette and the fop, who will emerge fully developed in *The Progress of Dulness*. The following mock-advertisement announcing the sale of Isabella Sprightly's estate is a foreshadowing of Harriet Simper:

> *Imprimis*, all the Tools and utensils, necessary for the trade of a Cocquet; viz. several bundles of darts and arrows, which are well-pointed, and capable of doing great execution, a considerable quantity of patches, paint, brushes and cosmetics, for plaistering, painting and white washing the face, and several dozens of *Cupids*, with all their appurtenancies, very proper to be stationed on a *ruby lip*, a *diamond eye*, or a *roseate cheek*.
>
> *Item.* As she proposes by certain ceremonies to transform one of her humble servants into an husband, and keep him for her own use, she offers for sale, Floris, Daphinis, Cynthis, Cleanthies, and several others whom she won, by a constant attendance on business, during the space of four years. She can prove her indisputable right to them, by certain deeds of gift, bills of sale and attestations, commonly called love-letters, under their own hands. They will be sold very cheap, for they are all either broken-hearted, or broken-winded, or in a dying condition; nay, some of them have been dead this half year, as they declare and testify in the above mentioned writings.
>
> N.B. Their hearts will be SOLD separate. (No. 3, October 26, 1769)

It may be said of Isabella, as Trumbull was to say of Harriet Simper, that "nurst in Folly's school," "She lov'd the chace, but scorn'd the prey, / And fish'd for hearts to throw away."[7] Whereas Harriet becomes the wife of the dullard Tom Brainless, Isabella "now retiring from business" chooses a husband from among her admirers and puts the rest up for sale.

Similarly the Meddler's account of how boys are trained up to foppery prefigures Dick Hairbrain. The country lad, after proper preparation, is sent off to college. His first acquaintance there, "who, ten to one is a rake, a coxcomb, or a gamester . . . makes a tool of him to execute his own purposes," whereupon he wastes his time and loses his ambition. The city lad, when he is fifteen or sixteen, "commences beau; is caressed by the Ladies, envied by all his brother-beaus and despised by all persons of sense and judgment; he spends his time in fashionable amusements, in gaming, in parties of pleasure, in 'squiring the Ladies to balls, plays and other places of resort, until in a few years, he becomes antiquated and is elbowed out by younger gallants . . . a most miserable creature, destitute and unworthy of notice and regard" (No. 9, January 15, 1770). Dick Hairbrain combines elements of the country and the city lad. A wealthy farmer's son whom college transforms into a coxcomb anxious to please the fair sex, he eventually runs through his fortune and becomes a "superannuated Beau . . . elbow'd out by younger Fops."[8]

One of the Meddler's contributors, the Schemer, contends that we Moderns "exceed the Antients in all the polite arts and sciences . . . dress, dancing, compliments, curses, drinking, swearing, gaming, poetry, fighting and dying, and, in a word, every qualification that belongs to a *gentleman* and a *man of honour*, in the modern acceptation of the words." His satirical explanation is heavy-handed: "All the elegance and beauty of dress have undoubtedly been added in modern ages. The antients have nothing to boast of, either in variety of fashions, or superfluity of decorations: they dressed for advantage and not for ornament. Necessity was their instructor, and plainness their model. . . . The art of cursing and swearing is almost wholly of modern invention. *Aristophanes, Plautus, Terence, Horace,* and a few more, who might perhaps have been gentlemen, had they lived in these days, do indeed make a few slight attempts in the practice; but they have not an oath, or a curse fit for the mouth of a modern gentleman." In "every polite and populous town" in America let there be erected two universities, "one for the education of gentlemen, and the other for the education of taylors. . . . In the college for the education of gentlemen, beside the usual officers, let there be a dancing-master, a fencing-master, a gaming-master, and above all, a professor of swearing: this post will require, a gentleman of superiour abilities and uncommon application, and may probably fall to some experienced seaman" (No. 7, December 21,

1769). The Schemer, anxious to counteract the view that "the world degenerates from that perfection, in which it was at first created," finds the moderns "superiour" to the ancients in manners. Although Trumbull was Connecticut born and bred, the manners in question sound English.

The Meddler, complying with a request for his views on good and bad breeding, presents a set of characters more vividly drawn than the members of his club. In contrast to Eusebius, who "places politeness, in such behaviour to others, as he would desire them to shew towards him," are three examples of how not to behave. The first is the fop Abaxus: "As soon as he rises in the morning, which is about eleven, he is attended by his valet, who spends about two hours in adjusting the back parts of his dress. . . . Then his barber passes about an hour in regulating his hair; after which he sometimes spares time enough to hurry down his breakfast; which being finished, he devotes about two hours of his time, to the contriving of fashions for the good of mankind, and then commits his important discoveries to paper. . . . When his hours of study, which he looks upon as the most advantageous and profitable part of his life, are over, he appears at the play house, or at any other assembly, where he may have an opportunity of shewing his accomplishments, either of dancing or dress." Licentio bullies his inferiors and is insolent to his superiors: "Yesterday, as soon as he was dressed, he rang the bell for his servant; after he had given him his orders, observing something in his gait or dress, which offended his good breeding, he followed him to his chamber-door, and being very well gifted in the art of kicking, with one stroke, laid him at the bottom of the stairs. Soon after he proceeded to a coffee-house, where the waiter happening to spill some coffee upon a gentleman's coat, he stepped up to him, and brandishing his cane in the genteelest manner, very politely knocked him down; then throwing him a guinea, marched off in triumph." Pephasio is awkwardly attentive to the fair sex: "When he first enters a company of ladies, he makes a most extraordinary bow; for beginning at the right hand person, he stares each one in the face, till he arrives at the left hand one, then bowing his head very low, turns it over his left shoulder. . . . one of the ladies dropping her fan, Pephasio in haste to pick it up, happened to step upon one corner of her apron: for which, with an appearance of much sorrow and confusion, he asked (if I am not mistaken) some thousand and odd pardons" (No. 4, November 2, 1769). These examples of ill breeding, Abaxus the fashion-monger, Licentio the bully, and the gauche Pephasio, are more vivid than Eusebius, who is the model of politeness.

As literary critic Trumbull was influenced by Lord Kames's *Elements of Criticism* (1762), which he read at Yale. "Upon a sense common to the species," writes Kames, "is erected a standard of taste, which without hesitation is apply'd to the taste of every individual. . . . We have the same standard for ascertaining in all the fine arts, what is beautiful or ugly, high or low, proper or improper, proportioned or disproportioned."[9] The criticism present in *The Meddler*, and later in *The Correspondent*, conforms with Kames's insistence on aesthetic uniformitarianism. Echoing the judgment of Addison who sought to establish "a Taste of polite Writing" by distinguishing between true and false wit (*Spectator* Nos. 58-63), Trumbull's Meddler writes, "True Wit depends upon genius and nature, the false upon labour or affection; true Wit is always accompanied with good-nature, politeness and a fine taste, the false with the grossest offences against modesty, good-manners or good-sense." Among the kinds of false wit that prevail in writing, and more especially in conversation, are "the art of talking unintelligibly," ridicule and raillery, and *double-entendre*. This last, "though mostly peculiar to the male sex, would not have so universally prevailed among them, had it not met with the approbation and encouragement of the female; since it is well known that their taste and opinion is the standard of politeness" (No. 2, September 18, 1769). It is clear from this discussion that Trumbull, like Addison in *Spectator* No. 62, agrees with Dryden who defined true wit as "a propriety of thoughts and words; or, in other terms, thoughts and words elegantly adapted to the subject."[10]

Among the dishes the Meddler prepares for his readers in the final number several consist of literary criticism. He describes "a late Poet" (Timothy Dwight) who "has filled his work with so much thunder and lightning, that upon reading it, I could not but compare his head to Vulcan's shop, in which an hundred

Cyclops were perpetually employed in forging thunderbolts."[11] To critics like Addison who blames Milton "for mingling allegory with reality, and introducing sin and death, as actors," in *Paradise Lost* (*Spectator* No. 297), the Meddler replies, "I leave it to the reader to judge whether, Sin and death only excepted, any other fictitious persons could properly be made the porters of hell-gate." And viewing Richardson's *Clarissa* as a conduct book, he advises, "If any Lady is desirous to know how to avoid the delusive snares of man, let her attend to the story and imitate the character of Clarissa; and if any man is desirous of learning how to deceive innocence, and betray unguarded female virtue, and in a word to become an incarnate devil, let him attend to the observations and imitate the character of Lovelace" (No. 10, January 22, 1770).

On one occasion Trumbull, sounding more like Swift than Addison, engages in humor for its own sake. The Meddler is handed a manuscript by "some learned Writer" consisting of miscellaneous essays. The first satirizes "those trifling projectors who trouble the world with pompous essays, upon subjects of no importance," like the study of words, points, and signs:

> We see many persons staring at a sentence or paragraph, not because they find any thing in it worth notice, but because it is ushered by a pointing hand and has the rear brought up by a sign of admiration. Hence we may judge what great advantages would accrue from introducing signs, to express every passion. . . . How many modern Comedies, although raked together with great labour of imagination, have been read over without a single smile, and for this reason only, that the authors of them were ignorant of any method or sign, by which to discover whereabouts the wit and humour lay? and how many Tragedies have failed of moving the reader, only for want of a few signs of crying inserted in proper places?

The next essay "ridicules and exposes those vain pretenders to science, who endeavour to explain and account for the mysterious works of nature, by the finespun imaginations of their own brain." One such pretender maintains that the tongue and fingers are the only channels "by which our ideas are let out of the brain. . . . If these channels are any way obstructed, they presently begin to swell, foam and ferment and press prodigiously against the skull; till with pushing by each other, fighting for place, crouding, sqeezing, and mixing with the brain, they breed such uproar and sedition in the head, that the patient cannot chuse but to fall into fits of raving and delirium, which after some continuance terminate in settled and downright madness." "Some persons have nevertheless been remedied by trepanning, which is cutting open the head, as when a cask is likely to burst, we ease it by boring a vent. . . . I have bought all the instruments and apparatus necessary for this part of Surgery, and am determined to send my servant with a gimlet, to perform the necessary operation upon every mad Author, Poet, Lover and Enthusiast of my acquaintance" (No. 5, November 13, 1769). This second essay, while neither ironical nor scatological, calls to mind "A Digression Concerning Madness" from *A Tale of a Tub* and the projects at the Grand Academy of Lagado wherein Swift satirizes pretenders to science.

The Meddler, while frequently clumsy and amateurish in execution, must indeed have stimulated an interest in belles-lettres at Yale. Except for the eighth number wherein the club members discuss enthusiasm and affectation in religion, this serial avoids controversy, depicting the coquette and fop so popular with eighteenth-century readers, castigating false wit, and satirizing trifling projectors. When the Meddler took leave of his readers at the end of the tenth number, "only desiring them to call in, and accept of another collation, next week," there was no hint that Trumbull was breaking off the series. A month later, however, he initiated a new serial, *The Correspondent.*

II

Assuming "the character of an universal Correspondent, to receive letters from all the world, to return suitable answers, and to patronize such writings, as nobody else would take any notice of," Trumbull's Correspondent promises to "vindicate [the World's] character from all . . . undeserved aspersions" and encourage "merit and virtue."[12] With an eye to the theological and philosophical disputation in which he would soon be engaged, he announces that sometimes he will "attempt to employ the style of humour and irony; since it is allowed by the greatest men of all ages, that ridicule is the best method of disgracing known falshood" (No. 2, March 2, 1770). Trumbull discontinued *The Correspondent* after only eight numbers, explaining later, "My leaving New Haven & engaging in an employment that left me no leisure for such amusements, made me soon drop the design."[13] He did not resume the series until three years later, by which time he had returned to Yale as tutor. Remembering how the first numbers so enraged "some Persons of eminence" that "they called the Author, all the *rogues, rascals, knaves* and *scoundrels,* that could be invented," the Correspondent now wishes "to avoid the character of a Party-satirist. . . . my design is to furnish, if I can, an entertaining series of miscellaneous essays" (No. 9, February 12, 1773). In spite of this profession he persists in making "satirical observations on the reigning follies and vices of the times" until finally his enemies threaten that "he is to be assaulted in private, caned, kicked and cudgelled; he is to have his nose cut off, his eyes knocked out, and his head beaten to a mummy; besides which, he is to be hanged, tarred and feathered, with several other punishments of so grievous a nature, that being employed at present in business more important, and engaged in amusements more agreeable, he declares that he hath neither leisure, nor inclination to undergo half of them" (No. 28, June 25, 1773). In a word, the Correspondent is a more contentious, less genial character than the Meddler, but no more sharply defined.

While the Correspondent ranges through the conventional subject matter of the periodical essay, he instructs the reader more and diverts him less than the Meddler had done. In the area of manners there are essays on the government of families,[14] flattery,[15] the art of begging,[16] and dunces. On the subject of dunces, three of whom Trumbull was just then portraying in *The Progress of Dulness,* the Correspondent wishes to vindicate the Egyptian god Theuth, inventor of the useful arts and sciences, who, finding that many of his countrymen are dunces, invents for them such pernicious arts as gaming, swearing, and debauchery. Theuth, ordering "all rogues, fools, simpletons, scoundrels and vagabonds in the kingdom" to convene "before his temple at the city of *Thebes*" on April 1, 1694, proceeds to lay down rules about ruffles, hairdresses and periwigs; shews them how to handle a cane, a fan, and a snuff box; unfolds to them the whole art of swearing and prophaneness, and gives them a compleat academy of compliments. He then produces a pack of cards, and a box of dice, and spends a long time, in explaining to them, the different kinds of gaming, and shewing them, how to calculate the chances of wagers. He directs them to the institution of clubs and lodges, and teaches them how to give out toasts, and drink bumpers. He gives some laudable hints about the erecting of brothels and concludes his instructions with a long explanation of the Freethinker's Creed.

Assuring them that "Sense, and Wisdom shall be out of fashion, and Honesty and Conscience shall be turned out of doors: And Coxcombs shall pass for Wits and Genius's, till the end of Dunces shall come," he commands the assembled company: "Retire then to your tents, ye Simpletons, game, dress, drink, revel, and carouse. Let your hearts be warmed with thankfulness, and your tongues sound forth the praise of *Theuth*. Let this day be remembered by your posterity as the period of gladness, and the first of *April*, as the anniversary of Fools" (Nos. 22-23, May 14, 21, 1773). Fearful for his own country's future, the Correspondent warns: "*America* seems designed by Providence for the last stage of Arts and Sciences; for their final seat when they have bid adieu to the other parts of the world. Great part of their train have already arrived. *Sense* and *Genius* came over with the first European Settlers; *Fancy* and *Invention* have begun to appear; But *Humour* and *Satire* having scarcely landed, the cultivation of the soil seems almost at a stand; *Folly* and *Dulness* have made great progress, and in many places there is danger least the Tares should over-run the Wheat" (No. 29, July 2, 1773).

When the second part of *The Progress of Dulness* ("The Life and Character of Dick Hairbrain") appeared, one of the Correspondent's friends, probably David Humphreys, asked, "Do you expect the world to mend? / Let me advise you better friend" (No. 32, July 23, 1773).[17] The Correspondent (Trumbull himself) replies:

> 'Tis true the world will ne'er be good!
> Nor is't our int'rest that it should:
> For what should sat'rists live upon,
> If all the fools and knaves were gone?

106

. . . .

T'our praise be't spoken, now for twenty year,
Rogues, cheats & fools were never plentier;

. . . .

Were there no fools beneath the skies,
What were the trick of being wise?

. . . .

While fools and knaves are nine in ten,
We'll pass for wits and honest men. (No. 33, July 30, 1773)

These lines reinforce the judgment made in the second part of
The Progress of Dulness, wherein Trumbull expresses satisfaction "that the present year hath borne a sufficient number of
fools to keep up the breed" and says of fops like Dick Hairbrain,

> As fire electric draws together
> Each hair and straw and dust and feather,
> The travell'd Dunce collects betimes
> The levities of other climes;
> And when long toil has giv'n success,
> Returns his native land to bless,
> A Patriot-fop, that struts by rules,
> And Knight of all the shire of fools.[18]

Trumbull is carrying on the campaign against dullness mounted
by Dryden and Pope in *Mac Flecknoe* and *The Dunciad*. These
essays and poems make it clear that, while the ostensible targets
are fops and coquettes, like Franklin in Silence Dogood's dream
vision of Harvard College, Trumbull, realizing the shortcomings in the Yale curriculum, is concerned that nonsense not gain
ground in America.

Morality, not noticeably present as a subject in *The Meddler*,
is often the concern of the Correspondent, who discourses on
greed,[19] knavery as a vocation,[20] lying and defamation,[21] pride,[22]
Negro slavery, and medical quacks. These last two subjects are
of particular interest in that they reveal Trumbull adapting his
material to an American audience. "We have a natural, moral,
and divine right of enslaving the Africans," asserts the Correspondent. "Is not the enslaving of these people the most
charitable act in the world? With no other end in view than to
bring those poor creatures to christian ground, and within hearing of the gospel, we spare no expence of time or money, we send

many thousand miles across the dangerous seas, and think all our toil and pains well rewarded.... And are they not bound by all the ties of gratitude, to devote their whole lives to our service, as the only reward that can be adequate to our superabundant charity!" At the end the Correspondent takes a broad view of the subject: "I would just observe that there are many other nations in the world, whom we have equal right to enslave, and who stand in as much need of Christianity, as these poor Africans. Not to mention the Chinese, the Tartars, or the Laplanders, with many others, who would scarcely pay the trouble of christianizing. I would observe that the Turks and the Papists, are very numerous in the world, and that it would go a great way towards the millennium, if we should transform them to Christians" (No. 8, July 6, 1770).[23] While Trumbull's Congregationalism helps explain the slur on Roman Catholics, it is difficult to reconcile this frontal attack on Negro slavery with his known conservatism and moderation. It is a sign of his youth that the irony in this essay lacks the subtlety, say, of Franklin's letter to the Philadelphia press, "On the Slave Trade."[24]

Medical quacks, like metaphysical writers and incompetent or hypocritical clergymen, engross the Correspondent's attention. In all countries, he declares, Death "hath a set of retainers to his business, whom the learned distinguish by the name of Quacks and Mountebanks."

> These Creatures know as little of physic, as of conjuration, are as poorly acquainted with the machinery of the human body, as of the air-pump, & are so far from understanding the operations of their potions, that they are entirely ignorant of the plainest principles of philosophy. Their stock and materials for setting up trade are, an old family-book of receipts, which they apply at a venture, as chance may be propitious; a portmantua, stuffed with herbs and roots, to which they have given some fantastical name, and in which they pretend to have discovered some unaccountable virtues; and an extraordinary gift of impudence, to extol the miracles of their medical applications, deride the practice of regular Physicians, and vent hard words of terrible sound, of which neither they, nor their gaping admirers know any meaning. (No. 14, March 19, 1773)

As for their education, "after devoting four years to the business of Idleness, they live perhaps six months with some one, who has had the same liberal advantages, and then sally forth into the world to help diseases kill mankind. . . . I am well satisfied, that if there were but one hundredth part so many diseases in the world, as Quacks have infallible cures, this life would be little preferable to that, which we may charitably conclude they will one time experience" (No. 26, June 11, 1773). Among the instances of quackery "that have fallen under my observation, in the practice of some among the most noted Physicians" in Connecticut, consider the following case:

> A Woman, three or four months advanced in a state of pregnancy, being troubled with some peculiar disorders, applied to a Physician, who had for a great number of years been celebrated in all parts of the country, for extraordinary skill in such cases. The old Doctor, when he arrived, found her in a very languid state; but bade her be of good courage, for he had cured hundreds in the same condition, and was acquainted with an infallible remedy, in these disorders. . . . he ordered a distilled liquor to be prepared from the *uterus, foetus & secundines* of a pregnant ewe; arguing that those parts, which had served such excellent purposes in a brute animal, would undoubtedly, by help of their experience perform the same good offices in the human body. I cannot omit, that the butcher, who was employed to procure the necessary ingredients, being something of an humourist, very wisely recommended to the Doctor, on the strength of his reasoning, to have the brains also saved out to be distilled for himself, and taken as a nostrum to promote medical knowledge. (No. 19, April 23, 1773)

The Correspondent is convinced that "these matters can never be properly regulated, but by the interpositon of the Legislative Authority of the Colony. Affairs of far less importance have been thought worthy their notice, and been the subject of a multiplicity of debates. A Lawyer shall not be allowed to practice in any court of judicature, till he have undergone a strict examination, and taken a solemn oath of faithfulness in his business and fidelity to his clients. . . . Very wise regulations are also established among the Clergy, and very just laws enacted to restrain an unbounded licence of Preaching." Surely, then, "some public examination of young Practitioners, some regular licence might be insisted on" (No. 21, April 30, 1773). Medical quacks, declares the Correspondent, are ignorant, ill equipped, contemptuous of regular physicians, and inadequately trained. The old doctor's home-made recipe for the pregnant woman domesticates and dramatizes such quackery. Serious and practical in his approach to this ever popular topic, the Correspondent urges that medicine, like the law and divinity, be regulated and its practitioners licensed. These three professions, as we saw in *The Humourist*, were associated one with the other in the mind of the eighteenth century. It is revealing that Trumbull the essayist, who would be studying law within six months, seldom attacked that profession as he often did the other two.

The Correspondent reflects philosophically on the blessings of folly,[25] love of esteem,[26] public spirit,[27] and what dying does for a man's reputation. "Dying is certainly the most expeditious way of gaining a reputation; it makes almost as great a change in a man's character, as his estate; it will transform a Scoundrel into a Gentleman, a notorious Cheat into a Man of Piety, and the most insignificant Scribbler into a great Genius." Consider the cobbler Samuel Snip:

> ... such was his increase of piety, that it may justly be affirmed, not a day passed, in which he did not as well amend the temper of his soul, as the shoes of his customers. . . . So great was the fame of his honesty and integrity, that he was often appealed to in disputes between his neighbours, & made arbitrator of several considerable wagers at the tavern & ale-house. . . . he sustained many honorable offices in this town. In the forty-sixth year of his age, he was solemnly set apart to the ecclesiastical office of a Sexton, which he exercised with much care and fidelity to his dying day. He kept the church in the utmost neatness, dug graves with great alacrity, and rang the bells with peculiar harmony and modulation. . . . He was for many years one of the School-committee for a certain district in the town; in which office, in conjunction with two Blacksmiths and a Barber, he was always particularly frugal of the public money, and engaged the cheapest school-master that offered himself for sale. . . . in the fifty-second year of his age and usefulness, he was, by a great majority of voices, raised to the dignity of a Corporal in the standing militia.

"And at last, full of days and full of honours, when, with *Caesar*, he had lived long enough both for nature and glory, to the unspeakable loss of his bereaved friends and his weeping country, this Glory of Sextons, this Flower of School-committees, this Ornament of Corporals, and Phoenix of Cobblers was snatched away by relentless Death, in the 81st year of his age"

(No. 11, February 26, 1773). This abstract reflection is concretized by the example of Samuel Snip who, long married to "Miss *Mary Titmouse*, only child and heiress to an opulent Soap-boiler," not only proves proficient and charitable in his vocation but serves the community with distinction in several offices. Here is another example of Trumbull's ability on occasion to accommodate his subject to an American audience.

The Correspondent hopes he draws his characters to life, but cautions "all those who find their own characters drawn, to take as little notice of it as possible, and remember that although the arrow be shot at random, among the flock, yet the bird that flutters is certainly known to be wounded" (No. 2, March 2, 1770). His gallery includes Xantippus the slanderer,[28] Dogmaticus the fool,[29] the dunces Castalio and Garrulas,[30] and the hypocrites Sombrio and Malicio. On weekdays Sombrio leaves the door open so that he may be seen at morning prayers, for he "is sensible that he shall never procure the reputation of performing secret duty, unless mankind find it out; and how shall they find it out, unless they catch him in the very act?" "On Sunday he takes his broad-brimmed hat and black wig, which is never profaned with powder, and, without any levity in his walk, proceeds to church. Being there comfortably built up in the faith by a nap, he returns home, thinking the people all the way spy in him nothing less than little Saint or Angel in embryo" (No. 13, March 12, 1773). In short, Sombrio is an example of a man who resorts to hypocrisy in an effort to gain a reputation, perverting religion in the process.

The fact that the Correspondent chose to instruct his readers more and divert them less than the Meddler explains why none of his essays are purely humorous and why only two focus on literary criticism. Aware that his satirical method has won him numerous enemies, he defends the use of personal satire under special circumstances. "The first is the case of personal injury. He, who endeavours to ruin my character, gives me an equal right over his own; and common sense will always justify the man, who exposes unprovoked slander, or revenges himself on a malicious aggressor." The second case "is when a man stands forth as the champion of injured innocence, against the assaults of open malevolence, or the ambush of secret slander." Finally, "when a Man's vices, by their nature and tendency, become hurtful to the public, every member of the society is injured by his conduct, and hath as just a right to expose his character, or designs, so far as they influence the morals of mankind, as he would have to remove a public nuisance." But "if it be in our power," adds the Correspondent, "let us expose the vice without naming the person, or dragging forth the character to public view" (No. 28, June 25, 1773). Trumbull's attempt to avoid personal satire in most circumstances helps explain why, when attacked by the Yale establishment for his unflattering portrait of Tom Brainless, he retreated in the second and third parts of *The Progress of Dulness* into the familiar and safer stereotypes of the fop and the coquette. His defense of the use of personal satire, like his views on true and false wit in *The Meddler*, is governed by the principle of aesthetic uniformitarianism. For the most part eighteenth-century practice observed his injunctions. Trumbull's own writings, both prose and poetry, always do.

In view of the epistolary nature of the periodical essay it is not surprising that the Correspondent should offer his thoughts on letter writing. "I shall at present remark on the serious, the complimentary, and the whimsical letter writer, the lady, the lover, and the satirist; and endeavour to point out in each which is ridiculous." Serious letter writers "are extremely apt to be well with help from above, to remain yours in the Lord, and to send salutations for compliments." The complimentary letter writer begins in a lofty manner, "Incomparable friend, I received your inimitable letter, and am eternally obliged to your condescending goodness, that you would demean your dignity to write to one, whose weak abilities are so far beneath the task of returning an equivalent answer." "The whimsical letter writer hates pedantry and affectation; he has heard that an easy, natural style is the chief beauty of letters; and thinks a sprightliness of imagination the only mark of genius. To avoid stiffness in style, he never finishes a period; to avoid method, he loses all connection; and to be witty, he strains at things so uncommon, that he deviates into the downright flightiness of nonsense." "The high bombast of love letters hath been so often exposed, that it may save a satirist the trouble; but the cringing submis-

sion of their usual style deserves equal notice." Here is how
such a letter would run:

> Madam, upon the strictest examination finding myself absolutely
> good for nothing, I have thought proper to offer myself to you:
> hoping that you will esteem me so highly, as to be willing to spend
> the rest of your life with me. As I have fallen entirely out of favor
> with myself, I doubt not of obtaining favor of you; and I think you
> cannot but be extremely obliged to me for the offer of an heart and
> hand, which I set not the least value on, and assure you are
> entirely unworthy of your notice. If you will be so kind as to
> accept of me on this representation, it will save me the trouble of
> dying for love, which I design otherwise to set about immediately;
> being resolved to get rid of myself, as soon as possible, either by
> marriage or hanging, both of which, it is said, go by destiny.
> (No. 34, August 6, 1773)

Nowhere else in *The Correspondent* does Trumbull display such
sensitivity to style, especially in his parody of a love letter. And
this at a time when letter writing was as highly esteemed in
America as in England. He reiterates the widely held view that
"letters should be only conversation on paper" and exposes the
absurdities present in a variety of epistolary styles, much as
Mather Byles and his associates had exposed bombastic and
grubstreet writing.

Trumbull, who planned to move to Boston in the fall of 1773,
has the Correspondent announce in July, "As the Copartnership
between the Correspondent and the Public will soon be dis-
solved, all persons, that have any accounts to settle . . . are
desired to send them in as soon as possible" (No. 33,
July 30, 1773). One contributor, chagrined at hearing this news,
praises the Correspondent for "the Plainness, the Freedom, the
Honesty, and Integrity of your Dealings; your prudent Choice of
Commodities; the Importance of your Fund; and the Regularity,
and Justness of your Accounts" (No. 35, August 13, 1773). Soon
word comes that "on Monday last, agreeably to his own predic-
tions, departed this life the noted Correspondent, who for some
time past hath existed in the public papers." Of his life all that is
known for certain is "that he died in the tenth year of his age."
Opinions differ as to the cause: Dr. Boltrope "affirms that he
died of the Catarrh, or dripping of the brains"; Dr. Philiatros,
"that he died of the *Caput mortuum*." "He was embalmed by his

friends, and the last offices will be performed to him, as soon as they have complied with the injunctions of his will, which he hath ordered his executor to publish in the next paper" (No. 37, August 27, 1773).[31] In his last will and testament, which brings the series to an end, the Correspondent bequeaths to the public all his "literary productions, which were composed for their own use and entertainment," adding, "I return my sincere thanks for the general kindness I have received from the Public, and desire only that the same goodness may still be extended towards my memory, that my writings may be read with candour, as they were composed without malevolence, and that a judgment of my character or designs may not be formed from the accounts of those men, who find it their interest and make it their business, by the most improbable falshoods to oppose, misrepresent and defame me" (No. 38, September 3, 1773).[32]

The Correspondent is a more ambitious serial than *The Meddler*, brought to a close less (it would seem) because Trumbull's invention was running dry than because he was preparing to study law in Boston. While frequently marked by attacks on church authority in Connecticut, it is clearly a literary serial, advancing the cause of belles-lettres as had *The Meddler*. In addition to such well-worn topics as dunces and medical quacks, topics which Trumbull manages to domesticate, are others less expected, notably the essay against slavery written at a time when almost the only anti-slavery advocates in America were Quakers.

Trumbull did not, by virtue of his essay writing, fulfill his early prophecy: "This Land her Steele and Addison shall view,"[33] but then he never claimed to be the American Addison. The Meddler and the Correspondent are thin disguises assumed by a young man who was unable, or perhaps unwilling, to put sufficient dramatic distance between himself and his readers. Of the conventions associated with the periodical essay Trumbull availed himself of only a few like aptronym, fictitious letter, and mock-advertisement. Like Franklin who initiated the tradition in America and Irving who presided over its demise, Trumbull began his career as a serial essayist. But whereas Franklin and Irving developed into wide-ranging prose writers, Trumbull found poetry to be his proper element. Nevertheless it is worth remembering that he served an apprenticeship as essayist and that these apprentice works not only illuminate the meaning of poems like *The Progress of Dulness* but left the essay serial in America permanently enriched.

VI. PHILIP FRENEAU

〔〕

PHILIP FRENEAU, like John Trumbull, made his literary mark as a poet. The fact that he too was an essayist is often overlooked. One critic has called Freneau "the Father of American Prose,"[1] a description that students of Franklin and Irving might wish to question. Another claims that he was "the most gifted prose writer [in America] between 1780 and 1800,"[2] a judgment that few closely familiar with the belletristic prose of these decades can challenge. Among the four hundred or so prose pieces he wrote in a career extending from 1770 to 1824,[3] four literary serials deserve to be better known: *The Pilgrim, Tomo Cheeki, Hezekiah Salem,* and *Robert Slender.*[4]

At the outset of his career Freneau sings of "godlike Addison" who "wrapt the soul of poetry in prose."[5] He read the *Spectator* as a boy and at Princeton had access to a wide range of essayists, Montaigne, Bacon, Dryden, and Defoe as well as Addison and Steele.[6] While Freneau the essayist frequently departs from the neutrality Addison had urged, he was strongly indebted to the *Spectator* and its descendants for his conception of the persona and other conventions like the fictitious letter, dream vision, and foreign visitor; for, although a liberal in politics and religion, he "was never quite to escape from conventional forms."[7] Like Franklin before him, Freneau was long associated with the rough-and-tumble world of journalism, working first to achieve national independence and later to consolidate the Republican party and help it to victory at the polls in 1800. The *Pilgrim* and *Slender* series, written to further these ends, are frequently partisan; *Tomo Cheeki* and *Hezekiah Salem,* produced at intervals in which he retreated temporarily from the heat of battle, are social and nonpartisan.

I

The *Pilgrim* essays appeared in the *Freeman's Journal* during the year following the British surrender at Yorktown.[8] The Pilgrim resembles Addison's Mr. Spectator in being an educated old bachelor who wishes simply to observe life. In the first number he gives an account of his "life, character and fortunes." Sole heir to his Swiss parents' little estate, he disposed of it in his twenty-second year and set up for a pilgrim in order "to gratify my curiosity at the expence of all nations." Having "spent upwards of thirty two years in this way of life," he came to North America ardently desiring "to see those far famed heroes, who with their swords have established the purest freedom, in direct opposition to the most barefaced tyranny." He inhabits a cave in a forest near Philadelphia, "perfectly sheltered from the severity of the winter and the violent heats of the summer season, with a small stream of water hard by," where "I am engaged in composing a voluminous treatise on an abstruse subject, De Anima Mundi," for which he has been collecting materials these thirty years. "I subsist wholly upon roots and vegetables [and] have not had an hour's sickness these forty years past. . . . I am in stature considerably above the middle size, of a very swarthy complexion much injured by the weather; am of an atrabilarious habit; walk with a staff of black ebony . . . constantly wear a pair of temple spectacles, [and] speak most of the languages of the known world, ancient and modern, with fluency."[9] His linguistic knowledge prompts the editor to remark shortly, "These pieces are penned in such a very strange, outlandish and perplexing hand, that we are persuaded the good Pilgrim has hitherto accustomed himself to write in the ancient Hebrew, Chaldean, or modern Coptic characters, rather than those used by the inhabitants of the American states" (No. 3, December 5, 1781). Urged by a correspondent Comus to leave his cave and come to the city where he can check for a while his melancholy by beholding "young gentlemen spending hours at the toilette; ladies building turrets upon their heads, and decking themselves off with thin silks and gewgaws in the midst of winter," the Pilgrim replies that Comus "has been strangely misled in supposing that my time passes heavily in this solitude." Those who rush to town "can hardly endure their own existence unless perpetually engaged in the hurry of business. . . . When such persons are compelled to be alone how wretched are they" (No. 6, December 26, 1781). When he does eventually come to town he is mortified to hear one of the company at a tavern, taking up the *Freeman's Journal*, vociferate, "there are some good political pieces in this paper, but this damn'd PILGRIM I believe will never have done; his writings contain neither sentiment, fire, wit, humour, information, amusement, argument nor sense; and I heartily wish him and his writings to the devil" (No. 13, February 20, 1782). Thereafter he goes "clad in the plain attire of an honest simple Whig Quaker" in order to remain unknown (No. 18, July 24, 1782). Unlike the leading character in so many American serials, we can visualize the Pilgrim because Freneau has paid attention to physical details.

While Freneau makes no attempt to develop a club, he does create a society through which the Pilgrim moves in town and country; notably the country parson, who thought me a ghost "when he first beheld me in my outlandish habit, walking toward the church yard, with my spectacles on." He and "the honest husbandman," another of the Pilgrim's rural neighbors, are men "of simple, upright, and blameless lives, strangers to all fantastical politeness, ceremony and insincerity. . . . neither of them have locked their doors by night for near forty years past" (No. 3, December 5, 1781). The parson "seems to have had a tolerable classical education," is abstemious and "a stranger to melancholy," and opposes slave keeping. "He has preached with such success against this execrable practice, that there are but one or two of his parishioners who are at present known to keep a slave under their roofs" (No. 4, December 12, 1781). The Pilgrim, who is disgusted by the sight "of a christian clergyman rolling in his coach, swelling with pride, associating only with princes and nobles, and courting the favour of kings and cesars," enjoys smoking a pipe and passing the evening with this humble, serene parson, "whom an ill-judging world stiles *Poor*" (No. 3, December 5, 1781).

Of all Freneau's serials, in none is the division between partisan and nonpartisan essays so sharp as in *The Pilgrim*. Not until he underwent the horrors of existence aboard a British prison ship and hospital ship in 1780 did Freneau experience war at first hand; thereafter he wrote with venom. *The Freeman's*

Journal, established at Philadelphia in the spring of 1781, carried his vitriolic verse against the English and the Tories; several of the *Pilgrim* essays are an extension of these poetic attacks. The Pilgrim, having been imprisoned and treated inhospitably in England, speaks from firsthand observation. Little wonder, then, that he charges the English with being cruel, arrogant, credulous, provincial, and factious. In England "thousands of unfortunate wretches are annually hurried out of the world for trifling thefts and other petty crimes." The English as a nation have so high an opinion of their own worth "that the very shoemakers, weavers and pedlars . . . suppose themselves, by some happy *privileges* of birth, to be nearly upon an equality with, and can swallow as much flattery as any crowned head in Europe or Asia" (No. 2, November 28, 1781).[10] "This island is also divided and subdivided into innumerable factions and parties. England despises Scotland for her poverty. . . . Scotland again stigmatizes her sister for gluttony, drunkenness, irreligion and pride. If an inhabitant of Wales makes his appearance in any town or city beyond his own district, in Britain, he immediately becomes an object of universal laughter. . . . If a native of Ireland travels to London . . . the company, if they pay any attention at all to his sentiments, it is only with a design to observe and ridicule the blunders they momently expect him to commit." In a word, the English "are lovers of discord, tyrannical, cruel, and enemies to peace and harmony" (No. 5, December 19, 1781).

Shortly the Pilgrim receives a letter from Jonathan Simple, "a round shouldered ill-looking" Englishman, challenging him to a duel with sword and pistols unless he publicly disavows his malicious misrepresentations. "Alas, Mr. Simple," replies the Pilgrim, "you have read my strictures upon your nation in a very unsuitable frame of mind." I am not the first to charge the English with being cruel and barbarous. "After a criminal is suspended to a gibbet, no nation but this takes him down when but half dead, rips up his bowels, tears out his heart, and throws it reeking with blood into his face!" What good can come from accepting this challenge? "Better would it be that ten, nay ten score of such persons as my correspondent should perish, than that one page of that bulky *folio* [*De Anima Mundi*] be lost to" the next generation. "I possess strength and activity enough to punish any one severely who may have the impudence to disturb or affront me in the manner he threatens. . . . Further, Mr Simple, I have a large dog [who] will by no means see me ill used without resenting it" (No. 7, January 2, 1782). "I am very glad that you did not axcept that there shallange from Mr. Simple," writes Eliakim Stout; "he kils you or you kils him; if he kils you, thers an end of you, if you kils him, you will be hang'd. . . . it maks no ods whitch is kiled, for let it be whitch it wil, we sha. never se that bigg book of yours about the *Animal Mundy*" (No. 9, January 16, 1782). Freneau's attack on the English gains immediacy by this heated interchange between Jonathan Simple, the Pilgrim, and Eliakim Stout.

After Yorktown the fate of the Tories was never in doubt; those who had not already so suffered faced confiscation and exile. Freneau, who had been outspoken against them throughout the war, now stepped up his attack. The Pilgrim meets a Tory in one of his travels, "a well dressed person, pretty well advanced in years, mounted on an elegant horse," who believes what he reads in Rivington's *Royal Gazette*. "Do you hear any thing new from Mr. Greene—or from count Rochambeau?" he asks. "The Royal Gazette adviseth that the former is killed and his army cut to pieces, and that the last mentioned has hoisted the French flag in Virginia and taken possession of that province in the name of the king his master. The same paper asserts that the French king intends to oblige us all to turn Roman catholics." Britain "is now thoroughly provoked—nothing could have happened more fortunate for her than the fall of lord Cornwallis and his army. The nations that have hitherto appeared indifferent to her fate, will now rise like a giant from his sleep, take an active part and settle matters entirely to her satisfaction. . . . seventy-five thousand Russian soldiers, embarked in four hundred transports, convoyed by thirty-eight ships of the line [may] be looked for on these coasts about the middle of April next." As the Tory rides off the Pilgrim concludes that men like him, who would pull down "this beautiful structure of liberty and virtue," the American republic, "may justly be compared to those unbelieving Jews . . . who wandered forty years in the wilderness and died there at last. . . . They wished rather to return and be slaves in Egypt, than assert their right to Canaan" (No. 10, January 23, 1782). One of the Pilgrim's correspondents proposes that words having "the disagreeable and ill-looking termination *-tory*" be banished: "there is, prohibi-tory, transi-tory, saluta-tory, moni-tory, his-tory, inven-tory, satisfac-tory, and in short so many *tories*, that I might proceed on with them till I had disgusted you as much as I am myself." It would be fatal to literature, replies the Pilgrim, if this proposal were adopted; for example, "by the simple trans-position of only one alphabetical character, the word tory itself is transmuted into TROY . . . without which Homer's Iliad is in a moment good for nothing." Then in a conciliatory mood he asks, "why should we hesitate to declare that there is no reason why the denomination *tory*, which at this day means an enemy to the peace, happiness, liberty and independence of the United States, may not in the course of a score or two of years, acquire an import directly contrary to what it now has, and imply a hearty friend to all four?" (No. 15, May 29, 1782).[11]

Counterbalancing his attacks on the English and the Tories, Freneau's Pilgrim pictures the present and future greatness of the United States: When Europe after many centuries discov-ered America, Britain among the rest banished her subjects to that distant continent. "These, with a mixture of adventurers from various nations at length humbled the savage tribes, and [rendered] this new country rich and flourishing." Whereupon Britain "claimed them as subjects, took them under her protec-tion, but said in her heart, 'They shall hereafter be my slaves.' . . .What a spectacle of derision do the infatuated Britons now exhibit to the world. . . . A little island situated on the ex-tremities of the ocean, [sending out] her fleets and armies, the flower of her youth, and her ablest commanders, who, the mo-ment they come within the vortex, the sphere of attraction of this huge, unwieldy body, the American world, are immediately swallowed up like straws in a whirlpool, and irrecoverably lost!"[12] "It is not easy to conceive what will be the greatness and importance of North America in a century or two. [Agriculture] will here probably be raised to its pinnacle of perfection, and its attendant, commerce, will so agreeably and usefully employ mankind, that wars will be forgotten, nations by a free intercourse with this vast and fertile continent, will again become brothers, and no longer treat each other as savages and monsters" (No. 8, January 9, 1782).

In actual fact most of the *Pilgrim* and *Philosopher of the Forest* essays avoid partisanship such as we have just seen. The Pilgrim determines at the outset to remedy the current neglect of "morality and refined sentiments" in the periodicals and proceeds to discourse on conventional subjects, notably manners. He sets forth the advantages of rural over city life[13] and the benefits of solitude,[14] expresses concern for the mistreatment of servants and horses,[15] and deplores dueling.[16] He exposes the fallacy in supposing that children educated for the learned professions are perforce happy and useful citizens. Bryan O'Krazie of Kilkenny writes him that having been appointed to a remote parish, he made the mistake of introducing a long Latin sentence into a sermon, "which I soon found disgusted my hearers almost beyond forgiveness," and quoted Pope's *Essay on Man* in another sermon, for which "I was calumniated for a papist, and soon had the bare walls and empty pews to preach to." Indeed, says the Pilgrim, "the untaught and illiterate shall sometimes do more for the advancement of true knowledge in an hour, than the crowds of sophists and professors could accomplish in the whole course of their lives. The illiterate man of invention is a Columbus, who ... boldly launches out into the immense ocean of ideas, and brings to light new worlds teeming with gold and diamonds," whereas "the scholar is the timorous and cautious pilot, who creeping along shores already discovered ... makes shift, in a bungling manner, to get from port to port" (Nos. 11 and 12, January 30, February 13, 1782). We have seen how Franklin and Trumbull pointed out the folly of wealthy parents who send their dull children to college since on such an education is a waste. Freneau extends the attack to middle- and lower-class parents. There is no guarantee, as the case of Bryan O'Krazie makes clear, that educating such children for the learned professions will render them happy and useful. A few years later, in "The Indian Student: or, Force of Nature," Freneau described how an Indian, enrolling at Harvard "Where learned men talk heathen Greek, / And Hebrew lore is gabbled

)'er," wonders unhappily why he ever forsook his native wood 'For musty books and college halls."

The Pilgrim is offended by foppery in Philadelphia, in particu-
ar "a little man with long thin legs, which may be aptly com-
)ared, when covered by his white silk stockings, to the perfo-
ated tubes of the earthen pipes in use among smoakers of
obacco." Fops exist in all ages and all countries. "The polite
:uropean, or the civilized American loaths, and laughs at the
Iottentot because he covers his head with a mass composed of
1ogs lard and cow dung, and yet the want of this filthy cap would
ender the African odious in the sight of his mistress! . . . a
:uropean or an American fopling is not a much less filthy or
idiculous object with his hair and coat plaistered, sprinkled and
)edaubed over with powder and pomatum, than the native of
he southern extremity of Africa, with the beforementioned
:urious *head dress*, so detested and abhorred by the people of
•ther countries" (No. 14, May 8, 1782). Here again, as in Trum-
)ull's writings, foppery comes under attack. As a spectator in
)hiladelphia the Pilgrim, who goes clad in plain attire and
:njoys simple country living, favors extravagance in female
ashions, for that is the way to catch a husband, but finds male
oppery less excusable.

The peace-loving Pilgrim, presenting an extract from the
l256th chapter of *De Anima Mundi*, moralizes on the irrational-
ty of war: "Every age has produced its CAINS, whom Divine
)rovidence . . . has often permitted to oppress, enslave and de-
)troy the more peaceable and well disposed part of the human
ace. . . . such were the Romans and Carthagenians, two
housand years since, such are the modern British in Europe, the
Malays in Asia, the Dahonims in Africa [and] the Mohawk
ndians in America." Thinking of the American Revolution still
n progress, he remarks, "Would not an inhabitant of another
)lanet, suddenly arriving here, pronounce all warriors lunatics
vhen he beheld them this hour tearing each other to pieces with
heir diabolical machines of destruction, and the next, smiling
1pon and embracing their vanquished opponent with all the
enderness of bosom intimacy and friendship!" "I am in doubt,"
:oncludes the Pilgrim, "whether a man that is constitutionally

a lover of fighting can be justly called *animal rationale* or not" (No. 16, June 19, 1782).

The most memorable character in the series is the Pilgrim's litigious old city neighbor, whose "head is full of chicanery, evasions, quibbles, distinctions without a difference, crotchets and catches." He has been reduced to near beggary by his perpetual lawsuits. The Pilgrim, inadvertently stepping on the old man's favorite spaniel, would have been sued for "an *action of battery*" and thrown in jail had not the man sighted one of his creditors and rushed in, barring the doors and windows (No. 17, July 3, 1782). As the Pilgrim passes his door, "two large flies stung [the old man] at the same instant, one upon the nose, the other upon his right leg. 'Sue them, said I, at law, for it is undoubtedly an *action of battery*' " (No. 18, July 24, 1782). The Pilgrim, asserting that "men are naturally enemies to each other," adds that "those who desire to keep whole bones and yet cannot help being at enmity with others, go to law." The old man is a case in point. Implicit in this character sketch is a slur on lawyers who prosper at the expense of such litigants.

The Pilgrim and *The Philosopher of the Forest* employ the well-worn conventions of the Addisonian essay. The persona of the Pilgrim as an observer of town and country life is sustained through the series, nor does he change when metamorphosed into the Philosopher; but the disguise is thin at times, especially in the partisan essays wherein the angry voice of the author is clear and unmistakable. The Pilgrim receives letters from Comus, Jonathan Simple, Eliakim Stout, Rachel Sleepless, Maria Flutter, Timothy Legible, Bryan O'Krazie, a Man of Feeling, Anti-Tory, Peter Steady, and Philequus. And the Philosopher has two dream visions; in the dream about fame the superintending spirit seizes the Philosopher "by the left hand to conduct me to the habitations of virtuous men, when the fright, occasioned by the sudden grasp of so formidable a spirit, awakened me just as the dawning of the day began to glimmer through the apertures of my cavern."[17] The style of this the earliest of Freneau's essay serials is formal and heavily latinate, unlike the relaxed, colloquial style of much of his later prose. Intrinsically it is the least interesting of his literary serials.

124

II

Tomo Cheeki, which makes effective use of the foreign visitor, appeared in 1795.[18] Tomo was a historical figure, "a *mico*, or chief of the Yamacraws, of the Creek Confederacy, who, in 1734, had been brought to England by Oglethorpe, presented to the king at Kensington, and feted in the British capital."[19] Freneau's first use in prose of the name Tomo Cheeki, and the germ of the future serial, occurs in his 1788 sketch of a splenetic Indian who abandons all thoughts of suicide when a trader offers to barter a keg of French brandy for his beaver skins.[20] In late July 1790 Andrew McGillivray, a half-breed chief of the Creek Indians, arrived in New York with thirty Creek sachems to sign a peace treaty. Freneau's immediate literary response to this visit was a short series of essays about one of these sachems, Opay Mico.[21] Five years later he undertook a much longer series, in which Tomo Cheeki (not Opay Mico) visits Philadelphia (not New York) to sign a treaty and writes his impressions of the city and its inhabitants.

Tomo Cheeki, like the splenetic Indian, is grave and melancholy. "While his fellow deputies were carousing in taverns and dramshops, he would walk into the fields and woods, smoke his pipe, divert himself with fishing and such other rural employments as he found most inviting and agreeable to his savage fancy." After he leaves Philadelphia his landlord admits that Tomo "was fond of cyder and small beer, slept but five hours out of the twenty four; rose constantly at the first dawn . . . eat sparingly . . . now & then noted down his remarks in his own language, expressed great disgust at the manners of civilized society,—and danced a whole hour, the evening before his departure, with a favourite squaw."[22] Tomo finds his landlord "cold, unconversable, and disobliging"; but "the woman of the house is a young handsome squaw, and has already obliged me with a pipe of tobacco" (May 30, 1795). We get little sense of the Philadelphia milieu through which Tomo moves, other than his disgust on first seeing "wigwams innumerable, of immense height and size" and his dislike of "these pebbled ways, these little lazy channels of putrifying water, this cracking of whips; the anxious discontented countenance of all I meet" (May 30,

1795). The story of how Moncachtape, a Yahoo Indian, "with a view of finding how far the woods extended towards the going down of the sun," journeyed to the Pacific, strengthens the "Indianness" of the series and makes Tomo a more credible character (July 11, 1795). As Tomo prepares to leave Philadelphia he views with a heavy heart the peace treaty he has signed, telling Opay Meeko, "These blankets—this brandy—these tomahawks and arms of thunder!—how slow are the white men in putting into our hands what the big council has demanded as the price of peace!" Here in Philadelphia we are "marked as an inferior, little race of men, and are considered the same as sticks and straws that are wafted on the face of the river, heeded by few, and neglected by all; while themselves are like the lofty ships that are seen afar from the hills." He retires "from the great village to pass away days by the side of the deep river, at a distance from men, the noise of their chariots, and the sound of their bells," and views with despair the future of his race.[23] Like the Pilgrim, Tomo prefers the simple rural life to the noise and clutter of the city. Freneau makes him the symbol of the doomed red man who sees through the blandishments of the white man.

In the first of several manners essays Tomo deplores men who drink so much that they become like beasts, but is afraid of "that man who was never known to transgress the bounds of strict sobriety in drinking. Such a man is cold and unfeeling. . . . Life should, in a certain degree, be chequered with folly, otherwise we . . . lose those pleasures which folly, when seasonably indulged, never fails to inspire" (June 20, 1795).[24] It is understandable that Tomo, who is "fond of cyder and small beer," should advocate a policy of moderation rather than abstinence. Elsewhere he smiles at the superstitions of white men. When he asks the master of a large ship what possible use a horseshoe nailed to the mast can be, the master explains, "I have sailed these five and forty years upon the deep seas, and never experienced any dangerous accident in such ships or barques as had this particular piece of iron attached to them; but constantly the reverse in those vessels wherein I neglected it." The white men "laugh at us for our credulity," remarks Tomo. "They despise us for believing in [our] good and bad *Manitous*. . . . they call us rude, savage and unenlightened, at the very instant when they themselves are putting their trust in HORSE SHOES!" (August 1, 1795).[25] Here, as throughout the series, Tomo exposes the hypocrisy of the white man who possesses the very traits he criticizes the Indian for.

In keeping with the convention of the foreign visitor, the natural life of the Indian is pictured as superior to the civilized life of the white man. Philadelphians commiserate with us, writes Tomo, "on account of what they call our savage way of life"; "we, in our turn, no less pity them for living cooped up in dark cages and narrow boxes, where they have scarcely room to turn or breathe." The artist sits "on his bench, pale as the grass beneath the thick spreading oak . . . restrained by an artificial necessity to his gloomy habitation," whereas a tree "will serve us for a house. Our largest wigwams are erected and finished in a day, and admit the light and air in abundance. . . . We hear not the voice of the tax-gatherer at our doors, to take away our bed of skins to support the luxuries of the proud, and governments that riot on the spoils of the poor. . . . Our manner of life renders us alert, cheerful, and courageous" (July 18, 1795).[26] Tomo writes Hopiniyahie, "an India Woman on the south side of the river O-conee," that he is sickened by the white man's fondness for seeing his own likeness. Passing through the streets of Philadelphia, he sees copies "in profuse abundance, suspended by way of sign from the houses; fixed over the doors as an invitation to come in; fastened to the walls in the nature of ornament; or attached to the glass windows as articles [of] sale. . . . What right have these white people to be staring down upon me from the walls of every house I enter?" But he realizes that such vanity exists in his own tribe; "otherwise why did you, my Hopiniyahie, persuade me to hang these trinkets to my nose, and suspend these little foolish drops of glass from my ears! why did I put on these mokkisons of many colours, and bear on my arm these strings of wampum of a dozen fantastical dyes! . . . the skin of a bear or a deer would have gained me more esteem from the wise and discerning than all the foppery, and all the splendid figures that you have lavished upon the blanket, which you gave me to put on!" (September 12, 1795). As the Pilgrim set forth the advantages of the rural life over the urban, so too Tomo. While disgusted by the vanity of Philadelphians, he is honest enough to admit that his own people are also vain. Nevertheless the Indian is depicted here and throughout the series as superior to the white man.

As the Pilgrim had moralized on the irrationality of war, so now Tomo Cheeki. When news reaches Philadelphia that Indians to the north and west are at war, a philosopher concludes *"that the whole race of red-men are therefore of a diabolical nature."* Whereupon Tomo asks, "is not blood and murder a trade with the white men also?" By abandoning the law of reason, under which he was originally "a mild, a beneficent, a humane creature, without wars," man "has become what he is—a mean, base, cruel, and treacherous being." "With these and other reflections, I laid myself down on my blanket to take a sleep," and dreamed I was in "a dismal valley, where all seemed horror, desolation, and disorder"; a person "of a dull melancholy visage, & with an extreme long beard" explains that this "is the world of perfect evil." Tomo asked why the inhabitants wore long beards. "Here, in hell, we have razors enough (answered he) and we all wish heartily to be shaved—but we devils will not trust each other for shavers." Shocked by this horrid speech, he woke up thinking, "How happy am I to reside in a town, among a species of beings who have barbers in every street, and where every man may entrust himself in the hands even of a stranger, without danger of having his weazon cut!" (June 13, 1795). So disproportionately long is the introduction that the dream itself comes almost as an afterthought to Tomo's discourse on war. While employing some of the familiar machinery (in this instance the valley is dismal, not fair), the dream is never developed, and the irony present in Tomo's waking thought is heavy handed.

In another dream Tomo hears a ship's Indian figurehead tell a crowd gathered at the wharf how the white man has persecuted his race: "Our habitations were once on the borders of the rivers of the ocean"; when we saw "your machines of death . . . we retreated from the shore to the Allegany, from the Allegany to the Ohio . . . you have at length followed us over the Ohio—you meditate to drive us beyond the Missisippi—to the lake of the woods, to the frozen desarts of the north, and to the regions of darkness and desolation." Consider "what were your feelings when only a few years ago, the great king on the other side of the water intruded upon your rights? . . . You yourselves are now, in your turn, become the oppressors. . . . Say not that you have purchased our territory. Was a keg of whiskey, some bundles of laced coats, or a few packages of blankets, an equivalent for the extent of a kingdom?" The missionaries you sent "to effect our conversion to your faith . . . have now quit us entirely, and given us up to the god of nature—you send armies in their room, not to convert, but to destroy us." "Being suddenly awaked by the yelpings of a wolf-dog, that sleeps at the foot of my blanket," Tomo loses "the remainder of this extraordinary speech" (July 25, 1795).[27] Although ostensibly a dream vision, this essay is in fact a monologue on the white man's mistreatment of the Indian; there is little attempt to set the scene, less certainly than in the dream about the world of evil. In these two essays Freneau casts the veil of the dream over his thoughts on war in a perfunctory, unconvincing manner.

Reflecting philosophically, Tomo warns one of his brother sachems at Philadelphia, who has applied for membership in the American Philosophical Society, not to be seduced by science: "Simpleton! . . . Why all this solicitude to be acquainted with the secrets of their philosophy?" In your extensive journeys, Tomo asks with mock sympathy, "could you no where have picked up some odd petrifaction—the tail of a fox—a tooth of the Mammuth— Could you not have caught a young alligator and dragged him captive hither, to ensure the success of your application?" What do you care whether the world is round; "were it as flat as a trencher—were it a cylinder—a cone—were it of the shape of a wigwam, it is still your home, your place of life and of death." Content yourself instead "with the knowledge of such things as really concern you, and will operate to your earthly good" (June 6, 1795). While not so clearly satirical as Hugh Henry Brackenridge's attacks on the American Philosophical Society in *Modern Chivalry*, Freneau is nonetheless questioning the value of such scientific investigations. Elsewhere Tomo agrees with a philosopher he was conversing with the previous night that the golden age, which Philadelphians think will return, is yet very far off. It was an age of shepherds, says the philosopher, a time when there were no wars and the earth produced "her fruits in abundance, without the aid of the plough share." "I see nothing but misery among these white men," concludes Tomo. "I see them enslaved and enslaving. ... I see jails, gallowses and jibbets." I see men, "perhaps for stealing a handkerchief, a hatchet, a blanket, or a bit of bread, tied to a post, stripped half naked, and whipped almost to death by the executioner with a merciless lash— Assuredly, their age of shepherds is yet very far off!" (August 29, 1782).

Later, reflecting on the fact that the history of the white man is "little else but murders, executions, treachery, and villainy," Tomo dreams "that the whole race of mankind are, after a time, to disappear from this earth, to be succeeded by a ruling animal more perfect, more grateful, and more agreeable to the upright mind of the creating patron of the Universe." In this dream vision the superintending genius of the world, having destroyed the human race, commands the inferior animals "to pass in review before him, and assign their pretensions, if any they had, to be the ruling animal in place of man, who was annihilated." All of the animals are found wanting. The elephant is "too heavy and unwieldy for an active governor," the horse subservient to the monkey on his back who directs him, the monkey "a compound of hypocrisy and grimace." The dog allowed himself to be worshipped in Egypt although "worship belongs to the Deity only"; moreover, he possesses sharp claws "calculated for war." The lion shows himself bloodthirsty by springing at a sheep and tearing him to pieces. So the genius determines to "form an animal in the outward resemblance of Man; the machinery within the head shall remain the same, but that of the heart shall be upon a new principle. The main spring shall be Benevolence, and every wheel in the system shall feel its efficacy." The forms of men and women who spring into being at the motion of his wand seem "to have no idea of war or contentions: the spirit of justice, benevolence, and every amiable virtue was prevalent within them." Tomo is on the point of asking the genius to transform him into one of these new beings "when I was awakened by my landlord with information that some letters had been received, addressed to me from the Indian

130

country" (October 17, 31, 1795). Even though Freneau fails to set the stage in detail, this dream vision is superior to the two earlier in the series, partly because he allows himself more space in which to work. The dream itself is carefully motivated, and interest is sustained by the procession of animals who plead their right to rule; the incident which brings it to an end is credible. This essay is clear evidence that when he tried, Freneau could develop and control this convention.

The appearance at the inn of Tomo's shipmaster friend who talked about horseshoes inspires the ordinarily taciturn landlord to mount the oaken table and describe the character of the retired sea captain: Having looked "about him with as much wildness and anxious concern, as a landsman would, that is left swimming for his life in the middle of the Atlantic . . . he, at length, agrees to be entertained by the week, or month, at some boarding-house, as near as possible to the wharves." But having "been so long accustomed to command, [he] cannot bear to be controuled by the landlady"; so at last he advertises for a wife: "She must be sharp built, with a long floor, and broad upon the beam—; handsome sheer, but not moon-sided. She must answer her helm well, and not miss stays, so as to oblige me often to wear her. I would rather, of the two, have her heavy rigg'd, as in our voyage through this life we have mostly stormy latitudes to sail in, and many a hard gale to encounter, &c. &c." After being married a month or two to an old seaman's widow who can "understand his jargon" and "endure the smell of pitch, tar, turpentine, and rosin," he makes plans to build a house. "With this view he purchases a lot of land as close as possible to the river's side, and where the yard-arms of the shipping may extend entirely over his roof. If the tides of the river come into his cellar, so much the better: this he calls bilge-water." Tomo's friend retires in tears, assuring him that this description "applied very well to most of the old men of his profession who had the good fortune to escape being swallowed up in the ocean, torn to pieces by great guns, or wrecked on unknown shores" (August 15, 1795). When he wrote this character sketch Freneau was himself a retired sea captain after several years in the coastal trade. He brings the type to life with deftly chosen nautical diction, just as in poems written a few years earlier he brings to life such other native types as "The Newsmonger," "The Drunken Soldier," and "The Roguish Shoemaker." His ability at realistic portraiture, to say nothing of his ability in such works as *A Journey from Philadelphia to New-York* to handle episodic narrative, suggests that he had the makings of a picaresque novelist.

Among American serials there is no more successful example of the foreign visitor than *Tomo Cheeki*. Although Freneau surely knew Addison's *Spectator* No. 50, wherein an Indian king makes "abundance of very odd Observations" about his stay in London, the contention of one critic that "Freneau's method is identical with that of Addison"[28] oversimplifies the case; it seems certain that he was also familiar with Montesquieu's *Lettres persanes* and Goldsmith's *Citizen of the World* and that he was influenced by their treatment of the foreign visitor as well. At any rate Freneau establishes the convention at once and sustains it, a fact which helps make *Tomo Cheeki* livelier than *The Pilgrim*. "Some years ago," he explains in the first number, "about thirty Indian chiefs of the Creek nation, attended by several squaws, came by land to Philadelphia, to settle a treaty of amity with the republican government of this country" (May 23, 1795). One of these chiefs, Tomo Cheeki, realizes that "in this place, during my abode in the great village, I am to pen down some notes for the information of my countrymen towards the south and the west" (May 30, 1795). After Tomo's departure from Philadelphia his landlord discovers "a large bundle of papers . . . in an old hamper in a corner of the room where he had lodged" and sells them for ten French crowns. "No person offered, that had a sufficient knowledge of the Talassee, or Creek language, to give only a tolerable translation," until one who had been a prisoner but had made his escape from the Creek nation is engaged and promises "to be true and faithful to his original, as far as the idioms of the two languages will allow. As these translated papers come to hand they will be inserted in the JERSEY CHRONICLE, for the amusement and information of the curious" (May 23, 1795). In letters home Tomo, as we have seen, makes observations on manners and morality at Philadelphia and offers philosophical reflections, all tending to elevate the Indian above the white man. The last essay, wherein Tomo informs Opay Meeko that he is returning to the Creek country, rounds out the series in a way Freneau had not done in *The Pilgrim*. Moreover, *Tomo Cheeki* is more relaxed and conversational than *The Pilgrim*, more diverting and less didactic.

III

Hezekiah Salem, over which signature Freneau composed a literary serial in 1797,[29] writes: "I am a native of the state of Connecticut. My father was a weaver of no mean degree." Resisting his father's arguments to follow the same trade, Hezekiah became a preacher instead; "no less than twenty five years did I pass in that benevolent occupation." Unluckily, though, he was "fond of playing at bowls"; at length a deacon, popping in unexpectedly, reported "that he had caught 'Hezekiah Salem, the grave preacher, playing at nine-pins on the bowling green!' " He was pronounced unworthy of his calling and dismissed. So "I sailed over to the east-end of Long Island in a canoe, with all my worldly appurtenances, consisting of a dog, a cat, a chest of old sermons and other writings, &c., seven pumpkins of the best and largest kind, a hoe, a spade, a straw bed, and some apparel of coarse sort and quality," where "I built a cabbin, or hut, near the seashore, and at my first settling, made frequent excursions in New England vessels on whaling voyages, in quality of steward, and, on occasion, harpoon-man. Weary, however, of the fatigues of the main great sea, I have reoccupied my hut, last year, and, by way of eschewing idleness, have, with some little exertion of ingenuity, adopted the trade of basket-making. I find this will maintain me comfortably (being an old batchelor) during my declining years" (October 25, 1797).

One of Hezekiah's whims is his love of pumpkins, a plant that flourishes in New England. "Perhaps nature did never make a more generous present to mankind, in the way of vegetation, for food, both of man and hog." It is said "that a spiritous liquor has been made therefrom that made some people, whom I will not bewray, talk rather *foolishly*." When a New Englander "sits down in his easy chair to reflect soberly and sedately, a pumpkin is the first object that strikes his attention." "If he makes a journey he is sure to pack some slices of pumpkin in his saddle bags"; "if he goes to sea, plenty of pumpkins is stowed into every hole and corner of the ship." But no more need be said here, "as I am told several learned treatises are soon to be published on the subject" (October 23). Another of his whims is how to get through a crowd. The best way, he finds, is "to eat a quantity of garlick" and fill his pipe with strong tobacco. "Smoking in a crowd, together with a strong breath of garlic, soon procures to a man, a little vacant circle, wherein he may stand at his ease, and as he advances, he remaineth still the centre of the circle" (October 31). Hezekiah delights in the melancholy music of a howling house. "In my time (and my years are not few in number) I have heard a great deal of music, sacred as well as prophane," but none so delights me, not the organ, the flute, or the clarinet, as "the *howling house*; where sitting pensively in a long winter evening, when the wind is to the eastward, and clouds impending, a melancholy sort of music plays through the eaves, and awakens the mind to contemplation" (November 13).

The bachelor Hezekiah, who as a minister spent much of his time in his study which held his "books, papers, and writings . . . penning down [his] reflections," recalls one of the inconveniences he suffered. Every week and sometimes oftener the housekeeper Grace Gibbons would

> intrude into my room of study with her washcloths, brooms, and scrubbing brushes to cleanse the walls and floors with a deluge of warm water. . . . Her scrubbings obliged me almost continually to be removing my large books from one end of the room to the other, a work of no small toil and difficulty: my papers became misplaced; my hints and heads of sermons lost or spoiled—and once, in consequence of her ill judged washings on a Saturday night, when she overwhelmed many of my choice papers, I had nearly been put to open shame the next day before the whole congregation, for the loss of some notes, on which I had depended, to eke out my discourse to two hours and a half in length.

Following the example of Plato, who "had written over the door of his academy at Athens '*Let no man enter here unskilled in* the Mathematics,' " "I placed over the door of my study room in capital letters, 'LET NO WOMAN *enter this room with broom, boonder, scrubbing brushes, filing-cloths, or Water* TUBS!' " (November 1).

Like the Pilgrim, Hezekiah when a minister turned away a challenge. He publicly rebuked one of his parishioners, "Benjamin Bigbones, a man of huge stature and forbidding countenance," for his "intemperate use of switchell, an undue mixture of molasses and water," whereupon "his countenance fell, and . . . he appeared confused; the eyes of the whole congregation being fixed upon him." Early the next morning he received a note from Bigbones requesting "that I would meet him with the accustomed weapons of fight on the morrow morning at five o'clock, in an obscure place on the other side of the river, to render him due satisfaction for the affront I had offered him in my last sermon." Knowing "little of the use of sword and pistols," Hezekiah concluded that it "would have been *out of character*" for him to duel and dispatched a note deploring the sneaking way in which dueling is carried on. He added, "I will e'en fight you on the great common of the town, where the men of the city, the old wives and the maidens may be assembled, by the ring of a bell, to behold the fight," and heard nothing further from Bigbones (November 10).

Admittedly the New Englander is treated humorously in this series, but it is overstating the case to call the character of Hezekiah Salem "a deliberate satire on the New England Yankee, whom Freneau had cause to hate."[30] The satire here is Horatian, not Juvenalian like the bulk of Freneau's Revolutionary writings. The matter is almost wholly whimsical, as though in anticipation of *Salmagundi*; the spectacle of Hezekiah beset by a scouring housekeeper, for example, calls to mind Launcelot Langstaff's antipathy to brooms. Indeed, it is almost impossible to dissociate the matter from the character of the old bachelor, Hezekiah Salem. The one exception is the final essay wherein he addresses himself to little men who, despite the examples of Lycurgus and Saul, "are an undervalued part of the species." Julius Caesar reminds us that though "the tall Germans despised my little Roman soldiers . . . yet Cesar conquered Germany." "Upon all occasions in life," concludes Hezekiah, "you will find yourselves big enough for any rational purposes, provided your souls are not as little as your bodies" (November 17). It may well be that Freneau broke off the series at this point because he realized that whimsy was giving way to didacticism.

IV

On March 25, 1799, Freneau over the signature "Robert Slender" initiated his most impressive and extensive serial in William Duane's *Aurora*, the foremost Republican newspaper of the day; he only brought it to an end on February 19, 1801, when it was finally determined that Jefferson had won the presidency.[31] The *Slender* letters are the most steadily partisan and least social of all Freneau's literary serials, and yet the character of Robert Slender and his Philadelphia milieu are full bodied and alive. Freneau's original Robert Slender of 1787 was a Pennsylvania stocking and tape weaver who at his death left a bundle of manuscripts containing, among other writings, an account of his journey from Philadelphia to New York in 1783.[32] The Robert Slender of 1799 is a Philadelphia cobbler who, if he can't use the initials A.M., D.M., LL.D., or F.R.S. after his name, will sign himself O.S.M., "ONE OF THE SWINISH MULTITUDE"; for he stands "unnoticed among the swinish herd," fulfilling his parents' prophecy that he "will never be a *great man*."[33] He is the familiar naïf, juxtaposed to his learned neighbors, the Latinist and the minister. Throughout the series Robert shows himself timid to the point of cowardice. During the Revolution, he admits, "I trembled for fear, and skulked into a corner, where I lay snug out of sight during the awful contest; and when Washington had gained the day . . . slipped out of my hiding-place, and talked, as well as I could, about Liberty, Independence, Freedom, and such like things" (19-20). Hearing that democrats ought to be executed without benefit of trial, he prepares to retreat again to his "old hiding-place" (30). He is also giddy-headed. Alarming rumors that prove untrue so perplex him that, as he says, "I have been, like the weathercock, the sport of every blast; like a tennis ball, bandied from hand to hand; now up and then down, for all the world like the ends of a balancing beam" (55).

We get our clearest picture of Robert, who guesses he is about forty, as he makes his way to the tavern:

> Having heard that there was a tavern at about the distance of a
> mile or so from my favourite country spot, where now and then a
> few neighbours meet to spit, smoke segars, drink apple whiskey,

cider, or cider-royal, and read the news—a few evenings ago, I put on my best coat, combed out my wig, put my spectacles in my pocket, and a quarter dollar. . . . so out I walks, with a good stout stick in my hand, which I always make a point to carry with me, lest the dogs should make rather freer with my legs than I could wish. But I had not gone more than half the way, when, by making a false step, I splash'd my stocking from the knee to the ancle.

Money, thinks Robert, "might with more profit be laid out in repairing the roads, than in marine establishments, supporting a standing army, useless embassies, exhorbitant salaries." Talking to himself about his search for a man in whom he might put his political trust, "by accident I looked up, and perceived to my surprise, that if I had gone but one step further, I would have actually knocked my nose against the sign-post—I declare, said I, here I am—this is a tavern indeed. I then felt in my pocket, if I had my quarter dollar, which to my joy I found—I then unbuttoned my coat, to shew my silk waistcoat, pulled my watch chain a good piece longer out of my pocket, fixed my hat a little better on my head—and then advanced boldly into the tavern" (128-31). We catch a glimpse of Robert's family as he prepares to flee to the country: "Phillis, Phillis, cried I, as loud as I could bawl, go and tell your mistress to make all the speed she possibly can, for we'll leave town before daybreak. Away ran Phillis—and in came Mrs. Slender, Why my dear all this haste? Why all this haste, replied I, that's a question indeed; do you think I am going to stay here to have my throat cut, to be whipped to death, or skivered like a lark? . . . I believe we can't go to-morrow, Patty has no shoes, the mantua-maker has not brought home my gown, and the barber has not your wig ready yet" (52-53). Robert Slender is the most memorable in the long gallery of characters Freneau created in poetry and prose, a seemingly naïve, excessively fearful cobbler who cuts a comic figure going to the tavern, muddying his stockings and almost bumping into a sign-post, then displaying his silk waistcoat and watch chain as he makes a grand entrance.

Gradually Robert's Republicanism asserts itself. He questions such recent Federalist actions as the Jay Treaty (August 18, 1795) and the Alien and Sedition acts (June 25, July 14, 1798), is critical of the clergy for their high-handed behavior and for mixing politics with religion,[34] and accuses the Adams administration of failing to condemn the British for executing the impressed seaman Jonathan Robbins who had led a mutiny.[35] Eventually he supports Thomas McKean, the Republican candidate in the 1799 Pennsylvania gubernatorial campaign, and rejoices at the election of Thomas Jefferson.[36]

In order to circumvent prosecution under the Sedition Act, Freneau resorts to irony, constructing mock-serious dialogue between the naïve Robert and his learned neighbors. The Latinist advises him, "let the cobler stick to his last," and proceeds to defend the Federalist position against all Robert's arguments to the contrary. Freneau, in parody of elaborate eighteenth-century dedications, has Robert, who despite the Latinist's advice is determined to commence an author, dedicate not only his works but his life "to the Freemen, the Lovers of Liberty, the Asserters, Maintainers and Supporters of Independence throughout the United States. . . . And if my plain told stories . . . can have the effect of calling up the republican spirits to a more ardent love of their country's rights—to more watchfulness, and stricter enquiry, I shall abundantly receive that which I expect" (iii-vii). Robert's espousal of Republican principles is seemingly offset here, as throughout most of the series, by his apparent naïveté and ignorance.

Freneau establishes at once the ground for his attack on Federalism and defense of Republicanism by having one who calls himself "The Monarchist" state that princes and governors stand above the law. The Monarchist argues on the authority of Pliny, Plato, Tacitus, and Plutarch "that princes are not bound to be, like other men, *virtuous*," maintains that the Alien and Sedition acts are aimed at those who "are inimical to all good government" and those who speak "against persons high in trust," and concludes, "Let us never judge governors by those rules by which we ourselves are to abide and be governed; but rest satisfied under whatever laws, decrees, or ordinances the rulers frame" (12-14). Robert is thunderstruck by the Monarchist's argument; but when he wonders about old Tories slipping into power, the pulling down of Antichrist, the Alien and Sedition acts, and the plans to influence the gubernatorial election, the Latinist advises him not to judge for himself but to trust the Federalists who love order and are enlightened, being "the admirers of the British government, firm supporters of the British Treaty, the Excise Law and Stamp Act, the Alien and Sedition bills, &c. &c." "Lord bless me," says an astonished Robert. "If these men think so, no doubt but they will soon strive to deprive the poor of the right of being electors" (23-24).

The Latinist exposes the naïveté of Robert's belief that all men, especially politicians, are honest and honorable unless he knows otherwise: "You think a republican form of government is best—I think a republican form of government is the *highest note in the gamut of nonsense.* . . . with all these gentlemen you will find it an established axiom—the end justifies the means—For proof of this, attend to the whole system of bribery, spies, fomenters of strife, secret service money, diplomatic skill, systems of alarm—and insincere negociations" (67-69). When Robert expresses hatred for the office and power of kings, the Latinist warns that "if the coalition of kings, emperors, seignors, and moguls, can prevail so as to establish a monarchy in France, which God in his infinite mercy forbid, our republic must undoubtedly fall: we must receive a king, one of the royal brood of Great Britain, and like spaniels lick the feet of godlike majesty." "God help us," says Robert, "I think I see the red coats once more march along the Delaware—I think I hear the groans of free-born Americans from the hulk of the Jersy prison ship . . . I see Burgoyne's Indian cantico . . . and behold more amiable Miss Crea's victims to their horrible cruelty" (88). Eventually, though, Robert wins the day in this dialogue with his learned neighbor. With regard to the Jonathan Robbins affair, for example, he declares that since "the days of priest-craft are at an end," the American government should "come plainly forward and acknowledge, that it cannot yield a sailor protection: or else let them resent such degrading behaviour with proper spirit, and so for ever put an end to the business." The Latinist expresses the hope that America will choose the latter course since "nothing so much encourages men to settle in any country, as a thorough belief that there they will be protected in their lives, property, and their invaluable privileges" (125-27).

Robert eventually wins out over the minister, too. When he declares that the orthodoxy the minister preaches "is neither agreeable to Judaism or Christianity," the minister leaps up and pronounces him "an infidel, a despiser of the clergy, constituted authorities, holy customs, and a dangerous man in society." Goody Rattle assures Mrs. Slender that her husband "is an infidel—a speaker against the clergy—a puller down of religion," and Robert has "once more to shut myself up in the house" and move "into the country among my friends, till the story blows over" (76-78). "Do please your reverence," asks Robert on a later occasion, "give me some mark by which I may know an infidel from a good Christian— Why, Robert, it is not possible to give you an external mark by which you may know an infidel—because it consists entirely in not *believing*. . . . you still wish success to the French, who are all infidels, the pullers down of all established religion, and good order, and speak against the friends of order and good government who openly avow their steady adherence to the christian religion." "What a fool I was," says Robert; "I tho't that true religion was like the French Republic, one and indivisible—but I see I was under a mistake. . . . what a number of religions are there in the world—and each contradicting the other tho—and yet all coming from the source. . . . I—I—I can't think of it any longer— with that I rose intending to throw away my segar, which was a bad one, into the fire—but in my confusion in went my spectacles—my staff was in my hand—the fire was immediately among the parson's legs. . . . by good fortune, I saved my spectacles—which I snatched up, and without saying a single word ran home, leaving the parson to brush his stockings as he saw fit."[37] The following year Robert again argues with the minister. To the minister's complaint, "You now pay little more reverence to our opinions, than to the opinions of a common tradesman—and a taylor, a carpenter, and even a cobler has the assurance to contradict a man, who has received a *liberal education*, and has been solemnly set apart for the ministry," Robert replies, "as long as the clergy fed the stock, with good sound doctrine, paid no adoration to great men, and made no observations on governments, the people respected them, as the ambassadors of Christ, and considered them worthy of the highest honor. . . . becoming men of the world, they ceased to be spiritual men. . . . thus the Clergy of all denominations have, said I, pulled down with their own hands the edifice, which once by better means was erected." "Robert, said his reverence, I find you daily go wrong; it serves no purpose to talk with you—I pronounce you incorrigible—the nonsense you have been talking is nothing to the purpose; you are ignorant of the scriptures, and to argue with a man so void of learning as you are, would be only demeaning myself."[38]

Freneau's ironic strategy also operates in ways independent of these dialogues, notably in Robert's fright at a horrific description of the aristocrat, a conversation with his cousin Simon Simple, his approving a scheme of punishment by baking, and the manner in which finally he throws his support to Thomas McKean. Robert is frightened by Federalist talk of conspiracy, burning, and invasion, but by nothing so much as a description he overhears in a tavern: "an aristocrat is headed like a lion, its body like a leopard, its feet like a bear, its tongue like that of a man, and its teeth like that of a panther. . . . one thing is certain, it was brought here from England. . . . Lord Dunmore was very intimate with it, and acted solely under its direction. . . . It was the aristocrat . . . that planned the campaign which rendered Burgoyne so famous. . . . It was also held in high esteem by General Howe." After the Revolution "the crafty creature put itself under the protection of the Society of Cincinnati. . . . he is admitted into the Senate chamber when the doors are shut, and is always present in the house of Representatives when the galleries are cleared." Running all the way home in fear of being attacked by this beast, Robert assures the editor "that the aristocrat meets me in my waking meditation, and is even present in my dreams" (44-47).

Robert's country cousin Simon Simple advises him not to meddle in politics. Your father Timothy Slender "always warned all his friends and relations, and particularly yourself, how that you should not upon any account have any thing to do with state affairs, but mind your own proper business, and get money as fast as possible" (58). A surprised Robert thanks Simon for this advice: "Have I indeed been meddling with politics? . . . I find I have been just in the station of the fellow in a play that my neighbour read to me the other night, who had been speaking *prose* all his life without knowing it. . . . Dear

Simon, you studied the law a little in your youth . . . tell me if I have written sedition— If I have not, they can't put me in limbo; and God be praised I am not an *alien*. But if you doubt in the smallest degree, put the house in readiness . . . and send black Titus down with Dobbin—we'll lose no time, but go up to you bag and baggage" (61).

When Robert, who is "wonderfully fond of new inventions," learns "of the baking of the poor soldier in Bristol," he says, "I have heard in England and Ireland, of gagging for impertinence, imprisonment, and sometimes flogging for drunkenness, ducking for slovenliness, shooting for desertion, and hanging for being an United Irishman; but BAKING [is] *vary* new—and shews the inventor to be an original genius." By way of improving on this invention I propose that the temperature and baking time be regulated according to the crime, ranging from five minutes at seventy degrees "for abusing a democrat, if a young man," to two hundred degrees "in cases of importance, and for desertion." "But the best of all useful ends which our oven would answer is, that *ten* or *fifteen*, or *twenty stout officers*, whether cavalry or infantry it matters not, could a-la-mode de militaire, *bake* a democratical printer in *such* a *well-heated oven*, and for such a *length* of *time*, that for the future he should never give them a single moment's uneasiness" (89-94). In this the most nearly Swiftian of the *Slender* letters Robert becomes a proposer, albeit not a modest one.

As the Pennsylvania gubernatorial campaign of 1799 drew to a close, Robert reveals his true colors. Arriving at the tavern in search of an honest man on whom he can fix his political faith, he hears an Alien outmaneuver a Citizen. The Alien says that whereas Thomas McKean was zealous for republican principles while serving in the Continental Congress and at the Constitutional Convention, the Federalist candidate James Ross "advocated the British treaty," "the alien and sedition laws," and a standing army; "the independent farmer and true American," declares the Alien, "may easily discern that, as soon as a standing army is strong enough, their liberty is no more" (135). Such persuasive arguments prompt Robert to send greetings "to the aristocrat, the democrat, the would-be-noble, ex-noble, the snug farmer, the lowly plebian, the bishops and clergy." He calls on "aristocrats and great men," "bishops and clergy," "old tories and refugees," and "supporters of the British treaty, alien bill, sedition law, [and] standing army" to "give a strong, true, and decided vote for James Ross." And on "democrats, soldiers of '76," "free born Americans," honest, independent, virtuous farmers, and "honest and industrious mechanics" to "give an honest vote for Thomas M'Kean" (138-41).

The existence of the Sedition Act forced Freneau to resort to a strategy that makes *Robert Slender* the most successful of his literary serials. In these letters he gives effective voice to his faith in Republican principles; unlike most of his political writings during the Revolution which were heavily invective, he here suppresses his anger by devising an ironic strategy at the center of which he situates a political naïf who is wiser than his professional neighbors. At first Robert seems to go along with their arguments for Federalism and orthodox Christianity, though from the outset he displays a stubborn common sense. He begins to throw off the mask when he professes to be surprised at having meddled in politics. Eventually he scores a political victory by forcing the Latinist to express the hope that the American government will take a stand against the British impressment of sailors like Jonathan Robbins, and a religious victory by getting the minister to admit in effect that the clergy have been mixing politics with religion. This serial is written in a more relaxed, conversational manner than *The Pilgrim* and even *Tomo Cheeki*; it is close in style and tone to *Hezekiah Salem* which, however, was a far less ambitious undertaking.

In 1788, speaking through Robert Slender, Freneau issued an early manifesto for American literary independence. Authors "are at present considered as the dregs of the community: their situation and prospects are truly humiliating," says Robert. Those "who have lately exported themselves from Britain and Ireland, and boast that they have introduced the Muses among us since the conclusion of the late war . . . are, however, excuseable in treating the American authors as inferiors; a political and literary independence of their nation being two very different things—the first was accomplished in about seven years, the latter will not be completely effected, perhaps, in as many centuries." The last of the rules Robert lays down for

143

authors requires that they not compromise their talents: "If fortune seems absolutely determined to starve you, and you can by no means whatever make your works sell; to keep up as much as in you lies, the expiring dignity of authorship, do not take to drinking, gambling or bridge-building as some have done, thereby bringing the trade of authorship into disrepute; but retire to some uninhabited island or desert, and there, at your leisure, end your life with decency."[39] It is arguable whether or not Freneau was, as Lewis Leary maintains, a literary failure. What is undeniable is that certain of his political and lyric poems and some of his essays, notably the *Slender* letters, were an attempt to declare literary independence and create the native literature he advocated.

VII. JOSEPH DENNIE

📖

FROM AN EARLY AGE Joseph Dennie read the essays of Steele and Addison and their English descendants and, as he remembered, "endeavoured to conform, with the most scrupulous care, to the purity of their standard."[1] A Harvard classmate recalled that Dennie's "acquaintance with the best English classics was uncommon at that period. His imagination was vivid and he wrote with great ease and facility."[2] Of special importance to his literary development was Laurence Sterne, whose major works were quickly reprinted in America: *A Sentimental Journey* in 1768, *Tristram Shandy* in 1774, *The Sermons of Mr. Yorick* in 1775. Dennie's Lay Preacher, picking up a "Shandean" sermon by the country clergyman whose company he enjoys during college vacations, remarks, "this sermon gave the first hint to that style of Lay Preaching, which I have, for some years, employed; [and] was a model of ease and sentiment in alliance."[3]

Joseph T. Buckingham, who served an apprenticeship at the newspaper office in Walpole, New Hampshire, when Dennie was editing the *Farmer's Weekly Museum*, offers us a portrait of Dennie which marks him, even at age twenty-eight, as a gentleman of the old school:

> He was particularly attentive to his dress, which, when he appeared in the street, on a pleasant day, approached the highest notch of the fashion. I remember, one delightful morning in May, he came into the office, dressed in a pea-green coat, white vest, nankin small-clothes, white silk stockings, and shoes, or *pumps*, fastened with silver buckles, which covered at least half the foot from the instep to the toe. His small-clothes were tied at the knees, with riband of the same color, in double bows, the ends reaching down to the ancles. He had just emerged from the barber's shop. His hair, *in front*, was well loaded with pomatum, frizzled, or *craped*, and powdered; the *ear-locks* had undergone the same process; *behind*, his natural hair was augmented by the addition of a large queue.[4]

In view of this portrait it is perhaps not surprising that Dennie, upon becoming editor, pledged himself to support the paper's conservative policy: "The political creed of this paper has already been so clearly manifested, that perhaps it is superfluous for the Publisher [David Carlisle] to avow the firmness of his Federalism. . . . he will defend the admirable constitution of the United States, and expose the nefarious schemes of the disorganizer and the Jacobin."[5] Nor is it surprising to hear Dennie tell his parents a few years later: "I am still a Bachelor, of 32, and, I believe, a *determined* one. I have no attachments, nor no intentions. I believe I may justly call myself an *old* bachelor."[6] Like Franklin and Freneau, he moved in the world of literary journalism, writing for a succession of newspapers and magazines in Vermont, New Hampshire, Boston, and Philadelphia and editing three of them: *The Tablet* (1795), *The New Hampshire Journal: Or The Farmer's Weekly Museum* (1796-99), and *The Port Folio* (1801-12). Unlike those writers, however, he did not engage in the hurly-burly of politics, but confined himself largely to genial essay writing, notably the *Farrago* and the *Lay Preacher* series.[7]

I

Dennie's first literary serial was *The Farrago*.[8] On January 4, 1794, midway in this series, he wrote his mother: "In the press of Obscurity, I knew that I should risque nothing either in censure or praise. The Public, however saw or fancied some merit;—and, as American essays have been hitherto unmarked except for flimsy expression & jejune ideas, they have allowed me the praise of reviving in some degree the Goldsmith vivacity in thought & the Addisonian sweetness in expression."[9] Looking back over nearly a century of periodical essay writing, Dennie was convinced that it continued popular with most readers. "To a lover of abstruse science, desultory essays may appear a minor species of literature," he writes in the first number of *The Farrago*. "But the majority of mankind are not scholars. . . . they content themselves with the simplest dishes of the literary banquet. Hence the currency of Essays. . . . Accordingly those who exclaim in the words of Armstrong, 'Peace to each drowsy metaphysic sage / And ever may all heavy systems rest,' have been allured to the temples of wisdom and virtue by the suavity of Addison, the sprightliness of Steele, and the sublime morality of Johnson and Hawkesworth" (February 14, 1792). Three years later he reiterates this conviction, with a Sternean emphasis: "Plain food daily grows into disrepute. . . . To gratify modern taste, every thing must be *high seasoned.*" While the literary adventurer resembles Addison's Spectator, he is not, like him, "only an observer in society, but cheerfully converses even with 'wayfaring men, though fools,' that he may learn some particulars of life's journey. . . . A lover of the desultory style, his effusions shall keep pace with STERNE'S—in digression and eccentricity, though halting far behind him in wit" (No. 23, May 19, 1795). Dennie's dejection at the discontinuance of *The Tablet* on August 11, 1795, must have been owing in part to the fact that it brought to an end the appearance of further numbers of *The Farrago*. Nothing came of plans at that time, or six years later, to have these essays published in book form.[10] Failures of this kind contributed to the literary eclipse into which he was to fall after his death.

Of the conventions associated with the Addisonian essay only the persona is notably present in *The Farrago*. We glimpse this unnamed character on a winter evening as he "hitches nearer the fire, quaffs another bumper of grape juice, and, as the rafters of his garret crack, repeats 'I like this rocking of the battlements' " (No. 15, February 10, 1794). As he sits puffing at his window, he overhears the vicar ask whether he is "dead, or only sleepeth?" and, in view of what he said in an earlier number about coquettishness, imagines that the ladies "exult at my exit from the EAGLE, and *protest,* that I was a *monstrous uncivil,* shockingly indelicate writer." He explains his four months' absence by saying that he has been too sick to write with the sprightliness expected of a periodical essayist; "during the languor of disease, when wit will not be at hand . . . he will not write a prescription of sleepy drugs for the public" (No. 17, July 14, 1794). He introduces an essay on worldly prudence with this whimsical self-portrait:

> A cloudy atmosphere and a fit of the spleen having confederated, and locked up all the powers of my invention and memory, I sallied out of my chamber, and sought for a key to liberate them,

that they might furnish a Farrago. I was proceeding, thrice gentle reader, to tell thee a story of "a king of Bohemia and seven castles," in the Shandean style . . . when, whom should I meet, in my flowery path, but one of "their worships and reverences," who . . . cried out, with a true critic's yell, "How now, madcap, whither do you wander? You are metaphor mad. . . . Why, what a curvetting palfrey, more restive than any in romance, is that same imagination, on whose neck you have thrown the reins. Do dismount my frantic friend, and stride some sober beast from our stable; or if, obstinately attached to your hobby, you will ride on, at least procure a martingale . . . ." This *alderman's* advice so damped my volatile spirits, [that] I returned to my desk, and, with chastised feelings, immediately wrote the following. (No. 21, April 4, 1794)

Elsewhere he promises to exercise moderation at all times: "All parties in the *State*, may read the moderate sentiments of a writer, who will neither factiously blow the trumpet of democracy, nor proudly stalk in the aristocratical buskin. All sects in the *Church*, may cheerily and charitably unite in the perusal of a work, intended to amuse as a speculation, not dogmatize as a creed. Though feminine foibles will be smilingly derided, yet, at the apprehension of a malignant satire from the author of the Farrago, not a heart need palpitate, a fan flutter, nor a tea table shake" (No. 23, May 19, 1795). In the final number he admits that his essays "have not . . . *a town air*. . . . I allude chiefly to rural events, and the scenes of my speculations are naturally laid in the country. . . . Instead of the rustling of silks, my rustical ears hear only the rustling of leaves, and the distant waterfall" (No. 29, July 24, 1802). This unnamed character, presumably a bachelor, lives a comfortable, easygoing life. Like Addison's Spectator who eschews controversy, he promises to "neither factiously blow the trumpet of democracy, nor proudly stalk in the aristocratical buskin." Although he claims that "not a heart need palpitate, a fan flutter, nor a tea table shake" at what he writes, he nonetheless incurs the wrath of the ladies.

While essays of character and manners are present in The *Farrago*, morality is all but absent[11] and philosophical reflection and criticism disappear altogether; in their place—and it is an indication of the growing subjectivity of the periodical essay at the end of the eighteenth century—appear two essays on nature. The most vivid of three character sketches is that of Meander (a thinly disguised self-portrait of the young Dennie halfheartedly studying law with Benjamin West of Charlestown, New Hampshire): "Were Sterne summoned to describe him, the eccentric wit would quote his Tristram Shandy, and affirm, that Meander was a mercurial sublimated creature. . . . he starts as many schemes, as a visionary projector. So entirely devoted is he to the cultivation of the Belles Lettres, that his graver moments, instead of being dedicated to Blackstone and Buller, are given to Shakspeare and Sterne. . . . Notwithstanding his enthusiastic fondness for the study of polite literature, even from that, he frequently flies off in a tangent; and the charms of the ladies and of loo, full often cause him to forget that there is a poet or novelist in our language" (No. 2, February 21, 1792). There follow excerpts from Meander's Journal, among them: "If I rise at the dawn, and study jurisprudence till noon, I shall have the satisfaction to reflect, that I have discharged my *legal* duty for the day"; "began to read a British statute; meanwhile . . . a couple of my college cronies were at a neighbouring inn, who wished me to make one of a select party. I complied"; "finding my spirits too sublimated for serious study, I beguiled the remainder of the afternoon, by writing a sonnet to Laura" (No. 3, March 6, 1792). This largely autobiographical sketch of an eccentric dilettante may explain why Dennie abandoned the law for belles-lettres.

Charles Cameleon, like Alcibiades and St. Paul, adjusts easily to the particular company and circumstance in which he finds himself. When at school, he "was equally the darling of the scholars on the first form, and the truants on the lower. . . . With the same facility, he could make correct Latin, and high-flying kites." He is now an eloquent, widely informed member of the bar. "An apothecary, hearing him harangue upon the superiority of Brown to Boerhaave, mistakes him for a regular bred physician. . . . Charles is intimately conversant with all the fathers of the church. . . . Among the ladies, he holds most gracefully ' 'twixt his finger and thumb, a pouncet box,' and chatters on Canterbury-gowns and French millinery. . . . To a lover of the fine arts, he quotes Hogarth's 'Analysis of Beauty'. . . . In a club of wits, he declaims Shakspeare, in the style of *Garrick*" (No. 14, January 27, 1794). Charles's chameleon-like qualities are his strength, not his weakness; he is depicted as a latter-day Renaissance man. Still another character is Aunt Peg. "Whether *my aunt Peg*, like Tristram Shandy's *aunt Dinah*, having been guilty of some back-slidings in her youth, has forfeited her right to respect from the family; or, whether certain envious prudes, as is their wont, have leagued, and look prim against her, when she appears, is a question, I cannot *sagely* solve. Certain it is, she is degraded from the rank of gentlewoman, and now keeps low and contemptible company. . . . *My aunt Peg*, like an English actress of scorched reputation, often exchanges the petticoats for breeches; and, disguised in male apparel, spouts farce and low comedy, in the *theatre universal*. . . . critical spectators are always dissatisfied with her style of acting. . . . pit, box, and gallery, hiss *'aunt Peg'* " (No. 16, March 3, 1794). Of the three characters Aunt Peg is the most Shandean. One suspects that she is happy with her lot in spite of the contempt in which she is held.

One manners essay pictures the dandy who not only "cuts a dash" but cuts his father to the heart by dropping "his coin, not into beggar's palms, but into tavern bars and taylor's shops. . . . He lately *lived away*, wore plated stockings, long quartered shoes, and . . . twined round his throat four yards of muslin." Now "his money's gone." "You affectionately anxious, grey headed fathers, whom I see stroking the flaxen locks of your prattling boy, pray that he may be a horse-jockey, and play all Fours with hutchers, across a tray—that he may become a scoundrel swindler, and cheat by system, that he may be surnamed BEELZEBUB, the prince of devils, rather than a *buckish blade*, who *cuts a great dash*" (No. 10, September 9, 1793). This beau runs through his money in an attempt to impress the ladies. Although he assures one of them that his moderate fortune will be compensated for by his affection, she rejects him with the words, "Affection is mighty pretty but—*it cuts no dash*." "My laurelled predecessor, the *Spectator*," begins another essay, "has assured us, that it was his delight, in his intercourse with mankind, to exercise his eyes, rather than his tongue." I am not of a mind with Addison "who, on all occasions, advocated and practised taciturnity. . . . It has been my misfortune to pass whole evenings with weak women and men, 'without a manly mind,' among whom, as Goldsmith tersely expresses it, there seemed to be a general combination in favour of stupidity. I have been compelled to sit, 'with sad civility, and an aching head,' and devolve the whole stream of chat among a circle, whose heads were as vacant as their faces, and whose tongues were as silent, as if mouldering in a charnel-house." I have prayed "that I might be confined in a milliner's band-box, and doomed to hear the clamourous click clack of feminine folly, rather than yawn for hours among silent starers, who, like puppets, acted in dumb shew" (No. 12, October 21, 1793). Unlike the taciturn Spectator the author of the *Farrago* is so desperate for talk that he longs to "smoke a smutty pipe with a *Dutch* burgomaster" or trade places with an oyster, "alternately opening and shutting his shell on a rock"; he prefers the idlest of chit-chat to the boring silence of the drawing room.

Dennie, whose insubordination at Harvard College led to a six-month suspension in December 1789,[12] thereafter bore his alma mater a grudge and on occasion gave vent to it. "When I was at college," begins one of the *Farrago* essays, "my mathematical tutor shook his head and dubbed me a stupid fellow. . . . I contented myself with studying the ways of men, and the works of Roman and English wits." Not all geniuses have excelled in mathematics. Shakespeare "was not only a novice in the doctrine of 'nought and carry one,' but frankly indulges a laugh of contempt at computation," and Swift "was refused, by the university of Dublin, a degree, because he lampooned Locke, and derided the aerial speculations of a mathematician." I do not wish to abolish "any branches of this recondite science," but "good-naturedly to deride that mode of education, which, neglecting, or partially studying, eloquence, poetry, history, the classics, and the world, devotes long and exclusive attention to things abstracted and foreign from men's business and bosoms" (No. 25, June 16, 1795). This essay affords us a glimpse of a wide-ranging campaign in late colonial times to modernize the college curriculum which was still closely bound to the medieval trivium, three philosophies, and four arts (which included arithmetic and geometry). Like Franklin and Trumbull, Dennie wanted modern languages and literature introduced into the curriculum.

The liveliest of the *Farrago* essays treats the conventional subject of dullness in a manner reminiscent at once of Swift and Sterne. It is my duty, announces the author, "to advance the cause of folly, by composing an essay, which . . . may disseminate dulness among my loving countrymen." Whereas in former times able men "were the pride of their own sex, and the favourites of the other," now there is no greater misfortune than to be born a genius. The ladies "have the same antipathy to genius, that they have to a toad." The author wishes to guard against "the future intrusions of Genius into good company" and "to qualify a man, at the age of twenty-one, to become a worthy member of the right worshipful society of fools." Therefore, agreeable to Sterne's hypothesis that children are sprightly or dull according to whether they are born of love out of wedlock or are the product of the marriage bed, he humbly proposes that Congress

> forthwith repeal all laws, which make the murder of bastards capital; and that, in committee of the whole, they seriously debate, whether it will not be expedient to bring in a bill to discourage abilities, and to advance folly, in which shall be offered to those benevolent damsels, who are fond of making children, a handsome premium to destroy them. . . . By the above expedient of premiums, young maidens being effectually prevented from fostering their love-begotten babes, the married ladies, on their part, without fee, or any reward, except that of conscious virtue, will assist, it is to be hoped, in the good work.

"Genius being thus literally stifled in the cradle . . . the conjugal caresses of their mates will become languid and joyless, and the sluggish marriage couch will grow so unelastic that, from it no Genius can spring."

> When infants actually appear with the panoply of folly girting their brains, let a milch-ass be straightway provided. . . . At the age of fourteen, or before, if he have towardly parts, let the hopeful boy be sent to some [foreign] college. . . . For those, who experimentally know how the talents of a learner are cherished here, and who have witnessed the erudition and urbanity of our university governors, cannot by any refinement of conjecture, suppose that I mean our own. Here, aided by careful tutors, he may grow in folly, as he advances in age, and on commencement day, he may add to his surname D.D. or distinguished dunce. . . . After a discipline, so goodly, he may rise with rapid steps, to the highest posts, in church and state. (No. 27, July 21, 1795)

The modest proposal that all bastards be murdered to ensure the extinction of genius, patterned to be sure on Swift, enlivens the overworked topic of dullness. Again the inadequacies of colonial colleges like Harvard are pointed up.

The subjectivity present in *The Farrago* is most apparent in the essays on the pleasures of winter (No. 15) and a morning in the country (No. 29). In the second of these the author relates how, having risen at dawn to read Rousseau, he climbed the mountain above his village and "contemplated the magic of Nature." An old peasant greeted him with a handshake "worth more than all the ceremonious civility of those, who hold . . . a fan," and said, "on these hills, Health and Husbandry are joint tenants with me and mine." Listening to his story, "I wiped the dew from my forehead, and a tear of regret from my cheek, and pensively quitted the mountain" (July 24, 1802). *The Farrago* is the earliest American serial to clearly manifest that loss of objectivity and growing preoccupation with self which marked the Addisonian essay in the second half of the eighteenth century and betokened the re-emergence of the familiar essay. This is owing in part to the fact that Dennie was of the first generation of American essayists to be strongly influenced by Sterne. Although Dennie's nameless persona possesses a dramatic identity distinct from his creator, the series several times becomes autobiographical, notably in the sketch of Meander and the attacks on collegiate education.

II

In a letter of January 4, 1794, Dennie told his parents that he had recently been appointed a lay reader at the Episcopal church in Claremont, New Hampshire, after delivering "the popular sermon of Sterne on the character of the Good Samaritan"; then he admitted, "I have the ready faculty of speech, but I doubt whether *profound* thought keeps pace with volubility of tongue."[13] Almost two years later, on October 13, 1795, the first of the *Lay Preacher* essays appeared in the *Farmer's Weekly Museum* at Walpole, New Hampshire, where Dennie had just settled.[14] On April 26, 1797, he told his mother how he had submitted "an Essay on 'Wine & New Wine,' and called it the

'Lay Preacher.' It had been objected to my earliest compositions [*The Farrago*] that they were sprightly rather than moral. Accordingly, I thought I would attempt to be useful, by exhibiting truth in a plain dress to the common people."[15] "The combination of moralist and essayist," writes Milton Ellis, "was one eminently suited to his character and temperament. 'As a preacher he could appropriately censure the follies, crudities, and shortcomings of his countrymen; as a *lay* preacher he was not debarred from rambling into politics, literature, and occasionally frivolous satire on manners and society.' "[16]

"Surrounded by plain husbandmen rather than by polished scholars," wrote Dennie in 1796, "the Author . . . has been more studious of the useful than the brilliant. To instruct the villager was his primary object. Hence, an easy and obvious style was indispensable. . . . The familiarity of Franklin's manner, and the simplicity of Sterne's proved most auxiliary to his design. He, therefore, adventured their union."[17] Later he characterized *The Lay Preacher* as "a series of essays, modelled after the designs of Addison, and the harmless and playful levity of Oliver Goldsmith"; the Biblical texts "are either a moral lesson, an economical precept, or a biographical picture. The topics, to which they are prefixed, are didactic, descriptive, or airy, as the gravity, or the humour of the hour prompted."[18] As the series was drawing to a close Dennie admitted:

> I hope that this style of speaking occasionally in the first person will be forgiven, even by the most fastidious reader, when he adverts to the custom of my predecessors. A periodical writer can hardly avoid this sort of egotism, and it is surely very harmless when its employer muffles himself in the mantle of concealment and in the guise, whether of a shrewd Spectator or a simple Lay Preacher, walks unobtrusively abroad. Mr. Addison and Monsieur Montaigne perpetually indulge this habit. . . . We are naturally curious thus to peep through the keyhole of a study, to see a writer in his elbow-chair, and to listen to his story with the fondness and familiarity of friendship.[19]

In a word, *The Lay Preacher*, like *The Farrago*, tends toward greater subjectivity than essays earlier in the century, a fact hinted at by Dennie's linking the tradition of Addison with that of Montaigne.

Although the reader glimpses Joseph Dennie beneath the

surface, his persona is nonetheless vividly and convincingly drawn. A woman-hater in his youth, the Lay Preacher has since made his peace with the ladies: "I pride myself that they still admit an old bachelor to their toilets, and that they will not refuse a dropped fan, though presented to them by a gray-headed gallant. If I hear the pleasing rustle of silk against my study stairs, I make shift to hide my spectacles, and at the expense of my gouty limbs, cheerfully resign my obsolete arm chair to the occupancy of the fair sex."[20] He is so addicted to tobacco that "often, when the consumptive state of my finances prevented the consignment of a thread bare coat to the tailor, or the stoppage of certain piteous rents in my black worsted hose, I have found a few solitary cents at the bottom of my exchequer, and was rich enough to contract for half a dozen cigars. ... I enjoined upon my bookseller to print the first edition of my sermons upon tobacco paper."[21] A splenetic author who drudges through life, he confesses: "At Clumsy College, where I had my education, governors and pupils stood for the most part idle.... To such a drowsy education the candid reader of these discourses must attribute the tediousness and insipidity of the Lay Preacher."[22] "If the Lay Preacher himself should, contrary to his own doctrine, be found snoring in his study while his neighbours are walking in their vocation, he gives them full permission to call a council and dismiss him from his office."[23] Five years later, though, this latter-day Spectator, now settled in Philadelphia, resolves "to shake off sluggishness ... to rise now and go about the city, in the streets, and in the broad ways."[24]

Feeling "a cordial regard for the established clergy,"[25] the Lay Preacher goes "with some degree of constancy to church," dressed in his best coat and linen.[26] He acknowledges "that he, like most sedentary parsons, is an awkward rider, and sits too much in his easy chair to sit gracefully on a horse."[27] Although some of his "friends reproach him for his labours in an age when few read, fewer remember, and none believe sermons,"[28] he "thinks it possible to provide useful and agreeable occupation, whether it rains or snows,"[29] and exhorts his readers, "Give the Preacher credit for the morality of his writings, exhibit that morality in your lives, and inquire not too cautiously whether his life and doctrine are coincident."[30]

Politically speaking, "there is a good, warm, well-made, easy garment, made to fit any one, called Federalism, which the Lay Preacher actually prefers to his canonicals, and prays may be constantly worn."[31] Talking politics with my neighbors, "I learn that certain restless and perturbed spirits, under the plausible title of 'Democrats,' are labouring anxiously to teach proselytes the soothing doctrines of liberty and equality. Liberty such as the fish-women of Paris enjoyed when they treated a Queen of France like a prostitute of the stews; and Equality such as a Legendre and Santerre could boast when the butcher's stall of the one, and brewer's dray of the other, were, in a Revolutionary government, on a level with the throne."[32] Being of Scottish descent, he possesses powers of divination. "Many democrats, confident of the potency of my art, have applied to me to ascertain if they were right in their hopes of a revolution, and the ultimate triumph of French arms, and French principles. I have ever made it a rule to resolve all such queries, by the rules of palmistry. But the hands of these gentlemen are either so dirty with the vileness of their occupations, or so filled with French crowns, or so closely clenched, to smite every person and every thing in their way, that it is an impossibility to discern the lines by which I can foretel."[33]

The Lay Preacher is the familiar figure of the old bachelor, ever welcome and gallant in the company of the ladies despite his addiction to tobacco. True to his name, he respects the clergy and attends church regularly, confident that his sermons will prove useful and agreeable. In time he exchanges his rural pulpit for one in Philadelphia and, like Addison's Spectator, goes "about the city, in the streets, and in the broad ways" gathering material for his next essay. A loyal Federalist, he cries down democrats, especially those spawned by the French Revolution.

"I confine myself to moral, economical, literary or political subjects," declares the Lay Preacher; "and to essay sublimer themes comports neither with my plan, nor with my sense of propriety."[34] Although Dennie characterized the subjects of The Lay Preacher as "didactic, descriptive, or airy, as the gravity, or the humour of the hour prompted," this series is more didactic and less lively than The Farrago. Being lay sermons, no fewer than twelve of these essays retell the stories of Biblical characters.[35] Manners is the subject of some of the livelier essays. Three of these focus on dress, the first on changeableness. "A new coat every month and a vest of a different pattern every hour are hardly sufficient, in the opinion of a jury of beaux, to excuse a man from presentment for high treason against the law of taste. . . . Customs which I copy, says the coxcomb, must be as changeable as the silk gown, or the temper, of a mistress. . . . The fashion of this world regulates our persons no less than our garb. . . . In the days of Cromwell and puritanism, fashion settled the length of countenance as well as the width of conscience. . . . In the merry days of Charles the Second and the profligate, behold the opposite extreme."[36] The second essay treats of immodesty in dress. "Where the semblance of *modesty* is wanting, there is strong ground to presume the absence of the virtue itself. . . . Is there worth in the female, who tramples upon what she has herself been educated to revere as good decorum, at the capricious instance of an idle fashion-monger? . . . A despicable courtezan, who commands the gallantries of a vitiated capital, is often known to lead one half the female world by her fantastic whimsies."[37] Slovenliness, especially that affected by authors, is the subject of the third essay. "I know a poet . . . who anticipates renown no less from a dirty shirt than from an elegant couplet. . . . he avers that a slouched hat is demonstrative of a well-stored brain and that genius always trudges about in unbuckled shoes. . . . If negligence be the criterion of genius, a critic will, in future, inspect a poet's wardrobe rather than his works. Slovenliness . . . is more inexcusable in men of letters than in many others, the nature of whose employment compels them to be conversant with objects sordid and impure. . . . I see no reason why an author should not be a gentleman, or at least as clean and neat as a Quaker."[38] The Lay Preacher, acknowledging "the vicissitudes and vanity of fashion" in both sexes and in all ages, nevertheless warns that dress reflects the character and ability of the wearer. Immodesty in dress, no matter how prompted, he declares, points to the absence of modesty itself. The Lay Preacher, who prides himself on cleanliness of dress, castigates writers, especially poets, who affect slovenliness, calling them "pretenders to authorship."

Again, as in *The Farrago*, Dennie gives vent to his lifelong animus against Harvard College. Writing on the text, "Great is Diana of the Ephesians," the Lay Preacher declares, "A degree conferred by a college is a Diana whose divinity many a dunce has acknowledged."

> Some have thought that the Cambridge Diana did not deserve to be worshipped by the learned world. I was once asked by an inquisitive foreigner, in what alcove of our University were deposited its own works [and] was compelled to reveal to him the nakedness of literature at Cambridge. . . . I informed him that the tutors, far from being eloquent like the orators of antiquity, were in general . . . raw boys. . . . That philosophy was pedlared out by the pennyworth, and the streams of learning, instead of being cheaply and easily conducted to each student, were sold, in their muddiest state, for a higher price than mineral water.

Some of the College Principals "were of such dubious taste as to reject from the College Library the works of Sterne and Swift, and . . . the best and brightest scholars, from Dr. Mayhew to the present time, were generally ignominiously punished for no other crime than that of volatility." The Lay Preacher concludes, "for a youth of lively parts and sanguine temperament, place him between the upper and nether mill-stone rather than on his knees before the leaden shrine of our Great Diana of Literature."[39] Continuing his campaign to improve the quality of college education, Dennie observes ironically that Diana is the goddess worshipped by many a Harvard dunce. As in The Farrago, he here stresses the fact that the study of literature is neglected, noting that Sterne and Swift are excluded from the college library.

Many more of the Lay Preacher essays, however, treat of moral subjects such as plagiarism,[40] fretfulness,[41] idle curiosity,[42] the folly of passion,[43] scandal,[44] harlotry,[45] and simplicity and sincerity.[46] An essay on slothfulness pictures the modern sluggard: "Dick Dronish lies in bed till eleven o'clock in a May Morning. . . . he always sleeps over his book and never displayed any vivacity in study except once, when he threw Dr. Franklin's works into the fire for saying that 'time was money.' . . . At four you see him exerting all his energies, crossing the street to a dram shop and loading a sot's pistol—with brandy."[47] Dick is "a modern sluggard in miniature" hung up in the first column of the Farmer's Museum to exemplify Solomon's question, echoed by the printer impatient for the Lay Preacher's copy: "Why stand ye here all the day idle?" Elsewhere the Lay Preacher admonishes parents for interfering in their children's love affairs, as Rebecca did in Jacob's. "In vain, Jacob, has some blooming, lovely virgin of Heth, caught thy youngling fancy . . . . Thou must hie thee to Padanaram and seek thee a wife, for if thou marriest one of these daughters of Heth, thy mother 'will be weary of her life.' " So "Jacob forsook his first love, and . . . married into the family of the wealthy Laban, as his mother had directed him." "Matrons of my country!" entreats the Lay Preacher, "ye proud Rebekahs of this land of equality,—Have ye never sent your Jacobs to Padanaram to seek them wives?"[48]

Dennie, who as editor of the *Port Folio* from 1801 to 1812 frequently engaged in literary criticism,[49] does so only once in *The Lay Preacher*, writing on Ann Radcliffe and the Gothic romance which was enjoying a vogue in America, Horace Walpole, declares the Lay Preacher, "was among the first of those, who, in the full blaze of the eighteenth century, chose to excite from the shades of gothic superstition the dreary phantoms of the cave and cloister. . . . He was followed by certain German writers, and by a lady, the plots of whose novels I am half inclined to forgive, from my admiration of the purity and grace of her language, and her descriptions of natural scenery, which she ever beholds with the eye of a painter. . . . A gallery, an unexplored chamber, a cottage on the shore, a cloister among the mountains, a distressed lady and a few drops of blood, these are the scanty materials of the modern novelist."[50] "In the works of Mrs. RADCLIFFE, and of all her imitators, mournful or horrible description predominates. . . . If I had a friend of exquisite sensibility, whose irritable nerves vibrated like the chords of music, I would lock up Mrs. RADCLIFFE's novels from his morbid curiosity."[51] "If our romances obtain a general currency, we may soon found abbeys and monasteries, running over with friars, 'white, black, and grey, with all their trumpery.' Raw head and bloody bones will become a fashionable fellow, and damsels and swains, even in broad day light, will see some strange figure or other, 'stealing slowly away into the distant obscure.' "[52] One of Mrs. Radcliffe's strengths, the Lay Preacher maintains, is her style: "What the ladies commonly call the *sentimental* part of a novel, she generally conceives more strongly and expresses with a vigour more masculine than the herd of writers in the same walk."[53] Another strength is the accuracy of her descriptions: "He, who counts among his books the romances of RADCLIFFE, will have no mean knowledge of the castles of feudal times, the vales of Arno, the shores of the Mediterranean, and the magnificence of Venice."[54] Determined to devote a sermon to literature, the Lay Preacher finds he must assume his critical spectacles five times before he has exhausted his subject. At the end he maintains that "the *Preacher*, regular or lay, in giving a literary opinion, neither breaks the tables of the law, nor departs from the character of the priesthood." Though praising Mrs. Radcliffe on some counts ("her descriptions may be embodied by the painter, and her periods may sooth the ear of a poet"), he denounces the Gothic romance, declaring, "We have been accustomed, ever since the Reformation, to laugh at legendary tales, and the monkish whimsies of a ruder age." He prefers sentimental and picaresque novelists like Fielding, Richardson, Smollett, and Burney who, he says, "laughed at witches and woods." Even as Dennie wrote, a young Philadelphian was establishing the Gothic tradition in America; *Wieland*, the first of Charles Brockden Brown's major novels, had just been published.

The Lay Preacher exhibits a partisanship not present in *The Farrago*. "When I first projected the erection of a Lay pulpit," declares the Lay Preacher, "it was my design, like my predecessors in periodical writings, to confine myself to familiar and domestic topics"; but "I cannot view . . . with ordinary and tempered sensibility . . . the madness of France, the rage of revolution, impatience of authority, the growth of faction and study of change."[55] The Lay Preacher, good Federalist that he is, attacks the French Revolution and its consequences in America, declaring: "it was reserved for French perspicacity to discover that Kings were necessarily worse than other men, and it was reserved for French steel to cut off heads, merely for being crowned. . . . in the enlightened eighteenth century, what prodigious discoveries have been made that there is no God and no government, but what the people can make."[56] "Philosophick encounters are, in effect, often as bloody, as the battles of

160

Buonaparte. One Helvetius, with several associates, many years since, opposed the settled opinions of the French nation. . . . Hawk eyed philosophy . . . looked down to the earth and beheld fishwomen, butchers, brewers. . . . they were Citizens Directors, they were Executioners, Jacobins, Devils, any thing but men." "I am persuaded," concludes the Lay Preacher, "thou wilt think with me that all the evils, all the atrocities of the French revolution originated in a false, impious and captious philosophy."[57]

Should I wish a Democrat or a Jacobin in Boston a happy new year, says the Lay Preacher, "he would instantly conclude that I mean a revolutionary one. He would imagine that my wish involved the abdication of Washington, the execution of Jay, and the introduction of the Guillotine."[58] Jefferson and Paine are two Americans peculiarly infected by Jacobinism: "professors of the new philosophy of France, and their servile devotees in America, taint every thing they touch . . . . Of this dangerous, deistical, and Utopian school, a great personage from Virginia is a favoured pupil. . . . At the seat of government, his abstract, inapplicable, metaphysico-politics are either nugatory or noxious. Besides, his principles relish so strongly of Paris and are seasoned with such a profusion of French garlic, that he offends the whole nation."[59] Paine "seduces many of you, my countrymen. You read his *Age of Reason*, and think the Bible a last year's almanac; you read his *Rights of Man* and think government slavery, and Washington an imposter."[60] Writing on the text, "No man also having drunk old wine, straightway desireth new: For he saith, the old is better," the Lay Preacher remarks: "How unfortunate for the benighted Jews, that Thomas Paine was then unborn, and did not print Common Sense, at the foot of the Mount of Olives. How many instructed readers would have staved to pieces their old wine casks, and, with an air of independence, swallowed huge draughts from the new."[61] When George Washington—in Dennie's eyes the chief bulwark against Jacobinism in America—died on December 14, 1799, the Lay Preacher eulogized: "It is an occurrence not less interesting, than extraordinary, that the departure of a single man should command the unaffected and indiscriminate lamentation of five millions of people. . . . His deeds, his fame and his counsel will endure, 'till 'the great globe itself; yea, all which it inherit shall dissolve.' "[62]

In spite of such partisanship *The Lay Preacher* is a literary serial, written by one who of all the American authors treated in this book conceived of himself first and last as an essayist. The subjectivity already noted in *The Farrago* is evident here also. In the thin disguise of a lay preacher, which in fact he was when he undertook the series, Dennie seeks to instruct and incidentally to divert his rural and later his urban audience with little sermons "in the first person," confining himself "to moral, economical, literary or political subjects," in a manner that combines the traditions of Montaigne and Addison. Frequently he abandons the neutrality urged by Addison to defend the Federalists and attack their opponents. Because a tone of familiarity and Sternean whimsy largely displace the dramatic point of view that characterizes the periodical essay, Dennie employs none of the Addisonian conventions except the persona.

Although on one occasion the Lay Preacher declared, "My readers must excuse the preceding rhapsodical and glowing paragraph, so foreign from the usual level style of the Lay Preacher,"[63] Dennie's style was in fact "overwrought and florid . . . often far above the nature of his subject."[64] The influence of Sterne is apparent in his tendency to digress. "Among the high privileges, which we digressive writers enjoy," he declares in *The Farrago*, "may be reckoned that, which Don Quixote gave his horse, to choose a path, and pursue it at pleasure. . . . When we begin an excursion, the Lord only knows how it will be prosecuted, or where it will end" (No. 24, June 9, 1795).

On September 6, 1799, as he was preparing to move to Philadelphia, then the literary as well as national capital of the United States, Dennie wrote his family, "In consequence of my perseverance in the cultivation of letters, I have greatly advanced my literary reputation, and, by my success and popularity in Lay Preaching, have, in my obscurity, been slowly and silently, but I hope surely fixing the basis of future character."[65] What he did not then know was that as editor of the *Port Folio*, the first important literary magazine in America, he would have little time to pursue his career as essayist. An appreciative obituary shortly after his death observed that it was Dennie's "own and the public misfortune, that his literary exertions were, for the most part, occasional and desultory—that his mind had never yet been seen in all its development—or occupied the high and ample space which its natural expansion would justify it in assuming."[66] Within a few years the man whom Timothy Dwight called "the Addison of the United States—the Father of American Belles Lettres"[67] would be all but forgotten.

VIII. JUDITH SARGENT MURRAY

⎣⎦

IN DECEMBER 1789 the editors of *The Massachusetts Magazine: or, Monthly Museum of Knowledge and Rational Entertainment* assured their readers that there had been nothing in their first volume "incompatible with pure morality, nor adverse to the grand principles of religion; neither has the blush of sensibility crimsoned the cheek, nor the lovers of wit received gratification at the pain of innocence."[1] The following month they published a poem by "Constantia," explaining that the author had used the signature some years before "in various pieces which were printed in the Gentleman and Lady's Town and Country Magazine, printed in Boston, and whose productions are known to her friends under that name."[2] "May we not hope," they asked, "that *Philenia, Constantia, Euphelia, Belinda* and *Almerine,* with the other daughters of poesy, will condescend to appear in the twofold robe of elegant prose and high wrought verse?"[3] Constantia was the pen name of Judith Sargent Murray, a Gloucester-born bluestocking, who began composing poetry and essays at an early age. Most of her work eventually appeared in the *Massachusetts Magazine,* one of the foremost American literary periodicals at the end of the eighteenth century. Of particular interest to us are her two serials which ran concurrently in the magazine from 1792 to 1794: *The Repository,* twenty-seven short moralistic essays, and—far more important—*The Gleaner.*

Although Judith Murray, who "had many pages prepared for the press," intended to continue publishing in the *Massachusetts Magazine,* she declared that during a suspension of the magazine (January-March, 1795), *"a serious accusation was preferred against me,* the nature of which, in my own apprehension, effectually barred my appearance in its pages."[4] Although she is not here explicit, it was her Universalist views which

164

Calvinist-minded readers of the magazine found offensive. John Murray, who settled at Gloucester in 1774 and whom Judith married in 1788, was the founder of Universalism in America;[5] "she was devoted to him and his religious interests and shared his preaching tours."[6] Under these circumstances it is not surprising that she should have openly espoused the Universalist cause. The Gleaner declares that, though not a theologian, "I cannot help regarding that plan as the most eligible, which represents the father of eternity, as benignantly planning, before all worlds, the career of a race of beings, who, however they were . . . plunged in a series of misfortunes, were destined, nevertheless, to progress on to a state of never ended felicity. . . . Methinks that system, which bounding the salutary operations of Deity, confines his gracious interference to an *elected few, while the many are consigned to perdition* . . . looks with a much more unfavourable aspect upon the moral walk, than the denounced sentiments of the Universalist."[7] In *The Repository* Judith Murray expresses her belief in universal salvation more eloquently: "What abundant thanks are due to the Redeemer for the manifestations of his tender love! How doth the assurance that his regards are universal . . . smooth the bed of pain, and remove the thorn from the pillow of the dying! . . . Are you not a sinner? Were you not lost? And is not Jesus Christ the Saviour, the benign, the compassionate Redeemer of sinners?"[8] The publication of such liberal theological views eventually precipitated "a controversy in which she was accused of using her essays in the magazine for Universalist propaganda,"[9] and after December 1794 no more of her writings appeared in the *Massachusetts Magazine*.

I

The Gleaner is Judith Murray's chief contribution, not only to the tradition of the essay serial, but to American literature as a whole.[10] The Story of Margaretta, a sentimental novel imbedded within this serial, is our special concern and will be considered shortly. But first let us look at the non-narrative portion of the series comprising four-fifths of the work. In these essays Mrs. Murray occasionally reveals a Federalist bias, imparting to the series a mildly partisan flavor. She praises John Adams (Nos. lv-lvi), to whom the work is dedicated, and George Washington (Nos. lxxvi-lxxvii)—the chief symbols of Federalism at this time—and is fearful lest factionalism, such as has recently desolated France, undermine the infant republic. The Gleaner, aware that *"federalism* was the basis, on which we were successfully building the superstructure of every thing useful, every thing virtuous, every thing ornamental," warns that "faction hath introduced its cloven foot among us; with astonishing effrontery it hath dared to lift its baleful head; and, drawing the sword of discord, it is preparing to sheath it in the vitals of that *infant constitution"* (I, xxvi, 253, 256). Later, in an essay *"written December 1st, 1796, during the important Contest which agitated the Public Mind, relative to a Successor to the immortal WASHINGTON,"* the Gleaner urges that reason, not factiousness, prevail at this juncture. Let us favor "a *Federal representative Republic"* rather than "a *pure unmixed democracy . . .* which is, in *all its parts,* the most friendly to the best interests of mankind" (III, lxxxvii, 180, 179).

Of greatest literary interest are the critical essays in *The Gleaner,* appearing at a time when American writers were uncertain how to develop a native tradition. A work like Royall Tyler's *The Contrast* (1787) reveals this uncertainty.[11] Judith Murray was particularly concerned about the future of American drama, especially in Boston where the legal ban on dramatic performance, imposed in 1750, was only lifted in 1792. In response to an appeal by the management of the Federal Street Theater she herself wrote two plays, *The Medium, or Virtue Triumphant* and *The Traveller Returned,* performed there in 1795 and 1796 and published in *The Gleaner* (Nos. lxx-lxxv, lxxx-lxxxiv). In *Virtue Triumphant* young Charles Maitland loves Eliza Clairville who, though poor, wins over Charles's father by her beauty and virtuous character. In the final scene Charles begs her, "Thus, on my knees, let me receive the heavenly investiture—thus pay my vows, and grateful worship at the blest shrine of bright TRIUMPHANT VIRTUE" (III, lxxv, 86). In view of this sentimental comedy it comes as no surprise to hear the Gleaner declare that "a *virtuous theatre* is highly influential in regulating the opinions, manners, and morals of the populace." Does it not exemplify "the lessons which the ethic preacher labours to inculcate?" He is convinced that "the theatre opens a wide field for literary exertions" (I, xxiv, 227, 228). Later, calling for literary independence, he asserts that "the stage is undoubtedly a very powerful engine in forming the opinions and manners of a people. Is it not then of importance to supply the American stage with American scenes?" Yet dramatic writers are not encouraged. "Tyler's plays are strangely neglected; and the finished scenes of the correct and elegant Mrs. Warren, have never yet passed in review before an American audience" (III, xcvi, 262). The Gleaner deplores the fact that, though America "has given birth to philosophers, politicians, and warriors of the first description" and to celebrated artists, she has as yet produced no literary genius comparable to Addison or Pope (III, lxix, 10).

The character of the Gleaner is one of the best rounded within the tradition of the literary serial in America. He introduces himself as "*rather* a plain man, who, after spending the day in making provision for my little family, sit myself comfortably down by a clean hearth, and a good fire, enjoying, through these long evenings, with an exquisite zest, the pleasures of the hour"; "ever since the commencement of your Magazine," he tells the editors, "I have been seized with a violent desire to become a writer. ... The smoothness of Addison's page, the purity, strength, and correctness of Swift, the magic numbers of Pope—these must all veil [sic] to me." He adopts "the name, character, and avocation of a GLEANER," a title that will prove "in many respects abundantly convenient; more especially should an accusation of plagiarism be lodged against me, my very *title* will plead my apology" (I, i, 13-16). Married at an early age to "a young woman of a mild and conceding disposition," he identifies himself as Mr. Vigillius (I, ii, 18). He is grateful to be living in an age of revolution; "over veteran foes we have been victorious; independence claps her wings; peace is restored; governments are formed; public faith established; and we bid fair to become a great and happy people" (I, iv, 39).

Like Addison's Spectator the Gleaner has "the advantage of mixing unnoticed, in places of general resort, with people of various descriptions"; nature has made him, too, niggardly of speech. At table in a public house he hears speculations as to who he really is. One of the company is certain he is a parson; another has heard that he is a student at Harvard College. A young barrister declares "that the Gleaner certainly bore strong marks of genius; that, to his knowledge, it was the production of a Connecticut pen, and it was well known that Connecticut was the land of essayists" (I, vi, 54-55). Later "an old lady, (taking off her spectacles, and laying down her knitting-work) informed me that she had been credibly assured, that the Gleaner had in fact never been married; that he was a young man, a dweller in Worcester, and that he never having had a *bit of a wife*, it was impossible to tell what to believe" (I, xii, 125). At the end of the first volume he confesses, "When I was first seized with the mania of scribbling, I very wisely endeavoured to combat it by much deliberate consideration, and many a salutary antidote." But "Ambition seized the reins—the die was cast— and helter-skelter round the world we drove. . . . There is hardly any thing I have so much feared, as the sands of oblivion; and that I might produce a stream of sufficient depth to fleet my little skiff, my faculties, diligently exercised, have been almost constantly employed" (I, xxxiv, 345, 347-48).

We encounter the Gleaner less often later in the work. Coming across a passage in Voltaire which reads, "*Miserable pamphlets!—the Gleaner!*—the Faultfinder, &c.—*Wretched productions! inspired by hunger, and dictated by stupidity and a disposition to lying! &c. &c.,*" he hastens to defend his own literary production: "To find my *boasted title* thus unexpectedly flashed in my face; and to meet it, too, *coupled with infamy*!!! . . . the candid reader, while he acquits me of an instance of *plagiarism*, so *impolitic* and so *absurd*, will not fail to sympathize with, and to vindicate *The mortified GLEANER*" (II, lvii, 238-39). Ever "solicitous to cultivate the good and amiable qualities of his readers," he "would endow them with that delicacy which trembles at the voice of accusation, and which, enwrapping itself in the mantle of propriety, is sedulously careful to avoid even the shadow of suspicion" (II, lxi, 266). One of his correspondents, Peter Laconic, advises him to "study plainness of speech," quoting his uncle Wiseacre to the effect that Mr. Gleaner "*always puts me in mind of a fresh-water spark, who* [being] desirous that the candle should be put out, thought proper to give his orders in some of his high-flown gibberish. *'Extinguish that nocturnal luminary,'* said he." Rachel Pliable, noting that "the Gleaner seems to prefer delineating the virtues," wishes he "would give us both sides of the question" and entreats him to "publish a few *invidious Gleaners"* (III, xcix, 296-97, 298). In short, the Gleaner, though not a bachelor, is the familiar character of the spectator, content to live simply but ambitious to write down in the manner of Addison, Swift, and Pope what he gleans from his observations of life in post-Revolutionary America. The guardian of Margaretta, he gives focus to this long series.

The Gleaner is finally unmasked when Judith Murray, over the signature "Constantia," informs the reader, "I appear before thee in *propria persona,* acknowledging myself to be that identical *Constantia,* whom possibly thou mayest recollect, as filling some pages in the Boston, and afterwards in the Massachusetts Magazine." She adopted the mask of the Gleaner because of "the indifference, not to say contempt, with which female productions are regarded," because it gave her the opportunity to make "myself mistress of the unbiassed sentiments of my associates," and because "I was ambitious of being considered *independent as a writer"* (III, 313-14).

II

As the eighteenth century drew to an end literary taste in England and America increasingly favored writers of sensibility like the novelists Sterne, Mackenzie, and Burney. Sensibility in the eighteenth-century American novel has been defined as "delicacy in perceiving and readiness in responding to emotional stimuli, particularly to the appeal of pathos."[12] The successful sentimental novel in the early national period was one which moralized at the same time that it appealed to the reader's sensibility. "Editors and publishers of periodicals, confronted by a popular demand for fiction and heedful of the loud clamor against its evils, adroitly contrived an editorial policy calculated to maintain their circulation as well as their self-respect," writes Herbert Ross Brown. "This was achieved by neutralizing stories with sermons, and historiettes with homilies, often printed in parallel columns. . . . At this profitable game of eating one's cake and having it, too, the *Massachusetts Magazine* became peculiarly adept. . . . The editors saw to it, however, that readers who suffered contamination had only themselves to blame."[13] Judith Murray, who as we have seen was one of the leading writers for the *Massachusetts Magazine*, hit upon the strategy of allowing the Story of Margaretta to unfold within the framework of a series of moral essays. We see this strategy most clearly in observations on the proper role of the novel in American life. During an interval between episodes in the story the Gleaner overhears a guest at a public house declare magisterially that "in his Margaretta, indeed, I took an interest, but he just popt her upon us, and very soon running himself out there, whip, in a moment, she was gone." Another guest counters that the Gleaner now withholds his Margaretta, "not altogether from poverty of genius, but from the fear of giving to his productions the air of a novel . . . and you know, Gentlemen, in what a frivolous point of view, the novelist, at this present, stands. . . . who would wish to debase the essayist . . . into a mere annalist of brilliant fictions"; yet "under proper regulations, the province assigned to the novel writer, might be productive of the highest utility" (I, vi, 56-57). Mary Vigillius, the Gleaner's wife, thinks it best to let young Margaretta read novels, but only "in her presence, hoping that she might, by her suggestions and observations, present an antidote to the poison, with which the pen of the novelist is too often fraught" (I, vii, 70). The Gleaner, aware of the evils produced "when a torrent of novels bursts suddenly on a girl, who, bidding adieu to childhood, hath already entered a career, to her of such vast importance," questions "whether there is not less risk in placing volumes of this kind in the hands of girls of *ten or twelve years of age*, than during that interesting period which revolves from *fifteen to twenty*." Novels "may very properly and advantageously constitute the *amusement* of a girl from *eight to fourteen years of age, provided always that she pursues her reading under the judicious direction of her guardian friend*" (II, xl, 64, 63).

Early American novelists thought it more important to satisfy the moralist than the literary critic.[14] In the Preface to *The*

Gleaner Judith Murray, confessing that her talents run more to amusement than to moral improvement, is nevertheless "*solicitous to obtain an establishment in the bosom of virtue.*" To this end the Story of Margaretta, itself steadily edifying as well as entertaining, is counterbalanced by didactic essays which relentlessly instruct the reader. For a notable example, in their study of history Mary Vigillius strives to impress on Margaretta the lessons to be learned from the example of great men and women like Aristides, Alfred the Great, Mary Queen of Scots, Henry IV of France, Charles I of England, Peter the Great, and William Penn (Nos. xlvi-liii). Elsewhere Judith Murray makes explicit her admiration for the sound morality in such sentimental novels as Richardson's *Clarissa* and Burney's *Evelina*. "Clarissa Harlowe," declares the Gleaner, "appears to me admirably well calculated as a useful companion for a female, from the first dawn of her reason, to the closing scene of life. . . . Love, in the bosom of Clarissa, was always subservient to virtue. . . . love, in the bosom of Clarissa, was what I wish, from my soul, it may become in the bosom of every female" (II, xl, 65, 67). Margaretta writes Mary Vigillius, "I pray God, that both you and my papa may be able to say of your Margaretta, as Mr. Villars of his Evelina, that she has amply repaid your care and affection, and that she is all which your fondest wishes had anticipated" (II, xliii, 95).

A favorite way to make the sentimental novel respectable was to insist that the story was founded on fact.[15] While Judith Murray does not go so far as Susanna Rowson, who subtitles *Charlotte* "A Tale of Truth," on one occasion she represents the Story of Margaretta as based on fact. In answer to a young woman just returned from New Haven who says that people there positively assured her that "they had never heard the name of Margaretta Melworth, until they saw it in the Magazine," a Yale graduate replies, "I was there at the very period, on which the Gleaner represents his Margaretta as having passed some time in the city of New-Haven, and I more than once saw that young lady at church, and in several private families; it is true that being then but a youth, (for it was my first year in the seminary) I was not very intimate with Miss Melworth, otherwise, I doubt not, I should have been made acquainted with every particular which he records" (I, xii, 125).

Judith Murray, like her contemporaries, realized that her readership consisted largely of women. Mr. Vigillius' account of Margaretta's attainments at age sixteen is directed first of all at the women in her audience:

> Of needle work, in its varieties, my wife pronounced her a perfect mistress; her knowledge of the English, and French tongues, was fully adequate to her years, and her manner of reading had, for me, peculiar charms; her hand writing was neat and easy; she was a good accomptant, a tolerable geographer and chronologist; she had skimmed the surface of astronomy and natural philosophy; had made good proficiency in her study of history and the poets; could sketch a landscape; could furnish, from her own fancy, patterns for the muslins which she wrought; could bear her part in a minuet and a cotillion, and was allowed to have an excellent hand upon the piano forte. . . . in the receipts of cookery she is thoroughly versed; she is in every respect the complete housewife; and our linen never received so fine a gloss as when it was ironed and laid in order by Margaretta. (I, vii, 70, 71)

It is also with an eye to this readership that Judith Murray has the Gleaner praise Penelope Airy for exhibiting the virtues of industry, order, and independence (Nos. xvii-xviii) and hold forth at length on the equality of the sexes (Nos. lxxxviii-xci).

In order to understand on how many counts it qualifies as a sentimental novel, albeit an unfinished one, the Story of Margaretta needs to be reviewed in some detail. At the end of the Revolution Mr. Vigillius (the Gleaner), then "an idle young fellow," journeys with his wife Mary to Charleston, where "the joy of the liberated citizens was unbounded" after seven years of war. The day after they take lodgings a young girl, "apparently about ten years of age," enters the breakfast room and tells the landlady that her "mamma" is very sick; Mary befriends the sick woman. A week later the dying woman tells the Vigilliuses her history. She is the eldest of two orphaned sisters, who retired "to a small town in the environs of London." Her sister married Charles Melworth, of whom she disapproved, and she, Captain Arbuthnot. After bearing a daughter named Margaretta Mrs. Melworth became sick, and news that her husband had been lost at sea hastened her death. She committed Margaretta to the care of Mrs. Arbuthnot, who accompanied her husband to South Carolina where he fought under Lord Rawdon. He died shortly, "a victim to the climate, and to the wounds which he received in the engagement, which took place near Shubrick's plantation." Now on her deathbed, Mrs. Arbuthnot makes the Vigilliuses Margaretta's guardians (No. ii).

The Vigilliuses leave Charleston and settle in a village near Boston. Mary sketches out "an extensive plan of education" for her adopted daughter. Margaretta, being put on her guard against pride and affectation, "prefers plain manners to all the glitter of a studied or laboured address." When she is sixteen the Vigilliuses decide it is time to introduce her "to a world, of whose deceptions we had been careful to warn her"; it is agreed that she shall spend a few weeks in New Haven as the guest of Mrs. Worthington, a friend in whom Mary has complete confidence (No. vii). A fortnight later Margaretta informs the Vigilliuses that "the gentlemen of New-Haven appear to me to be friendly, and hospitable" and that the ladies "are remarkably fond of cultivating flowers." Scarcely had she arrived at Mrs. Worthington's when Mr. Sinisterus Courtland appeared in the drawing room; "three days afterwards he declared himself my lover." Although Mrs. Worthington assures her that Courtland "is a gentleman whose addresses no lady need blush to receive," Mr. Vigillius, sensing that the man is "base, designing, and however incongruous these qualities may seem, improvident also," shudders at the prospect of his modest fortune "being squandered by a spendthrift, while my daughter, and her descendants, were left pennyless!" Mary, assuring Margaretta of the love she and her husband bear her, warns her that a man like Courtland "will steal into the confidence of the unsuspecting virgin, obtaining what he conceives an unalterable and undivided ascendancy over her mind." She urges her to turn her attention instead to Edward Hamilton, a family friend: "I know not the youth who can equal him for gentility of mein, and beauty of person" (No. viii).

Mr. Vigillius goes to New Haven on business and when he returns home, Margaretta dutifully accompanies him; he notices, however, that the "cheerfulness, which had so long presided in her bosom, had taken its flight, and . . . the rose upon her cheek visibly gave place to the lily of her complexion." He and Mary are determined, if they cannot "bend her to our wishes, to follow her through all the vicissitudes her unfortunate preference might involve, with every alleviation which we could furnish." When Courtland appears in the village, he is given "every decent opportunity of advocating his cause"; "we thought best to await some fortunate crisis, holding the *unquestionable facts* of which we were possessed, relative to Courtland, as our *dernier resource.*" Under no circumstance do the Vigilliuses want Margaretta to marry until she has turned nineteen. For Edward Hamilton, who is "every thing amiable," her feelings are only sisterly; Mary points out "the absurdity of holding a character in great estimation, and highly accomplished, as a brother, which we should at the same time regard with reluctance as a conjugal companion." Margaretta tells Miss Amelia Worthington, however, that she wishes she had never seen Courtland; distressed at Hamilton's appearance ("the bloom hath forsaken his cheeks—the lustre of his fine eyes is no more"), she asks Amelia to help her "discharge as I ought, with becoming decency, a daughter's part," enclosing a poetic invocation to duty (No. ix).

Shortly Hamilton, "upon pretence of business," goes away. Courtland continues to pursue Margaretta, who experiences a severe conflict between duty and inclination. Until exposed by Serafina Clifford, Courtland claims to be the author of a poem Hamilton wrote on Margaretta. Just as Mr. Vigillius wonders whether he has judged Courtland too harshly, Margaretta cries out: "Never more do I wish to behold the man. . . . I am convinced that he is poorly mean, that he is capable of the most deliberate baseness." Mr. Vigillius, now determined to expose Courtland, informs him "that, as Miss Melworth is not in fact, our daughter, she is not by nature entitled to our inheritance"; whereupon Courtland, in "anger, disappointment, and the deepest chagrin," says he cannot marry a young lady who "doth not seem to have *any* well grounded expectations." Margaretta writes Amelia that "thanks to the unworthiness of Courtland, my liberated heart is at this moment lighter than a feather"; I discovered that "his soul was not formed for pity or for sympathy" and that "his air was haughty and forbidding." However, "I owe him no ill-will, and I am only solicitous that no unhappy young body, not patronized and directed, as I have been, may fall a victim to the wiles which an enemy so fascinating may prepare for her" (No. x).

No sooner has Margaretta sent this letter than she receives one Amelia wrote several days earlier, relating the pathetic story of Frances Wellwood, a defenseless orphan with a £2,000 patrimony, who succumbed some years before to Courtland's professions of unbounded love and secretly left New Haven with him. Now appearing in the Worthington breakfast parlor, she tells how he stripped her of honor, patrimony, furniture, and library and how "for some months past she hath been reduced to the necessity of parting with her clothes, and of availing herself of her skill in needle work, for the subsistence of herself and three sons, whom she hath borne to Courtland." Enclosed in Amelia's letter is one from Miss Wellwood importuning Margaretta to help her, for her children's sake, "reclaim a husband, who, not naturally bad, hath too long wandered in the dangerous paths of dissipation." Margaretta assures her that Mr. Vigillius, a friend of her father's, will undertake her cause. Courtland, humbled by his confinement in the county jail, readily agrees to Mr. Vigillius' proposal that he make Miss Wellwood his lawful wife (No. xi).

Edward Hamilton, who has been abroad, returns the night Courtland and Miss Wellwood are married; "he could think of no one but Margaretta," who is now nineteen (No. xii). "No sooner was she assured of the confiding friendship of her Edward, than she yielded up her whole heart." In the interval before her marriage admirers crowd about and assail her with "the perniciously enervating and empoisoned airs of adulation," but she receives them "in a manner which was truly worthy of approbation"; "she was not ambitious to enlist a train of danglers." She and Edward are married and their first-born is a boy (No. xiii).

Shortly Mary Vigillius tells her husband, *"All is not right at Margaretta's."* Whenever she visits Margaretta unexpectedly, she always finds her in tears, even though she and her son are in good health and Edward is "still the pensively pleasing and entertaining companion." Bewildered by this behavior, Mary writes Margaretta, "I pity the mind which prefers not the calm rational affections that succeed, to all the hurricane of the passions." Margaretta explains that soon after their marriage Edward began to exhibit "marks of a growing and deep-felt inquietude" and to look at her "with a fixed, and melancholy attention." Our son "is as dear to him, as the vital spark which warms him to existence—*but alas! this is the sum total of my enjoyments!*" I accidentally learned "that all those hours of which he has robbed me, were devoted to Serafina!" When I proposed that she come to live with us, she all too readily accepted. "The fine eyes of Serafina are often drowned in tears, and the grief of Hamilton seems to know no bounds!" I came upon her letter to him containing the words: *"Can Edward consign Margaretta to ruin? Can he be forgetful of the interest and well-being of his infant son?"* In agony I turned toward the window, only to behold "Edward and Serafina, arm under arm, walking down the gravel-walk of our little flower garden." Mary advises Margaretta to "persevere as you have begun—Mr. Hamilton is a man of sense and feeling; he will rouse to a recollection of your virtues, and your *reward* will be great" (No. xx).

The mystery is solved when Margaretta rushes into the Vigilliuses' apartment in "the mania of joy." She tells them that, determined to demand an explanation, she saw Edward and Serafina alone and, entering the room unobserved, overheard Serafina say sorrowfully: "O Edward! why are you thus un- kindly persevering? False sentiments betray you. My attach- ment to you is closely interwoven with my existence. I stand upon the brink of a precipice, down which your unyielding obduracy will not fail to plunge me! Again I assure you, that my happiness or misery is involved in yours! If you become an exile from your country, doubtless I shall be the companion of your flight." Upon hearing these words, Margaretta faints and, when she is revived, is temporarily deranged. "Hamilton, agonized beyond expression, in the frenzy of the moment, would have put a period to his existence; but by Serafina, who is ever present to herself, he was wooed, and awed to some degree of composure." When they are alone, Serafina tells Margaretta that she is Ed- ward's illegitimate half sister, born of their father's indiscretion while abroad, and that Edward, though nearly bankrupt, has refused the tender of her fortune which would reinstate him;

176

"he styles himself a wretch who hath deceived and betrayed you" and "meditates absconding from America." At this disclosure Margaretta regains her senses and is reunited with Edward (No. xxi).

When Edward asks Mr. Vigillius' advice "in regard to the line of conduct which the untoward state of my affairs renders it proper for me to pursue," Mr. Vigillius tells him, "*Justice* must be your guide." In order that your possessions may be secured to your children, you must prepare a full statement of your liabilities and assets; "you must not fail to discharge, to the last farthing, every just demand which can be made upon you" (No. xxiii). Although the months following Margaretta and Edward's reconciliation pass quietly, Mr. Vigillius knows that "the bursting storm, the tremendous and uprooting hurricane must succeed." Mr. Seymour, "the generous young man who had extricated Hamilton from his difficulties," fails for "some thousands" and is made a prisoner in his own house while creditors go over his accounts. Serafina still cannot prevail on Edward to accept her fortune. "In concert with Mr. Hamilton," Mr. Vigillius immediately takes steps "to place the property in his possession, beyond the reach of *any single* creditor." When he argues that Edward "might perhaps entirely retrieve his affairs" by making two or three voyages, Margaretta, far advanced in her second pregnancy, begins to change color; "the lily and the rose seemed to chase each other upon her now mantling, and now pallid cheek," and she sinks "breathless into the arms of that passionately beloved, and truly afflicted husband, who hasted to prevent her fall." "Can you condemn my Edward to bondage, perhaps to irretrievable slavery?" she cries. "Do you not recollect the British depredations? Do you not recollect the ruthless and unrelenting rigour of that fate which awaits the captive, doomed to wear out a wretched life under the galling yoke of an Algerine despot?"

On the eve of Edward's departure a stranger appears and, embracing Margaretta, exclaims, "It is a *father's* arms that are at length permitted to enfold his long lost Margaretta!!!" Mr. Melworth assures his daughter that "riches, more than thou canst want, are in my gift," sufficient to satisfy every creditor and rescue Mr. Seymour from bankruptcy (No. xxviii). Seated in the happy family circle, he tells his story. When his ship bound for the East Indies was wrecked, he managed to save himself and was eventually picked up by an English ship. He returned to England to find his wife dead. When Mrs. Arbuthnot gave out a report that Margaretta was dead too, he went to sea again and "became a citizen of the world." One day there caught his eye the *Massachusetts Magazine* for March 1792, which carried the first installment of the Story of Margaretta; immediately he took ship for America to hunt for his daughter. "Already our young people have resumed their elegant family seat," concludes Mr. Vigillius; "this very morning, the second day of July, one thousand seven hundred and ninety-four, witnessing the birth of a daughter to Margaretta, hath seemed to complete our family felicity" (No. xxix). Thus ends the first volume of *The Gleaner*.

In the second and third volumes Judith Murray adds a few episodes to the Story of Margaretta. Old Timothy Plodder and young Bellamour both wish to marry Serafina Clifford. Plodder tells Mr. Vigillius, "if you will absolutely and *bona fide* clear Miss Clifford, and the heirs lawfully born of her body, *from all claims whatsoever, which the Hamiltons may, on any future emergency, find it convenient to lay to her estate* . . . she shall forthwith become my *true* and *lawful* wife *until death*." Bellamour, although he has never seen her, knows she is charming; "you may inform Edward Hamilton, that I have a handsome estate in possession; it is true, it is encumbered with a few mortgages." Monima Castalio proposes a third candidate; "I have *wagered* two five-dollar bills with Miss Primrose," she informs Mr. Vigillius, "that you will, out of hand, marry Mr. Melworth to Miss Serafina Clifford" (No. xxxvii). Mr. Vigillius, while pitying Mr. Plodder his bachelorhood, tells him it is too late "to begin that career, which should at least commence in the meridian of our days," and announces that "the name of Clifford is now absorbed in that of Seymour." Seymour, when Melworth has discharged his debts, visits Hamilton-Place, woos and wins Serafina, and builds Seymour-Grove nearby. Margaretta gives birth to a third child, Mary-Augusta (No. xxxviii).

Margaretta relates how her friend Miss Hayden rushed into the room in dishabille and asked to read Mary's last letter. I refused, says Margaretta, knowing "she does not *spell properly*, and she reads very badly, with the very *tone of voice which you, mamma, dislike."* Moreover, she "cares for nothing but running about from place to place. She was a *whole month* in making a shirt for her father, and it was *ill made* after all. They say she lays in bed *until nine o'clock*! . . . She thinks herself handsome; but *one of her eyes is plainly a darker blue than the other."* Mary chides her for such uncharitable remarks: "Your account of Miss Hayden is so *foreign from your usual style.* . . . you endeavour to detract from those personal charms, which Miss Hayden is generally acknowledged to possess!! . . . Detraction is the first-born of envy. . . . *Beware* then, my child, of its blighting influence." Seek Miss Hayden and condescend "to solicit a reconciliation" (No. xli). Chagrined at having behaved so ungenerously, Margaretta hastens to apologize; Miss Hayden "immediately rose from her chair, and, throwing her arms about my neck, she burst into tears!" "I have to acknowledge your mild submission, sweet discretion, and affectionate duty, as the richest solace, both to your father and myself," says Mary. "Nothing is more disgusting than an overweening self-sufficiency and presumptuous pride, particularly in young persons" (No. xlii).

We last see Margaretta "relieving a desolate female, whom Providence has thrown under her protection." This woman, bereft of husband, children, and fortune in a succession of catastrophes, tells Margaretta her story. Born in Belfast, she came to Maryland at the close of the Revolution and married a young doctor. Smallpox broke out in the West Indies where he set up practice; "I was brought to the verge of the grave—and my babes—my darling babes—became the victims of the despoiler!" When the blacks on the island revolted, her newborn boy "perished in the general wreck" and her husband was murdered trying to defend her. She was nursed back to health, came to Boston "pennyless, and a stranger," and turned to Margaretta as a last resort. "Could I reach Ireland, my pecuniary wants would know an end; but this I have not the means of doing. . . . I have endeavoured to obtain support by my needle . . . but ill health impedes my efforts." The ever-compassionate Margaretta places "within her reach, the *power* of ameliorating those ills which had made such large inroads on a mind so deeply stricken" (No. xcviii). With this episode the unfinished Story of Margaretta breaks off.

Literary taste has of course changed since Judith Murray's time; consequently most present-day readers will find contemporary enthusiasm over *The Gleaner* excessive. One of her contemporaries thought the work "not half so much praised and encouraged as it ought to be" and was persuaded that a generation hence "the Gleaner will be as universally read and admired, as the works of our Addison, and will be a very able competitor, to the spectator."[16] "Happy talents, Constantia, are confessedly thine!" exclaimed another. "Had mines of gold been thine; and hadst thou, with the generous patriotism thou hast so eloquently commended, dispensed them for the public weal, they had been but trifles, when compared with the rich, valuable presents thou hast made to thy country!"[17] We read the Story of Margaretta more dispassionately and put it down with the realization that Judith Murray made a tangible, though modest, contribution to the early American novel. She shrewdly chooses to focus on the years when female sensibility is most acute. From the time she meets Courtland at age sixteen until her reunion with her father Margaretta's heart is constantly aquiver. Although she experiences the familiar conflict between inclination and conscience, unlike Clarissa Harlowe and Charlotte Temple filial duty prevails and she is never actually seduced. Because she is not told at the time of her marriage that Serafina is her husband's half sister or that he is near bankruptcy, she suffers an anguish that brings on temporary insanity. But she also knows moments of joy, such as getting free from Courtland, learning that her husband and Serafina had the same father, and being reunited with her long-missing father. Whereas Clarissa and Charlotte are dishonored and die a lingering death, when last seen Margaretta is the happy, useful wife, mother, and citizen. Like Pamela's, hers is the story of virtue rewarded.

"Sinisterus" Courtland, though a less artful charmer than Lovelace, resembles him in being the seducer not of Margaretta, but of Frances Wellwood. He has designs on Margaretta's fortune and, had he won her love, would undoubtedly have

deserted her as he did Miss Wellwood. However, he is reclaimed
by the woman he seduced and makes her his wife, thus becoming an example of the reformed rake, like Montraville who wept
"over the grave and [regretted] the untimely fate of the lovely
Charlotte Temple." Edward Hamilton, Courtland's rival in love,
has but one fault, an inability to manage his business affairs.
From their first meeting it is clear that he and the equally
virtuous Margaretta, whose character is marred only by the
single time she judged a friend uncharitably, are made for one
another.

Although the voice of Mr. Vigillius (alias the Gleaner) is heard
throughout the series, the Story of Margaretta is told, like many
other sentimental novels, largely through letters, in particular
those that pass between Mary Vigillius and her ward Margaretta. Since the periodical essay traditionally employed letters from and to correspondents, the epistolary form of the Story
of Margaretta is easily fused with *The Gleaner* as a whole. By this
fusion the balance between an appeal to sensibility and to
morality is firmly established so that Judith Murray can eat her
cake and have it.

IX. WILLIAM WIRT

⃞

FOR THE LATE-EIGHTEENTH-CENTURY VIRGINIAN "the only fitting peace-time pursuits outside the management of his
estates were law, politics, or statecraft. Most of the creative
energies he possessed went into the political pamphlet, oratory,
or personal correspondence."[1] William Wirt was atypical: a
lawyer by profession, "he had ever some literary project in hand,
to which he gave a portion of his time."[2] Entering practice in
Culpeper County at the age of twenty, he described his library as
consisting of "no other munitions than a copy of Blackstone,
two volumes of Don Quixotte and a volume of Tristram
Shandy,"[3] a statement which suggests that in addition to studying law he had familiarized himself at an early age with belles-
lettres. We know, for example, that while at the grammar school
of the Reverend James Hunt of Montgomery County, Maryland,
he "read, or as he put it, *devoured*, all the dramatic poets available in Mr. Hunt's library. And *Tom Jones* was his 'bread and
meat.' "[4] There also he encountered the works of Addison. His
British Spy declares, "Were I the sovereign of a nation, which
spoke the English language, and wished my subjects cheerful,
virtuous and enlightened, I would furnish every poor family in
my dominions (and see that the rich furnished themselves) with
a copy of the Spectator; and ordain that the parents or children
should read four or five numbers, aloud, every night of the
year."[5] But "Wirt's own taste, though he admired Addison, ran
chiefly to the later eighteenth-century writers: Gray, Young,
Ossian, Sterne, and Burke."[6] Especially Sterne. Seated on a
gravestone at Jamestown, the British Spy brushes aside melancholy and thinks of "the whimsical pages of Tristram Shandy:
that book which every body justly censures and admires alternately; and which will continue to be read, abused and devoured, with ever fresh delight, as long as the world shall relish a

oyous laugh, or a tear of the most delicious feelings" (187).[7]

By 1800 Wirt had settled in Richmond where during the next decade, chiefly in collaboration with like-minded professional men and planters who "saw that the new nation must have a literature of its own,"[8] he engaged in a series of literary projects. Three of these, published first in local newspapers, then in book form, were essay serials: *The Letters of the British Spy, The Rainbow,*[9] and *The Old Bachelor.*

I

In the late summer of 1803, "to while away six anxious weeks which preceded the birth of my daughter,"[10] Wirt published ten essays under the title "The British Spy."[11] *The Letters of the British Spy*, the title given the book edition, follows Addison, Lyttelton, and Goldsmith in employing the foreign visitor. Wirt introduces the misplaced manuscript, though less convincingly than Freneau had done in *Tomo Cheeki*. We are informed that it "was found in the bed-chamber of a boarding-house in a seaport town of Virginia" and that it "seems to be a copy of letters written by a young Englishman of rank, during a tour through the United States, in 1803, to a member of the British parliament." The landlady describes this boarder (the British Spy) as "a meek and harmless young man, who meddled very little with the affairs of others" (97). The Spy tells his parliamentary friend that although he has resided in Richmond for six months, he "suspended writing until a more intimate acquaintance with the people and their country should furnish me with the materials for a correspondence." Now ready to begin, he explains his pseudonym: "Under my assumed name, I gain an admission close enough to trace, at leisure, every line of the American character; while the plainness, or rather humility of my appearance, my manners and conversation, put no one on his guard, but enable me to take the portrait of nature, as it were, asleep and naked. Beside, there is something of innocent roguery in this masquerade, which I am playing, that sorts very well with the sportiveness of my temper" (99-100). Hereafter Wirt halfheartedly sustains the illusion that the author is British. Once the Spy refers to himself as "a plain son of *John Bull*" (214), and on several occasions the reader is reminded of the Spy's nationality in pointed footnotes.[12] "I adopted the character of a British Spy," Wirt later explained,

> because I thought that such a title, in a republican paper, would excite more attention, curiosity and interest than any other: and having adopted that character, as an author, I was bound to support it. I endeavored to forget myself; to fancy myself the character which I had assumed; to imagine how, as a Briton, I should be struck with Richmond, its landscapes, its public characters, its manners, together with the political sentiments and moral complexion of the Virginians generally. I succeeded so well that in several parts of the country, particularly in Gloucester, and in the neighborhood of Norfolk, the people went so far as to declare that they had seen the very foreigner, (and a Briton he was, too,) who had written the letters.

Then, mindful of the resentment which his portraits of John Marshall, Edmund Randolph, and John Wickham in the series had aroused, Wirt added, "Unfortunately, however, in my zeal to support my adopted character, I forgot myself too far in some of the letters."[13] Although Wirt announces that his Spy is an Englishman visiting Richmond, he never breathes life into this Spectator-like character as Freneau does into Tomo Cheeki. Because the disguise is thin, we are never made to feel the Spy's nationality and his observations and judgments sound for all the world like those of a Virginian at the turn of the century.

Although a letter to the editor explains, "Persons of every description will find in [these letters] a light and agreeable entertainment; and to the younger part of your readers they may not be uninstructive" (98), clearly the *British Spy* letters are intended primarily to instruct and only incidentally to entertain. Wirt, as a young married man busy establishing himself professionally and socially in Richmond, addresses himself "more to the rising generation than to that which is passing away."[14] Examining the Virginia scene, the Spy remarks on social and economic inequality, the evolution of the North American continent, the mistreatment of the Indian, lack of public spirit, and, most important of all, eloquence. Although Virginia "plumes herself most highly on the democratic spirit of her principles," the Spy discovers "a species of social rank . . . which arises from the different degrees of wealth and of intellect tual refinement." "This inequality struck me with peculiar force in riding through the lower counties on the Potomac," he observes. "Here and there a stately aristocratic palace, with all its appurtenances, strikes the view; while all around, for many miles, no other buildings are to be seen but the little smoky huts and log cabins of poor, laborious, ignorant tenants" (100-102). It is perhaps arguable that these observations are such as a status-conscious Briton might deliver.

The discovery of the skeleton of a whale below the surface of a farm near Williamsburg seems to the Spy indisputable evidence "that the whole of this beautiful country was once covered with a dreary waste of water." The topography of Virginia, extending from the Blue Ridge to the Atlantic, "tends to confirm the ingenious theory of Mr. Buffon; that the eastern coasts of continents are enlarged by the perpetual revolution of the earth from west to east, which has the obvious tendency to conglomerate the loose sands of the sea on the eastern coast; while the tides of the ocean, drawn from east to west, against the revolving earth, contribute to aid the process, and hasten the alluvion. . . . If Mr. Buffon's notion be correct, that the eastern coast of one continent is perpetually feeding on the western coast of that which lies before it," some day "the present sickly site of Norfolk [will] be converted into a high and salubrious mountain." Facetiously the Spy adds, "I apprehend, however, that the present inhabitants of Norfolk would be extremely unwilling to have such an effect wrought in their day; since there can be little doubt that they prefer their present commercial situation, incumbered as it is by the annual visits of the yellow fever, to the elevation and health of the Blue Ridge." With Shandean whimsy he concludes, "Who could have believed that the skeleton of an unwieldy whale . . . would have led me such a dance!" (114-31). "An Enquirer" (George Tucker) replies, "This hypothesis, which the British Spy has partially adopted, is liable to many objections, which, to me at least, are insuperable. . . . we have not yet arrived at that certainty which will satisfy the inquirer [and therefore] we must be contented to acknowledge that this great phenomenon is, yet, unsolved" (149, 158). This letter reminds us of the then current vulcanist and neptunist theories concerning the formation of continents. A dilettantish Wirt, thinly disguised as the British Spy, is led by news of the discovery of the skeleton of a whale to subscribe with Buffon to the latter theory.

Returning from a visit to the Indian town Powhatan, the Spy recalls the mistreatment of the Indian. Virginians "have no right to this country. They say that they have bought it—bought it! Yes;—of whom? Of the poor trembling natives who knew that refusal would be vain. . . . Poor wretches! No wonder that they are so implacably vindictive against the white people." If I were president of the United States, vows the Spy, "I would glory in going to the Indians, throwing myself on my knees before them, and saying to them, 'Indians, friends, brother, O! forgive my countrymen!' " Such magnanimity "would go further to bury the tomahawk and produce a fraternization with the Indians, than all the presents, treaties and missionaries that can be employed. . . . Magnanimity can never be lost on a nation which has produced an Alknomok, a Logan, and a Pocahuntas" (163-68). As Tomo Cheeki discourses on the white man's mistreatment of the Creeks in Georgia, the British Spy deplores similar treatment of the Indians in Virginia and urges magnanimity.

Viewing the remains of the English settlement at Jamestown, the Spy reflects on "what a nation, in the course of two hundred years, has sprung up and flourished from the feeble, sickly germ which was planted here!" But Virginia, "as rapidly as her population and her wealth must continue to advance, wants one most important source of solid grandeur . . . public spirit; that sacred *amor patriae* which filled Greece and Rome with patriots, heroes and scholars. There seems to me to be but one object throughout the state; *to grow rich*." Lacking public spirit, Virginia still needs highways, public buildings, even a great university. The College of William and Mary has only been "endowed with a few despicable fragments of surveyors' fees, &c."; meanwhile the youth there are permitted "to run riot in all the wildness of dissipation" (191-94). These remarks are addressed to the rising generation in Virginia who, thinks the Spy, are too concerned with growing rich. The call for a public university seems an anticipation of the founding of the University of Virginia. A few years later Wirt's Old Bachelor would re-emphasize the need for public spirit.

As a man of little formal education who, overcoming an early speech defect, rose to the top of his profession and became attorney general under James Monroe and John Quincy Adams, Wirt valued eloquence from an early age. His views were largely shaped by Hugh Blair's *Lectures on Rhetoric and Belles-Lettres* (1783); Blair's ten lectures on eloquence deal successively with the nature of eloquent discourse, its history, its ancient and modern kinds, the six parts of the oration, the invention and disposition of proofs, the pronunciation or delivery of the speech, and the means to self-improvement in public address. [15] Eloquence is a recurrent topic throughout Wirt's literary career, culminating in *Sketches of the Life and Character of Patrick Henry* (1817), the work for which he is best remembered. Four of the ten *British Spy* letters focus on eloquence, more particularly on the oratory of Patrick Henry, James Monroe, John Marshall, two Richmond lawyers, Edmund Randolph and John Wickham, and the blind Presbyterian preacher James Waddell. When Marshall, Randolph, and Wickham and their families took umbrage at the portraits the Spy drew of them, Wirt felt it necessary to apologize: "If the letters of the British Spy . . . have given pain to the gentlemen described . . . there is no man in the community disposed to regret it more sensibly than the man who furnished those letters for publication" (238). [16]

Deploring the fact that eloquence "has few successful votaries" in America, the Spy makes three general observations about American orators: "First, They have not a sufficient fund of general knowledge. Secondly, They have not the habit of close and solid thinking. Thirdly, They do not aspire at original ornament." "In reading an oration," he continues, "it is the expanse and richness of the conception itself, which I regard, and not the glittering tinsel wherein it may be attired." Emphasizing the importance of sympathy, the Spy quotes Francis Bacon to the effect *"that there should be some transmissions and operations from spirit to spirit without the mediation of the senses."* Patrick Henry (whom Wirt never heard) commanded attention because he possessed this power. "I am told," says the Spy, "that his general appearance and manners were those of a plain farmer or planter of the back country; that, in this character, he always entered on the exordium of an oration; disqualify-

ing himself, with looks and expressions of humility so lowly
and unassuming, as threw every heart off its guard and induced
his audience to listen to him, with the same easy openness with
which they would converse with an honest neighbour: but, by
and by, when it was little expected, he would take a flight so
high, and blaze with a splendour so heavenly, as filled them
with a kind of religious awe, and gave him the force and authority of a prophet" (132-45).

Monroe's "sober, steady and faithful judgment has saved him
from the common error of more quick and brilliant geniuses,"
says the Spy, adding prophetically, "it would be matter of no
surprise to me, if, before his death, the world should see him at
the head of the American administration." Marshall possesses
"the faculty of developing a subject by a single glance of his
mind, and detecting at once, the very point on which every
controversy depends. . . . All his eloquence consists in the apparently deep self-conviction, and emphatic earnestness of his
manner; the correspondent simplicity and energy of his style;
the close and logical connexion of his thoughts; and the easy
gradations by which he opens his lights on the attentive minds
of his hearers" (175-81). The Spy, learning "that the bar of
Virginia was, a few years ago, pronounced by the supreme court
of the United States, to be the most enlightened and able on the
continent," singles out two Richmond lawyers. Edmund Randolph's "character, with the people, is that of a great lawyer and
an eloquent speaker. . . . he is a man of extensive reading, a
well-informed lawyer, a fine *belles lettres* scholar, and sometimes a beautiful speaker." John Wickham's "temper and habits
lead him to the swelling, stately manner of Bolingbroke. . . .
Instead of giving a simple, lucid and animated view of a subject,
[his method] overloads, confounds and fatigues the listener"
(207-14).

The best known of the *British Spy* letters, and the most popular throughout the nineteenth century, is the portrait of James
Waddell. The Spy, journeying "along the eastern side of the Blue
Ridge," comes upon "a ruinous, old, wooden house, in the
forest," which he recognizes as "a place of religious worship."
Curious to hear the preacher, the Spy entered and "was struck
with his preternatural appearance, he was a tall and very spare

188

old man; his head, which was covered with a white linen cap, his shrivelled hands, and his voice, were all shaking under the influence of a palsy; and a few moments ascertained to me that he was perfectly blind." When during the communion service he said, "Father, forgive them, for they know not what they do," his voice grew faint and "he raised his handkerchief to his eyes, and burst into a loud and irrepressible flood of grief," whereupon "the whole house resounded with the mingled groans, and sobs, and shrieks of the congregation." When the tumult subsided, he delivered a sentence from Rousseau ("Socrates died like a philosopher, but Jesus Christ, like a God!") in such a slow, solemn manner that the Spy experienced "a kind of shuddering delicious horror! . . . I have never seen, in any other orator, such a union of simplicity and majesty. . . . Guess my surprise, when, on my arrival at Richmond, and mentioning the name of this man, I found not one person had ever before heard of *James Waddell*!!," even though he lives only eighty miles away (195-202).[17] The popularity of this portrait was owing not only to the high value nineteenth-century Americans placed upon eloquence but also to the pathos it evoked. The spectacle of the preacher pausing midway in the sentence from Rousseau and lifting his sightless eyes to heaven was calculated to appeal to contemporary readers.

In his final letter the Spy relates that, stopping at a country inn to refresh himself, he called for a book while his meal was being prepared. The landlord "brought me a shattered fragment of the second volume of the Spectator, which he told me . . . had been sleeping unmolested in the dust of his mantel-piece, for ten or fifteen years." "Is it not strange," the Spy asks his friend in parliament, "that such a work should have ever lost an inch of ground? . . . What person, of any age, sex, temper, calling, or pursuit, can possibly converse with the Spectator, without being conscious of immediate improvement?" I regret "that such a book should be thrown by, and almost entirely forgotten, while the gilded blasphemies of infidels, and 'the noontide trances' of pernicious theorists, are hailed with rapture, and echoed around the world" (240-43). Although such enthusiasm might seem to place this serial squarely in the Addisonian tradition, a recent critic suggests that the essays of *The British*

189

Spy "owe equally as much to Goldsmith and Blair in their critical principles and general choice of subjects. In their style they have been warmed by the pre-Romantics such as Macpherson and Gray and by the whimsy of Sterne."[18]

The British Spy, like *The Farrago* and *The Lay Preacher*, is dramatic evidence that the Addisonian essay in America had all but run its course. Not only is the subjectivity we saw in Dennie present here, as witness the pathetic portrait of Waddell, but also elements of the travel essay then enjoying a vogue on both sides of the Atlantic, notably descriptions of the Virginia scene in the letters of inequality and the mistreatment of the Indian. The only Addisonian convention employed is the foreign visitor and this in so casual a manner that Wirt, not the Spy, seems to be the speaker.

Contemporary judgments of *The British Spy*, while often severe, help account for the work's popularity. "The letters bespeak a mind rather frolicksome and sprightly, than thoughtful and penetrating," said Wirt self-deprecatingly; "and therefore a mind qualified to amuse, for the moment, but not to benefit either its proprietor or the world, by the depth and utility of its researches. The style, although sometimes happy, is sometimes, also, careless and poor; and still more frequently, overloaded with epithets. . . . Upon the whole, the work is too tumid and too light; yet these, perhaps, are the very properties which gave it the degree of admiration which it excited. . . . Certainly I shall write no more Spies; 'too much pudding,' &c."[19] A review of the 1812 London edition largely confirms Wirt's judgment: "The style possesses a liveliness, and a force, which fix the attention; though the first occasionally degenerates into flippancy, and the last swells into bombast.—When we lately reviewed a work from the United States [*Salmagundi*] we had the pleasure of being able to congratulate that country on the growing honours of its literature; and the present composition, although destitute of the humour which embellished its precursor, possesses a firmer and a higher tone."[20] In actual fact, *The Letters of the British Spy* proved so popular that it went through no fewer than ten American editions in the author's lifetime.[21]

II

Wirt did not keep his promise to "write no more Spies." On December 24, 1810, he told Dabney Carr of a new literary project that was afoot: "He [Richard E. Parker] was with me the other evening, and I imparted to him our project of a series of moral and literary essays, with which he was delighted, and agreed to contribute, provided I would sit at the helm, to preserve the unity of course and character, and expunge, alter or reject, any thing he should send which did not meet my approbation. . . . I mentioned to him, that you and Frank [Dabney's brother] would contribute, and he is very anxious to know you both. . . . Before he went, we agreed . . . that the Sylph would not do. So I have hit upon another, the Old Bachelor."[22] Two days earlier, on December 22, the first of the *Old Bachelor* essays had appeared.[23] *The Old Bachelor* was a collaborative effort, as the letter above makes clear, presided over by Wirt and enlisting the literary services of Virginia friends that included Dabney and Frank Carr, Dr. Louis Girardin, Richard E. Parker, George Tucker, and Major David Watson. It seems certain that Wirt, who created the character of the Old Bachelor (Dr. Robert Cecil), wrote all or part of sixteen numbers in the series.[24]

Peter Hoffman Cruse, Wirt's early biographer, suggests that Wirt undertook *The Old Bachelor* to answer Thomas Ashe's misrepresentation of America in *Travels in America* (1808), a review of which he read in the *Edinburgh Review*.[25] The broader purpose of the series, however, was *"virtuously to instruct, or innocently to amuse"* the reader and to work a reform of manners and morality in town as well as country.[26] The Old Bachelor, addressing himself like the British Spy to the rising generation, seeks "to awaken the taste of the body of the people for literary attainments" and to "see whether a groupe of statesmen, scholars, orators, and patriots, as enlightened and illustrious as their fathers, cannot be produced without the aid of such another bloody and fatal stimulant [as the Revolutionary War]" (No. 12, February 2, 1811).

Although its immediate concern is for the well-being of the youth of Virginia, *The Old Bachelor* is undeniably a literary serial, more Addisonian in manner and matter than *The British*

Spy. In particular, the persona is much more fully developed. "I am upwards of six feet high and as thin as that knight whom Cervantes has immortalized," declares the Old Bachelor. "My locks have been bleached by the snows of sixty winters. My nose and chin have sallied out, like two doughty champions, to meet in mortal combat; and . . . must soon have a meeting, in spite of my teeth: While my mouth recedes from the field in dismay, and its corners retreat to my ears" (No. 8, January 15, 1811). Once a year for the past twenty-five years he has tried and lost his suit with "every age from fifteen to forty; and every complexion from the Italian Brunette, to the dazzling and transparent white of Circassia." He hobbles on a cane as a result of wounds received at the Battle of Brandywine. As a young man he failed in law, medicine, and divinity:

> . . . when I came to the bar of my country, I found that I was like a seventy four gun ship aground in a creek; while every pettifogger, with his canoe and paddle was able to dodge around and get a-head of me. . . . Alas! my medical career was a very short one; for the first patient submitted to my skill, was my own beloved mother [who] expired in my arms. . . . my abortive efforts to shield my fellow creatures from death were now converted into an exertion to teach them how to die. . . . although, at last, I did not feel myself authorized to enter the sacred desk in the character of a teacher, yet I shall never regret my having fortified my own faith against the assaults of sophistry and qualified myself to silence the cavil and witticisms of the infidel. (No. 1, December 22, 1810)

Exempted from having to pursue a learned profession, he was fortunate in having sufficient means "to follow my own taste, in delivering myself up to the pure and simple pleasures of the country and the uncloying charms of general literature" (No. 2, December 25, 1810).

The Old Bachelor is "not distinguished by dirt, tobacco and brandy on the one hand; nor, on the other, by uniform and elaborate tidiness and closeness . . . instead of cats and dogs, I have two boys and a girl, the orphan children of a favorite sister." Alfred is studying law and Galen medicine, while Rosalie has the run of his library and laboratory. His farm, lying at some distance from Richmond, "is situated in a fine and healthy part of the country, has been laid out with great skill and taste by my manager . . . and commands a most extensive and beautiful prospect." Previously he lived in a small wooden cottage. Now, however, being "subject to the most extravagant starts of enthusiasm," he took his promise to care for his sister's children so seriously that he constructed a stone house, "turreted and built with walls of cannon proof," standing on a cliff. Originally he planned "to fortify it with cannon and to surround the base of the crag with a moat and draw bridge. But before the work could be compleated the fit had gone off" (No. 2, December 25, 1810).

Persuaded by Alfred and Rosalie "that a course of moral and literary essays . . . would do great good in this country," the Old Bachelor decided to commence author (No. 3, December 29, 1810). "I am an old-fashioned old fellow, whose earnest desire is to amuse and serve you," he informs the public, after the manner of Sterne. "If you choose to be my reader you must be content, as I am, to follow the wanderings of my mind, in its own way; and to drop, resume and continue a broken subject, just as occasion and fancy prompts" (No. 13, February 7, 1811). Midway in the series one of his correspondents admonishes him: "we think you are, like the Rambler, too often and too long mounted upon stilts. . . . You must come down from your castle and your cliff, and mix with us folks in our own way." Be it therefore resolved "That Doctor Cecil, the author of The Old Bachelor, do change his style oftener, than usual, on pain of being displaced; and when he cannot instruct, that he do make us laugh, on the like pain" (No. 15, March 5, 1811). The Old Bachelor (Dr. Robert Cecil), distinguished by his quixotic appearance and behavior, is an important addition to the growing gallery of bachelors that appeared in American serials. Try as he may to win a wife, this Revolutionary veteran has been constantly disappointed in love. Having failed in the respected professions, he possesses the means to live as a dilettante and now turns author.

Another Addisonian convention that figures prominently in *The Old Bachelor* is the fictitious letter. Early in the series the Old Bachelor declares, "I shall cheerfully relieve the dullness & monotony of my own productions, by any virtuous sport of wit or fancy which may be furnished by another" (No. 5, January 5,

1811). However, "nothing will find its way to the public under the sanction of The Old Bachelor, but what is calculated . . . to promote the cause in which he has embarked: *virtuously to instruct, or innocently to amuse*" (No. 11, January 26, 1811). He trains his nephews Galen and Alfred to be correspondents by teaching them "rather to think correctly, than either newly or finely" (No. 7, January 12, 1811). Other correspondents include the Quaker Tim Lovetruth, Obadiah Squaretoes, Arthur O'Flannegan, Richard Vamper, Peter Schryphel, Stephen Micklewise, Romeo, John Truename, Diogenes, and Susannah Thankful.

In *The Old Bachelor*, as in *The British Spy*, instruction is more important than entertainment. Education was the principal topic Wirt and his friends set themselves when they undertook the series, though in time they wearied of it and turned more and more to other topics. Good Republicans all, they asserted the Jeffersonian ideal of an aristocracy of virtue and talent. The Old Bachelor, deploring the practice of intriguing for office, exhorts young Virginians: "Make yourselves capable of serving the people; of serving them greatly and effectually; make yourselves worthy of their love and confidence by the perpetual exhibition of a pure, a virtuous and an useful life, and you will then possess *that popularity which follows*. . . . We are now, I believe, at the bottom of the moral wheel; or, at least, as low, I hope, as we shall ever sink. Much depends on the young men who are at this time preparing to come forward" (No. 14, February 26, 1811). Recalling the Revolutionary generation, he wishes to stimulate his countrymen "to a generous competition with their forefathers in those great qualities which exalt the soul and ennoble the mind" (No. 22, July 5, 1811). Because *"the virtues of this country are with our women"* (No. 5, January 5, 1811), we should not neglect their education. At present, however, "the important interval between twelve and eighteen is unprofitably consumed in spoiling paper with colours, producing discord on the Piano, and dancing out of time to the violin. . . . After all this misapplication of a young lady's time, she is transferred from the romping boarding school to the solitude of the country, to yawn with disconsolate fatuity over the fragments of her broken instrument, and the faded landscapes of her youthful limnership, and we console her by deriding her ignorance of Greek and Mathematikes."[27]

Many people say that they are too poor to educate their children when in fact they are simply indifferent. "Boots, bonnets and brandy must be had at any price; but learning may shift for itself" (No. 25, August 20, 1811). The children, too, are at fault, having "contracted habits of idleness, that more fatally even than poverty, frustrate the effect of latent powers, and smother the seeds of great abilities" (No. 26, December 21, 1811). Tim Lovetruth, distressed by this *"moral stagnation,"* proposes a system of public education in Virginia (No. 8, January 15, 1811). The Old Bachelor endorses this proposal and calls for "a board of education, under the control of the Legislature, and a national Press, for the diffusion of moral and physical knowledge, through all the classes of society" (No. 12, February 2, 1811). Looking beyond the state level, his nephew Alfred opposes the idea of a National University but suggests many ways short of this in which the federal government can advance general education: "Government may, in the first place, become the pioneer of literature. It may employ learned men to make voyages of discovery for the objects of science, and take exact surveys of our interior country and maps and charts of our coasts and harbours." It may "print school books and distribute them at an inconsiderable expence. . . . In every large town and even in every considerable village, reading rooms, well selected libraries, laboratories and philosophical apparatus might be furnished at public expence. . . . At the seat of government. . . there might be a very large and extensive national library" (No. 28, December 24, 1811). These observations are addressed to the rising young men and women of Virginia with whom the Old Bachelor feels the future rests; he wants them to emulate the noble qualities of the Revolutionary generation by educating themselves for moral leadership and holding public office. In particular, he shares Trumbull's concern about the inadequacy of female education in America.

Among the moral subjects examined in this series are industry, avarice, and patriotism. The Old Bachelor, recalling what an old Swiss peasant told him ("industry is the mother of virtue and health, and these are the parents of happiness; as idleness is

195

the mother of vice and disease, the immediate parents of human misery"), observes mischievously, "In this class of victims to a busy indolence, next to those who devote their whole lives to the unprofitable business of writing works of imagination, are those who spend the whole of their's in reading them" (No. 4, January 1, 1811). Underscoring the importance of observing the golden mean, he relates the story of the virtuous young Henry Morton whose father, because his own youthful dissipation led to poverty, overcomes Henry's instinctive generosity and teaches him to be avaricious (No. 13, February 7, 1811). John Truename, who declares that "if ever there was a truehearted Virginian, I must be one for I never was out of the state in my life," dates his love of country (and hatred of the British) from the time his father fought and died at Yorktown (No. 21, April 5, 1811).

In one of several manners essays a Pennsylvania German farmer, Peter Schryphel, recommends that the Old Bachelor send his nephews to Richmond "to get some knowledge of men and manners." When my father and my wife died, writes Peter, I provided myself "with a pair of handsome horses and a new suit of clothes, for myself and my valet," and "set out for Richmond." "The first thing which struck my attention, next to the ceaseless stir and bustle in the streets and the shewy elegance of the shops was the smoothness and polish of manners which I could not but contrast with the coarse simplicity of my neighbors and country men." Shopkeepers "took particular pains to accommodate me—told me what was fashionable or otherwise." One of the city dignitaries "took the trouble to procure me a ticket to a ball given by the citizens to the members of the Legislature. . . . I can truly say, I never passed so agreeable an evening in my life" (No. 15, March 5, 1811). Elsewhere the Old Bachelor praises the natural conversation of men like Benjamin Franklin: "Look from the tinkling cymbals of the present day to such a colloquial character as Doctor Franklin! . . . he never shone in a light more winning than when he was seen in a domestic circle." "In these days of modern refinement and illumination," however, "the artless simplicity and innocence of nature are gone!" "Who, for instance, would exchange the sweet simplicity and ease of Montaigne or Sterne, for the stiff affectation and elaborate pomp of Shaftesbury? Or," he adds with avuncular pride, "the vital grace and sweet enchantment of my Rosalie's natural manner, for all the arts and ambuscades of the most practised coquette?" (No. 17, March 12, 1811). An unnamed correspondent illustrates "the ruinous and detestable practice of gaming" by relating his brother's history. "My brother was affectionate, and open, and generous, in his character, and highly sensible to whatever was honourable; but he was wild and heedless, and violent in his passions." Discovering a proficiency for gaming, he not only lost his own fortune but eventually "dissipated nearly all the remains of our father's estate, and involved himself inextricably in enormous debts." He also took to drink. One stormy December night his wife and children, "drenched with rain and shivering with cold, and still more with terrour," fled to my house to avoid his brutality. A few months later "a disease to which he had been long subject, and which proceeded from his intemperance, terminated his miserable existence."[28]

The most memorable character in the series is Obadiah Squaretoes, who charges that the Old Bachelor's essays "have introduced anarchy and misrule" into his household, "where order and good government reigned before." Obadiah explains that, having taken to wife "the blooming daughter of a neighboring farmer," "no vagaries about the rights of women, or the equality of the sexes, ever disturbed her quiet brain." He and his wife define the extent and limits of the education of their six daughters:

> ... it consisted of reading, writing and arithmetic to the rule of three—The Bible & Testament, the Whole Duty of Man, and the art of cookery, by Mrs. Hannah Glass made up their library—all beyond was forbidden ground. ... with our three eldest, we succeeded completely—aye, shew me, who can, three more notable and house-wifely women than Bridget, Winifred and Dinah— Girls that can turn their hand to any thing—Milk a cow, iron a shirt, mend a stocking or make pudding—and I defy any one to catch them idling over a book; except on Sundays, and then strictly within the pale of the law; none of your novels, or histories, or such.

"Of my three younger daughters, would to Heaven, I could say as much; but they have blasted all my hopes. ... This misfortune I owe, partly, to my own imprudence, but more particularly, Mr. Bachelor, to the baleful influence of your essays." His wife's sister, "a true town lady, with all the airs and graces, and high flown actions, and delicate sensibilities of the tribe," persuaded him against his better judgment to permit her to take his daughter Grace to the city and "show her some thing of life." When she returned he scarcely knew her. "Instead of the plump, rosy-cheeked country girl, with health and life, and activity in every muscle—I saw a thin, maciated, *delicate* figure, with cheek of snow, & languid step moving slowly towards us—all the warm habiliments of the country, the comfortable petty coats, the snug pocket—thrown aside, and in their place, a thin muslin dress." What was worse, "I found my lady's mind more metamorphosed than her body—she had been reading novels, plays and histories—nay I even caught her one day delivering lectures to her younger sisters, on the 'Rights of Women,' a book which she had met with in her aunt's library." He reasserted his authority over her, and "things seemed to be getting right again, when you, Mr. Bachelor stepped in, and ruined all my hopes." One morning he found her reading aloud from a newspaper "while my two youngest, were sitting round her devouring her words, and the tears trickling down their cheeks. . . . It was your 5th number, Mr. Bachelor . . . your foolish story of a Roman woman, Agrippina." When he snatched the paper and called her to account, Grace said: "Father, I respect your authority within reasonable limits . . . but you expect too much, when you suppose that I will go, or can be carried all lengths—I am now 18, capable, if ever, to think for myself, and I hope that in this free country, women have some rights—the law which you have read . . . is gothic, obsolete, and I deny its authority. . . . the Old Bachelor—God bless him!—came to my rescue—he wakened my curiosity, he roused my energies, he warmed my ambition and determined me, at all hazard, to proceed in the career of knowledge." Since she is determined to persevere in this course and his wife sides with her, Obadiah calls on the Old Bachelor to "repair this injury" (No. 9, January 19, 1811).

The Old Bachelor replies that women have an equal right to knowledge. "There is no man who respects the establishment of family rules more than I do," he assures Obadiah, but these rules "must have reason to command my respect. And what reason can there be in annihilating a girl's mind?"

> There is such a thing as a progress in mind and manners, insepara-
> ble from the nature of man, to which every sensible father will pay
> some attention in the education of his children. . . . The passion
> for knowledge is natural to the female character; it will be grat-
> ified at any risque. . . . are we acting a christian part, when by the
> wretched system of education which we have adopted for them,
> we cover the rising glory of female genius with a cloud and hide its
> splendor from the world forever? . . . Are we not playing off upon
> them the policy of the Roman Church; and practically confessing
> that it is only while we can keep them in ignorance, that we can
> expect them to acknowledge our boasted supremacy?

Referring to his essay on industry, the Old Bachelor adds, "if Mr. Squaretoes can vanquish his antipathy to newspaper essays, so far as to read my fourth number, he will see, in the example of my friend Bianca, that The Old Bachelor is no advocate for the excessive use of novels, nor for the neglect of domestic duties." Thereupon he instructs Grace to perform her household duties "for her own sake as well as the honor of the Old Bachelor, whose disciple she professes to be" (No. 10, January 22, 1811). Obadiah Squaretoes is a male chauvinist who prides himself on having trained his daughters according to his own lights, only to have his household upset by Grace's enlightened view, for which he holds the Old Bachelor responsible. What enhances the portrait of this old-fashioned father is our strong sense of the domestic circle in which he moves; his boast, for example, that Bridget, Winifred, and Dinah can "milk a cow, iron a shirt, mend a stocking or make pudding."

At the end of the series Wirt, writing with greater care than he had in the earlier newspaper numbers, turned to his favorite topic, eloquence. The Old Bachelor complies with Alfred's request that in view of "the woful state of eloquence" manifest in the pulpit, legislative assembly, and at the bar, he share with the young "the fruits of [his] observation and experience on this head." Young men in Virginia, he declares, mistakenly suppose that success depends wholly upon inspiration. In actual fact, "genius is only the diamond in the quarry; it is labour and art that must bring it forth, purify it, polish it, and invest it with the radiance which constitutes its beauty and worth." As the example of Cicero proves, he who wishes to excel in eloquence "must keep forever in view the glorious pre-eminence at which he aims, and be willing to sacrifice to it every consideration of personal ease and pleasure."[29] Deficiencies in American public address are many and obvious: "we are fatigued and distressed by the dissonant raving and screaming of a voice strained above its natural key . . . or we are deafened with the bellowing of a Bedlamite . . . or we are lulled to sleep by the chiming reciprocation and alternate monotony of a frog-pond." Upon seeing the tragedian Cooper enact the dagger scene in *Macbeth*, "I found that I had been bereaved of my breath—my sinews and my muscles had been strained to a painful extremity—and I felt my hair descending and settling on my head, for it had been raised by sympathetick horrour." Our public speakers would do well to model their behavior after actors like Cooper. "Who is not disgusted with the stiffness, the formality, the slow, mechanically measured enunciation, the nasal melody, the affected mouthings, or the coarse rusticity, the ear-crucifying sing-song, and the delirious raving and shrieking, which, too often, degrade the pulpit and defeat the very purpose of the institution."[30] Eloquence was highly esteemed in early nineteenth-century America, nowhere more so than in Virginia. Wirt, who had praised the oratory of Henry, Monroe, Marshall, and Waddell in *The British Spy*, here impresses upon young Virginians the importance of cultivating whatever oratorical abilities they possess. As the Spy was moved by the preaching of James Waddell, so is the Old Bachelor by the acting of Thomas Cooper whom he holds up as a model.

While Wirt's is the controlling hand, *The Old Bachelor* was a joint venture involving at least six of his friends, all anxious to cultivate native literature. It is more clearly a literary serial than *The British Spy*, the more fully developed persona being evidence of its greater objectivity; while the Old Bachelor expresses views with which Wirt and his associates were generally in agreement, we accept the fiction of the persona and his exchanges with numerous correspondents as we do not the character of the British Spy. If instruction looms larger than entertainment, still there is more in this series to divert the reader than in *The British Spy*, most notably the trials of

Obadiah Squaretoes. In view of the emphasis on education early in the series and on eloquence late, it must be admitted that the underlying purpose of *The Old Bachelor* was to train up "a groupe of statesmen, scholars, orators, and patriots, as enlightened and illustrious as their fathers" who lived in Revolutionary times. As it turned out, it proved to be the last clear example of the literary serial in America.

Learning midway through the series that a book edition of *The Old Bachelor* was being contemplated, Wirt confided to Dabney Carr on March 23, 1811: "If I had realized the idea that my good name, fame and reputation were at stake, I would have taken care to write to the best advantage—in rural privacy, for instance, and only in the happiest moments of inspiration, after having, by previous meditation, exhausted upon it all my retail shop of thought. Instead of this I have been dribbling on, with a loose pen, carelessly and without any labour of thinking, amidst incessant interruptions—and with the printer's devil at my elbow, every half hour, jogging me for more copy."[31] He was disappointed that the series had apparently not had the intended effect: "I wrote in the hope of doing good, but my essays dropped into the world like stones pitched into a mill-pond; a little report from the first plunge; a ring or two rolling off from the spot; then, in a moment, all smooth and silent as before, and no visible change in the waters to mark that such things had ever been."[32] Wirt's contemporaries and posterity, however, regarded *The Old Bachelor* highly. He heard it reported that President Madison "thought Mr. W's pen, at least, ought to redeem us from the censures of the Edinburgh Reviewers."[33] A critic reviewing the 1818 Baltimore edition declared that these essays constitute "one of the most successful experiments which has been made in this department of letters, since the era of Johnson."[34] And Wirt's major nineteenth-century biographer called *The Old Bachelor* "the best of all his literary compositions,"[35] a literary judgment that seems just today.

Shortly before *The Old Bachelor* appeared in book form in 1814, Wirt, for whom such literary projects were a necessary activity though always kept subordinate to the practice of law, confessed, "I am afraid that both the Old Bachelor and the British Spy will be considered by the world as rather too light and *bagatellish* for a mind pretending either to stability or vigor."[36] If this seemed to him a just appraisal, we can be grateful that William Wirt "dribbled on" and produced these two serials. Early southern literature is the richer for them.

X. WASHINGTON IRVING

NEW YORK CITY in the period following the Revolution developed a self-consciousness that enabled it to outdistance Philadelphia in the early years of the nineteenth century and become for a time the literary capital of the nation. Even before the turn of the century there arose literary clubs devoted to original compositions in prose and poetry.[1] Two of Washington Irving's older brothers were active in the Calliopean Society. William Irving, a prominent merchant whom Paulding characterized as "a man of great wit, genius, and originality,"[2] became president of the Calliopean Society in 1791. Dr. Peter Irving was elected first vice-president the next year; William Dunlap remembered him as one of the gentlemen who in 1796 "were regular frequenters of the New-York theatre, enjoyed its productions as men of education and lovers of literature, and wished to correct the abuses existing in the costume, demeanour, and general conduct, of the actors on the stage."[3]

James Kirke Paulding, who would collaborate with Washington and William Irving on *Salmagundi*, was bound to the Irving family not only by literary interests but also by marriage; his sister Julia married William Irving in 1793, and the couple took James into their home when he came to New York from Westchester County as a young man of 18 or 19. Remembering Goldsmith's *Citizen of the World* as the book that "possibly gave a direction to my whole life,"[4] Paulding was early attracted to a career in letters. "Oh—may all the glory and success attend the noble art of scribbling!" he wrote a friend on August 14, 1802. "What would become of me without the solace it affords?"[5] It is likely that he wrote essays for Peter Irving's *Morning Chronicle* (1802-1805).[6] From the time he contributed to *Salmagundi* there existed a tension in his style between satire and sentimentality.

Washington Irving, whose acquaintance with Paulding ripened into friendship at least as early as the time of their association on the *Morning Chronicle*, wrote with greater geniality and always with an "eye to the *picturesque*."[7] In his earliest journals, written during the four years separating the two serials, the *Oldstyle* letters and *Salmagundi* papers, his prose style matured rapidly. Nathalia Wright states that whereas the New York journal (1803) "foreshadows his later writing: general fluency, with particular tendencies toward a pictorial technique in describing landscapes and toward low-keyed satire of pretense and pomposity," the style of the European journal (1804-1806) is "decidedly more confident. . . . not only the type of scenic description in *The Sketch Book* but its whole range of literary genres—reverie, scenic description, character sketch, narrative, historical account—are found in the journal."[8] Invective too, though it all but disappeared in later works, marks his early style. A recent editor has argued convincingly that Irving contributed twelve pieces, and possibly as many as forty-five, to *The Corrector*, a New York newspaper of March-April 1804 that supported Aaron Burr in his unsuccessful bid for the governorship of New York.[9] Even though Irving would write political essays for *Salmagundi* which closely resemble these *Corrector* pieces in tone and topic—for example, the Mustapha letters in Nos. 11 and 16 and "On Greatness" in No. 15—he was speaking from the heart when he declared on February 2, 1807, "I have rather shunned than sought political notoriety."[10]

For all his traveling and long sojourns abroad, Irving always identified himself with New York, the city of his birth. "The bay; the rivers & their wild & woody shores; the haunts of my boyhood, both on land and water, absolutely have a witchery over my mind," he wrote Henry Brevoort from Paris on December 16, 1824. "I thank God for my having been born in so beautiful a place among such beautiful scenery."[11] He realized his dream of being able "to return home, nestle down comfortable . . . and have wherewithal to shelter me from the storms and buffetings of this uncertain world,"[12] when in 1836 he moved into Sunnyside, north of the city.

I

In much the way that young Benjamin Franklin began his literary career by publishing the *Dogood* papers in his brother's newspaper, nineteen-year-old Washington Irving published the *Oldstyle* letters (though not surreptitiously) in his brother Peter's *Morning Chronicle*.[13] And as Franklin broke off when his "small Fund of Sense for such Performances was pretty well exhausted," Irving ended his serial abruptly after the ninth letter. The fact that Jonathan Oldstyle does not fulfill the promise he makes at the beginning of the eighth letter to describe in a subsequent number the ball he visited with Quoz and Dorothy indicates that Irving was not then planning to discontinue the series. Irving may have been thinking of this promise when in the opening number of *Salmagundi* he described the "New-York Assembly."

Jonathan Oldstyle is so conventional an aptronym for the old bachelor as probably to have occurred instinctively to Irving. An "odd old fellow" (3) who favors old-fashioned dress and deportment, Jonathan laments "the degeneracy of the present times" in which wives consider themselves totally independent; "what husband," he declares, "but will look back with regret, to the happy days of female subjection" (7). A regular theatergoer, he prefers the old style of acting to the new. When his country neighbor calls John Hodgkinson's interpretation of Gondibert in George Colman's *Battle of Hexham* "first rate acting," Jonathan replies, "you should have seen an actor of the *old school* do this part; he would have given it to some purpose; you'd have had such ranting and roaring, and stamping and storming; to be sure this honest man gives us a *bounce* now and then in the true old style, but in the main he seems to prefer walking on plain ground to strutting on the *stilts* used by the tragic heroes of my day" (17). Jonathan moves between home and theater in a domestic circle that includes Jack Stylish, the son of his old-fashioned Aunt Barbara and her husband Squire Stylish; his sister Dorothy, with whom he is seen "calmly enjoying [his] toast and coffee" (32); the honest old countryman whom he meets attending the playhouse for the first time; and Andrew Quoz, the correspondent who seeks to educate Jonathan in the ways of actors and critics.

Jonathan is far less discomfited by the inconveniences of being single than by the indignities he suffers at the theater. Sitting in the pit before the play begins, he is "a little irritated at being saluted aside of my head with a rotten pippin" thrown by one of the gallery gods but manages to hold his temper. Later he is almost suffocated "by a host of strapping fellows standing with their dirty boots on the seats of the benches" (12, 15). He barely escapes the lounging room when the young gentry threaten to "smoke his wig" and "twig his silver buckles." Most humiliating of all, one of the actors in a farcical afterpiece suddenly exclaims, "And as to *Oldstyle*, I wish him to old nick" (23, 24). In taste, habits, and dress Jonathan Oldstyle is a relic from the eighteenth century, an old bachelor tolerated by his family but not at the theater. He sees himself for what he is, but has no desire to adopt modern ways.

Letters of Jonathan Oldstyle, Gent., to give the serial its book title, is wholly social, three of the essays focusing on manners, the other six on theatrical criticism. Whereas many serialists devoted the first number to stating their purpose and introducing the dramatis personae, Irving has Jonathan turn at once to the conventional topic of dress and deportment, then and now. In place of "very high crowned hats with very narrow brims, tight neckcloth, tight coat, tight jacket, tight small clothes, and shoes loaded with enormous silver buckles: the hair craped, plaited, queued and powdered," declares Jonathan, recalling his youth, "we now behold our gentleman, with the most studied carelessness, and almost slovenliness of dress; large hat, large coat, large neckcloth, large pantaloons, large boots, and hair scratch'd into every careless direction." Then young men knew how to deport themselves at a ball ("nothing more common than to see half a dozen gentlemen knock their heads together in striving who should first recover a lady's fan or snuff-box that had fallen"). Now "our youths no longer aim at the character of *pretty gentlemen*: their greatest ambition is to be called lazy dogs—careless fellows—&c. &c. Dressed up in the mammoth style, our buck saunters into the ball-room in a surtout, hat under arm, cane in hand; strolls round with the most vacant air; stops abruptly before such lady as he may choose to honor with his attention; entertains her with the common *slang* of the day, collected from the conversation of hostlers, footmen, porters, &c. until his string of smart sayings is run out, and then lounges off, to entertain some other fair one with the same unintelligible jargon" (3,4). Given his predilection for the old style, Jonathan would if he could turn back the clock and re-establish the fashions and the good breeding that prevailed when he was young.

While acknowledging that in general "times are altered for the better," Jonathan holds up his Aunt Barbara and Squire Stylish as models of deportment: "*her* conduct was always regulated by *his*—her sentiments ever accorded with his opinions. . . . The squire was the most attentive and polite husband in the world: would hand his wife in and out of church, with the greatest ceremony—drink her health at dinner with particular emphasis, and ask her advice on every subject—though I must confess he invariably adopted his own—nothing was heard of from both sides but dears, sweet loves, doves, &c." But Jonathan knows that a modern couple, "accustomed to treat one another with the utmost carelessness and neglect," will laugh at such behavior. "The wife now considers herself as totally independent—will advance her own opinions, without hesitation, though directly opposite to his—will carry on accounts of her own, and will even have secrets of her own with which she refuses to entrust him" (5-7). One reason Jonathan favors the old ways is that then wives were subservient to their husbands, as Aunt Barbara is to Squire Stylish. He shudders to think of modern wives who, scorning such behavior, stand up to their husbands and get their own way.

Learning from Quoz that the New York legislature has passed a law imposing penalties for dueling, Jonathan exclaims, "Spirit of chivalry, whither hast thou flown!" Dorothy, too, mourns "to see the last spark of chivalric fire thus rudely extinguished," and wonders how challenges can now be conveyed.

> Nothing more easy, said friend Quoz:—a man gives me the lie— very well: I tread on his toes in token of challenge—he pulls my nose by way of acceptance: thus you see the challenge is safely conveyed without a third party.— We then settle the mode in which satisfaction is to be given; as for instance, we draw lots which of us must be slain to satisfy the demands of honor. Mr. A. or Mr. B. my antagonist, is to fall: well, madam, he stands below

in the street; I run up to the garret window, and drop a brick upon his head: If he survives well and good; if he falls, why nobody is to blame, it was purely accidental. Thus the affair is settled, according to the common saying, to our mutual satisfaction.

Jack Stylish protests that Quoz's project is "a vulgar substitute" and wishes to see the law amended so as to require duelists to secure a license from the *"Blood and Thunder Office,"* "give two or three weeks notice of the intended combat in the newspapers," "fight till one of them [falls]," and admit the public "to *the show*." Approving of Jack's plan, Jonathan informs the editor, "Our young men fight ninety-nine times out of a hundred, through *fear* of being branded with the epithet of *coward*; and since they fight to please the world, the world being thus interested in their encounter, should be permitted to attend and judge in person of their conduct" (32, 34-35). This ironical attack upon a custom then passing out of favor, crude though it is, helps flesh out the character of Jonathan who, as a man of the previous century, would have approved of dueling.

From at least as early as 1798 when the Park Theater near Broadway opened its doors, Irving frequented the theater. He was "more than the mere gentlemanly theater-goer; he was a hanger-on at stage doors and in greenrooms, as in London a score of years later; he was at once the intimate and the critic of the actors."[14] It is no surprise, therefore, to find him at the outset of his literary career devoting so much space to aspects of the theater: audience, musicians, actors, critics. Entering the playhouse, Jonathan is "much amused with the waggery and humor of the gallery, which, by the way, is kept in *excellent* order by the constables who are stationed there. The noise in this part of the house is somewhat similar to that which prevailed in Noah's ark; for we have an imitation of the whistles and yells of every kind of animal." "I found the ladies in the boxes, as usual, studious to please; their charms were set off to the greatest advantage; each box was a little battery in itself, and they all seemed eager to out do each other in the havoc they spread around. An arch glance in one box was rivalled by a smile in another, that smile by a simper in a third, and in a fourth, a most bewitching languish carried all before it" (12-13). Jonathan complains that whereas once "people went to the theatre for the sake of the play and acting," now "it begins to answer the purpose of a coffee-house, or fashionable lounge, where many indulge in loud conversation, without any regard to the pain it inflicts on their more attentive neighbors" (16). "I had marched into the theatre through rows of tables heaped up with delicacies of every kind—here a pyramid of apples or oranges invited the playful palate of the dainty; while there a regiment of mince pies and custards promised a more substantial regale to the hungry. I entered the box, and looked round with astonishment—not a grinder but had its employment. The crackling of nuts and the craunching of apples saluted my ears on every side" (22). Jonathan paints a vivid picture of the behavior of American theater audiences in his day: the unruliness of those in the gallery, the affected manners of the ladies in the boxes, and, what distresses him most of all, the noisy eating throughout the playhouse.

The musicians, says Jonathan, "came crawling out of their holes, and began with very solemn and important phizes, strumming and tuning their instruments in the usual style of discordance, to the great *entertainment* of the audience. What tune is that? asked my neighbor, covering his ears. This, said I, is no tune; it is only a pleasing *symphony*, with which we are regaled as a preparative. For my part, though I admire the effect of contrast, I think they might as well play it in their cavern under the stage. . . . What I heard of the music, I liked very well (though I was told by one of my neighbors that the same pieces have been played every night for these three years;) but it was often overpowered by the gentry in the gallery, who vociferated loudly for *Moll in the wad, Tally ho the grinders,* and several other *airs* more suited to their tastes" (14). "I think you complain of the deficiency of the music," Quoz tells Jonathan; "and say that we want a greater variety and more of it. But you must know that, though this might have been a grievance in old times, when people attended to the musicians, it is a thing of but little moment at present.— Our orchestra is kept principally for form sake. There is such a continual noise and bustle between the acts that it is difficult to hear a note; and if the musicians were to get up a new piece of the finest melody, so nicely tuned are the ears of their auditors, that I doubt whether nine hearers out of ten would not complain, on leaving the house, that they had been *bored* with the same old pieces they have heard these two or three years back" (20). A generation later there were still complaints about the music heard at the Park Theater. In a newspaper letter "The Tune in Book Number Six" recalls "being of a lively disposition" thirty-six years before; in time, though, the tune came to be "played on all occasions, farce or melo-drama, tragedy, comedy, or pantomime," so that now "I am a by-word in the pit. People insult me by eating apples, and crack jokes and peanuts on me with a total forgetfulness of my original charms. The managers, and not I, are to blame for my long sojourn and constant repetition in the orchestra."[15]

Andrew Quoz, parodying Shylock's "Hath not a Jew Eyes?" speech, defends actors:

> Ods-bud, hath not an actor eyes and shall he not *wink*?—hath not an actor teeth and shall he not grin?—feet and shall he not stamp?—lungs and shall he not roar?—breast and shall he not slap it?—hair and shall he not *club* it? Is he not fed with plaudits from the gods? delighted with thumpings from the groundlings? annoyed by hisses from the boxes?
> If you censure his follies, does he not complain? If you take away his bread will he not starve? If you starve him will he not die? And if you kill him will not his wife and seven small infants, six at her back and one at her breast, rise up and cry vengeance against you? (21)

"The world, my friend Oldstyle, has ever been prone to consider the theatrical profession in a degraded point of view," says Quoz, setting forth the rights of actors. "Why the actor should be considered inferior in point of respectability to the poet, the painter, or any other person who exerts his talents in delineating character, or in exhibiting the various operations of the human mind, I cannot imagine" (27). An actor is

> competent to judge of his own abilities—he may undertake whatever character he pleases—tragedy—comedy—or pantomime—however ill adapted his audience may think him to sustain it. He may rant and roar, and wink and grin, and fret and fume his hour upon the stage, and "who shall say him nay?" He is paid by the manager for using his lungs and limbs, and the more he exerts them the better does he fulfil the engagement, and the harder does he *work* for his living—and who shall deprive him of his "*hard-earned* bread?" . . . an actor has a right whenever he thinks his

author not sufficiently explicit to assist him by his own *wit* and *abilities*; and if by these means the character should become quite different from what was originally intended, and in fact belong more to the *actor* than the *author*, the actor deserves high credit for his ingenuity. And even tho' his additions are *quaint*, and fulsome, yet his *intention* is highly praise worthy, and deserves ample encouragement. (28, 29)

In support of Quoz, who declares that "few of our modern critics can shew any substantial claim to the character they assume," Jonathan exclaims that "the Critics are the most 'presumptuous,' 'arrogant,' 'malevolent,' 'illiberal,' 'ungentleman-like,' 'malignant,' 'rancorous,' 'villainous,' 'ungrateful,' 'crippled,' 'invidious,' 'detracting,' 'fabricating,' 'personal,' 'dogmatical,' 'illegitimate,' 'tyrannical,' 'distorting,' 'spindle-shanked moppets, designing villains, and upstart ignorants' " (30, 31). Jonathan's castigation of critics was prompted by a flurry in the New York press involving the author James Fennell, the actor John Hodgkinson, and the editors William Coleman and James Cheetham. Although Fennell claimed to be sole author of *The Wheel of Truth*, a farce performed at the Park Theater, Hodgkinson who played the chief role was suspected of having introduced the character Littlewit as an actor's revenge on drama critics. Cheetham defended Hodgkinson against Coleman's attack upon him, calling his opponent "Mr. *Cole*-man or more properly Mr. *Black*-man."[16] When Hodgkinson finally declared, "I had no agency whatever in the production of the 'Wheel of Truth,' " Colman replied, "I have done you an injustice in attributing to you some considerable share in its authorship."[17] At this point Jonathan, who had been warned against critics by Quoz, began "to doubt the motives of our New-York Critics" and launched into this diatribe.

Jonathan, constituting himself a critic, offers suggestions for every department of the theater:

I would recommend,
To the actors—less etiquette—less fustian—less buckram.
To the orchestra—new music and more of it.
To the pit—patience—clean benches and umbrellas.
To the boxes—less affectation—less noise—less coxcombs.
To the gallery—less grog and better constables—and,
To the whole house—inside and out, a total reformation. (18)

Two months after Jonathan called for a total reformation of the playhouse, the Park Theater was closed for a short time. "During the recess," reported the *Morning Chronicle* of February 23, 1803, in its review of the reopening two days earlier, "the backs of the boxes have been re-colored with a lighter blue, and the benches newly covered. These are the only improvements that could be made in so short a space of time." In the summer of 1807 the interior was extensively remodeled.

Irving's maiden effort at age nineteen, *Letters of Jonathan Oldstyle, Gent.*, is less impressive than Franklin's *Dogood* papers written at age sixteen, chiefly because in the eighty years separating these works the influence of the *Spectator* had grown progressively weaker. Irving, who would parody the tradition of the essay serial in *Salmagundi* and abandon it altogether in *The Sketch Book*, at the outset of his career acted reflexively rather than originally in choosing Addison for his model. The only Addisonian conventions employed in the *Oldstyle* letters are the persona and the fictitious letter. However, Irving does adhere to a dramatic point of view more faithfully than his near contemporaries, Dennie and Wirt, as witness the vivid glimpses we are given of Jonathan's home life and the New York theater. One would not guess that in less than twenty years the author of this serial would turn familiar essayist.

In 1825, at a time when the success of *The Sketch Book* and *Bracebridge Hall* was helping establish Irving's literary reputation on both sides of the Atlantic, John Neal characterized the *Oldstyle* letters, which had just been reprinted in American and English editions, as "boyish theatrical criticism . . . from the rubbish of old printing-offices. . . . Nevertheless, there is a touch of Irving's quality in these papers—paltry as they are: A little of that happy, sly humour; that grave pleasantry, (wherein he resembles Goldsmith so much); that quiet, shrewd, good-humoured sense of the ridiculous, which, altogether, in our opinion, go to make up the chief excellence of Geoffrey [Crayon]—that, which will outlive the fashion of this day; and set him apart, after all, from every writer in our language."[18] Irving, thinking even more poorly than did Neal of this juvenile work, withheld it, as he did *Salmagundi*, when preparing an authorized edition of his works in the 1840s.

II

Drawn together in the first years of the nineteenth century by a love of literature and the desire for conviviality were a group of young New Yorkers which included William, Peter, Ebenezer, and Washington Irving, Peter and Gouverneur Kemble, Paulding, Henry Brevoort, Henry Ogden, David Porter, and Richard McCall. Gouverneur Kemble opened Mount Pleasant, an old family country place on the banks of the Passaic near Newark, to this group who were known by such names as the "Nine Worthies," the "Lads of Kilkenny," the "Ancient and Honorable Order," and the "Ancient Club of New-York." When in the city they would sometimes "riot at Dyde's,"[19] a public house near the Park Theater. *Salmagundi* grew spontaneously from the activities of this club in town and country, Mount Pleasant serving as the model for Cockloft Hall.

Of more immediate importance to the *Salmagundi* authors than the essays of Steele, Addison, Johnson, and Goldsmith and their younger contemporaries in America were the writings in certain American magazines at the turn of the century. Dennie's *Port Folio*, which appeared weekly in the period 1801-1807, not only reprinted essay serials like *The Farrago* and *The Lay Preacher* but included departments of art, drama, fashion, fiction, music, poetry, politics, and travel. John Howard Payne's *Thespian Mirror* (1805-1806) carried a theatrical register of New York productions, biographical sketches of contemporary actors and actresses, selections from British and American writings on drama, and dramatic anecdotes. Charles Brockden Brown's *Literary Magazine and American Register* (1803-1807) published original essays on such topics as female dress, marriage, and punning. At the beginning of 1807 there appeared five numbers of *The Town* (January 1, 3, 7, 9, 12), a short-lived New York magazine which helped precipitate the first number of *Salmagundi* a fortnight later and which makes it clear that the *Salmagundi* authors set out to parody the tradition of the literary serial rather than take it seriously. Will Wizard's essay on "Theatrics" and Anthony Evergreen's on the "New-York Assembly" in the first number of *Salmagundi* and Anthony's essay on "Fashions" in the third number are satirical responses to *The*

Town's serious criticism of a recent performance of *Macbeth* at the Park Theater, an account of a recent gathering of the City Assembly, and a note on London female fashion.

Between January 24, 1807, and January 25, 1808, there were published at New York twenty paper-covered numbers of *Salmagundi; or, The Whim-Whams and Opinions of Launcelot Langstaff, Esq. & Others*. The expression "whim-wham" is synonymous with Laurence Sterne's "hobby horse"; what Sterne says of Uncle Toby can be said likewise of the characters in *Salmagundi*: "When a man gives himself up to the government of a ruling passion,—or, in other words, when his HOBBY-HORSE grows head-strong,—farewell cool reason and fair discretion!"[20] More than any earlier American serial *Salmagundi* is a collaboration throughout its length, its principal authors being Washington Irving and Paulding, two fledglings still in their twenties; they interested William Irving in the venture and would probably have enlisted Peter Irving too, had he not recently gone to Europe. "The thoughts of the authors were so mingled together in these essays, and they were so literally joint productions," cautions Paulding in the Preface to the 1835 New York edition, "that it would be difficult, as well as useless, at this distance of time, to assign to each his exact share."[21] The work quickly proved to be a bestseller, a monetary fact grasped more readily by the publisher, David Longworth, than by the authors for whom it was a spontaneous, imaginative expression of the literary and social conviviality they were then enjoying. That the *Salmagundi* authors were more interested in diverting the public than in instructing it is established in the first number by their promise to teach parents "how to govern their children, girls how to get husbands, and old maids how to do without them" (73). Indeed, they might well have said after Sterne, "I write a careless kind of a civil, nonsensical, good-humoured *Shandean* book, which will do all your hearts good—And all your heads too,—provided you understand it."[22]

Salmagundi is an appropriate title; Webster defines the word as "a heterogeneous mixture; a medley; potpourri." At the outset Launcelot Langstaff, the chief persona, apportions the duties among himself and his fellow editors, naming fashion Anthony Evergreen's department and criticism Will Wizard's, reserving for himself the freedom to range widely. The second number introduces Pindar Cockloft, from whose mill the poetry in the series will issue. Mustapha Rub-A-Dub Keli Khan makes his appearance in the third number, supplying the first of nine letters to friends back in Tripoli. Beginning in the fourth number the traveler Jeremy Cockloft entertains the reader with accounts of his tours of New Jersey, Pennsylvania, and Broadway, in parody of British travel writers like Sir John Carr and Isaac Weld. In short, each number of *Salmagundi* is a potpourri consisting of two or more distinct pieces in prose and poetry.

In place of the club frequented by bachelors in the essays of Defoe, Steele, Addison, and Goldsmith, the social center of the world of *Salmagundi* is Cockloft Hall, a snug pastoral retreat near New York where Launcelot Langstaff, Anthony Evergreen, and Will Wizard spend much of their time as house guests of Launcelot's cousin, Christopher Cockloft. "In the south-east corner of the house," Launcelot informs the reader, "I hold quiet possession of an old fashioned apartment, where myself and my elbow-chair are suffered to amuse ourselves undisturbed, save at meal times" (131). Anthony, Will, and I "are none of those outlandish geniuses who swarm in New-York. . . . we write for no other earthly purpose but to please ourselves" (69-70). Although "in his youth he was forever in love" (154) and was something of a prankster (once he "smoked out a country singing-school with brimstone and assafoetida," 249), now Launcelot stays close to his elbow-chair. He "inherited from his father a love of literature, a disposition for *castle building*, a mortal enmity to noise, a sovereign antipathy to cold weather and brooms, and a plentiful stock of whim-whams" (156).[23] Launcelot declares, "I can sit in a corner, indulge in my favourite amusement of observation, and retreat to my elbow-chair, like a bee to his hive, whenever I have collected sufficient food for meditation" (201). What he longs for most is a serene old age: "When a man is quietly journeying downwards into the valley of the shadow of departed youth, and begins to contemplate in a shortened perspective the end of his pilgrimage, he becomes more solicitous than ever that the remainder of his wayfaring should be smooth and pleasant, and the evening of his life, like the evening of a summer's day, fade away in mild uninterrupted serenity" (266).

Launcelot says that though Anthony Evergreen "has slowly and gradually given into modern fashions, and still flourishes in the *beaumonde*, yet he seems a little prejudiced in favor of the dress and manners of the *old school*" (71). He deplores the "dancing mania" (76) which holds sway in New York and describes a near accident which befell a Frenchman at the Assembly: "One of these jack-o-lanthorn heroes ... unfortunately wound himself—I mean his foot—his better part—into a lady's cobweb muslin robe; but perceiving it at the instant, he set himself a spinning the other way ... and extricated himself, without breaking a thread of the lady's dress!" (77). Anthony calls all modern music "but the mere dregs and draining of the ancient" and longs to hear "the chant of the naiades, and the dryades, the shell of the tritons, and the sweet warblings of the mermaids of ancient days!" (81). Scornful of modern dress, he offers the local milliners his own "receipt for a full dress": "take of spider net, crape, sattin, gymp, cat-gut, gauze, whalebone, lace, bobbin, ribbons, and artificial flowers, as much as will rig out the congregation of a village church; to these add as many spangles, beads, and gew-gaws, as would be sufficient to turn the heads of all the fashionable fair ones of Nootka-sound" (95). In taking leave of the ladies Anthony makes a final plea for domestic simplicity: "we have endeavoured to lure them from the mazes of a dissipated world ... and to restore them before it is too late, to the sacred asylum of home" (309).

Will Wizard is more whim-whamsical than Launcelot or Anthony. "I never in my life," says Launcelot, "met with a man, who rode his hobby-horse more intolerably hard than Wizard" (271). Will's department being theatrical criticism, he is pleased with Mrs. Villiers' acting in *Macbeth*, but thinks "she would have given greater effect to the night-scene, if, instead of holding the candle in her hand ... she had stuck it in her night-cap. This would have been extremely picturesque, and would have marked more strongly the derangement of her mind" (74). Having written a favorable review of a performance of *Othello*, Will explains in a postscript, "Just as this was going to press, I was informed by Evergreen that Othello had not been performed here the lord knows when; no matter, I am not the first that has criticised a play without seeing it, and this critique will answer for the last performance, if that was a dozen years ago" (141). Will's behavior in public is frequently bizarre and unpredictable. Anthony describes how at a ball he helped "himself to a quid [of tobacco] in face of all the company" (124) and then "thundered down the dance like a coach and six . . . now running over half a score of little frenchmen, and now making sad inroads into ladies cobweb muslins and spangled tails" (126). Christopher Cockloft's "prime favorite and companion is Will Wizard, who is almost a member of the family, and will set before the fire, with his feet on the massy andirons, and smoke his cigarr, and screw his phiz, and spin away tremendous long stories of his travels, for a whole evening, to the great delight of the old gentleman and lady, and especially of the *young ladies*" (134). An antiquarian at heart, Will "takes great delight in ransacking" the Cockloft library which consists of "specimens of the oldest, most quaint, and insufferable books in the whole compass of english, scotch, and irish literature" and "ponderous tomes in greek and latin," modern works being "thrust into trunks, and drawers, as intruding upstarts" (270). "It was a sight, worthy of a man's seeing," says Launcelot, "to behold Will, with his outlandish phiz, poring over old scrawls that would puzzle a whole society of antiquarians to expound, and diving into receptacles of trumpery, which, for a century past, had been undisturbed by mortal hand" (270-71).

These three bachelor editors complement one another, Anthony and Will writing about fashions and the theater and Launcelot serving as jack-of-all-trades. Like Jonathan Oldstyle they are gentlemen of the old school, especially Anthony who abhors the fashionable waltz and Will whose antiquarian taste prompts him to ignore modern books. The elbow-chair at Cockloft Hall serves as the city desk where material for the next number is assembled by Launcelot, who for all his Sternean whimsy is less dogmatic than Anthony and less mercurial than Will.

"Whim-whams," declares Launcelot, "are the inheritance of the Cocklofts, and every member of the household is a humorist *sui generis*, from the master down to the footman" (132). So it happens that Christopher Cockloft, present proprietor of the Hall, "lost most of his children when young, by the excessive care he took to bring them up like vegetables. . . . he sprinkled them every morning with water, laid them out in the sun, as he did his geraniums. . . . The consequence was, the poor little souls died one after the other, except Jeremy and his two sisters, who, to be sure, are a trio of as odd, *runty*, mummy looking originals as ever Hogarth fancied in his most happy moments" (130). Jeremy completed his education at Columbia College, "where he became exceedingly expert in quizzing his teachers and playing billiards. No student made better squibs and crackers to blow up the chemical professor; no one chalked more ludicrous caricatures on the walls of the college; and none were more adroit in shaving pigs and climbing lightening rods" (101). Upon graduation Jeremy, being "seized with a great desire to see, or rather to be seen by the world" (102), spent three or four months visiting strange places like Albany and Philadelphia. Launcelot, finding Jeremy's "notes and hints for a book of travels which he intends publishing" (102), proceeds to entertain the public with extracts. As for Jeremy's sisters, "BARBARA the eldest, has long since resigned the character of a belle," but Maggie "seemed disposed to maintain her post . . . until a few months since, when accidentally hearing a gentleman observe that she broke very fast, she suddenly left off going to the assembly, took a cat into high favor, and began to rail at the forward pertness of young misses" (134-35).

The Cockloft family, says Launcelot, "has been fruitful in old bachelors and humorists. . . . My cousin Pindar is one of its most conspicuous members—he is now in his fifty-eighth year—is a bachelor, partly through choice, and partly through chance. . . . From sixteen to thirty he was continually in love. . . . The evening of his thirtieth birth-day . . . he was seized with a whim-wham that he was an old fool to be in love at his time of life." Since then he has lived at the Hall, "writing odes, sonnets, epigrams, and elegies, which he seldom shows to any body but myself" (83-84). Launcelot assures the public that Pindar's poems will "tickle, plague, please and perplex the whole town" (85). He "is like a volcano, will remain for a long time silent without emitting a single spark, and then all at once burst out in a tremendous explosion of rhyme and rhapsody" (169). In a poem picturing the dames of the teapot, Pindar warns young maidens against that great unloosener of tongues—tea:

> In harmless chit-chat an acquaintance they roast,
> And serve up a friend, as they serve up a toast,
> .   .   .   .
>
> The wives of our cits of inferior degree,
> Will soak up repute in a little *bohea*;
> .   .   .   .
>
> But the scandal improves, (a refinement in wrong)
> As our matrons are richer and rise to *souchong*.
> With *hyson*—a beverage that's still more refined,
> Our ladies of fashion enliven their mind,
> .   .   .   .
>
> If I, in the remnant that's left me of life,
> Am to suffer the torments of slanderous strife,
> .   .   .   .
>
> Condemn me, ye gods, to a newspaper roasting,
> But spare me! oh spare me, a tea table toasting! (300-302)

Pindar, Launcelot's constant companion in his autumnal expeditions from Cockloft Hall and one (says Launcelot) "who still possesses much of the fire and energy of youthful sentiment . . . makes me feel young again by the enthusiasm with which he contemplates, and the animation with which he eulogizes the beauties of nature displayed before him. . . . when I see a hale, hearty old man, who has jostled through the rough path of the world, without having worn away the fine edge of his feelings, or blunted his sensibility to natural and moral beauty, I compare him to the evergreen of the forest, whose colours, instead of fading at the approach of winter, seem to assume additional lustre, when contrasted with the surrounding desolation" (268-69).

Two other members of the family lived out their lives in single estate. Charity Cockloft, as Launcelot explains, "died of a frenchman!" She "departed this life in the fifty-ninth year of her age, though she never grew older after twenty-five."

My aunt, though a great beauty, and an heiress withal, never got married. The reason she alledged was that she never met with a lover who resembled sir Charles Grandison, the hero of her nightly dreams and waking fancy. . . . the fates had ordered that a french boarding-house, or *Pension Francaise*, as it was called, should be established directly opposite my aunt's residence. . . . she beheld a little meagre, weazel-faced frenchman, of the most forlorn, diminutive and pitiful proportions, arrive at neighbour Pension's door. . . . From the time of this fatal arrival my poor aunt was in a quandary. . . . she never held up her head afterward,— drooped daily, took to her bed in a fortnight, and in "one little month" I saw her quietly deposited in the family vault—being the seventh Cockloft that has died of a whim-wham! (164-68)

Uncle John, whose chamber Launcelot now occupies, "died a bachelor, at the age of sixty-three, though he had been all his life trying to get married. . . . The truth is, my uncle had a prodigious antipathy to doing things in a hurry. . . . On this whim-wham, he proceeded: he began with young girls, and ended with widows." Once he courted Pamela, "the daughter of a neighbouring gentleman farmer, who was reckoned the beauty of the whole world. . . . my uncle had as good as made declaration, by saying one evening very significantly 'that he believed that he should soon change his condition,' when, some how or other, he got a tremendous *flea in his ear*, began to think he was *doing things in too great a hurry*, and that it was high time to consider." While he was a month thinking it over, Miss Pamela married an attorney's apprentice. "The young people in the neighbourhood laughed a good deal at my uncle on the occasion, but he only shrugged his shoulders, looked mysterious and replied, 'Tut boys! *I might have had her*' " (198-200).

Of all the characters in American serials none are more whimsical than the Cocklofts: a father who brings his children up like vegetables, a son who makes the grand tour of such remote places as Albany and Philadelphia, a bachelor uncle who explodes into verse, another who hates to do things in a hurry, a maiden aunt who dies of love for a Frenchman. This family, the joint creation of Paulding and Washington Irving, seems lifted from the pages of Sterne. The world of Cockloft Hall, where Christopher plays host to his cousin Launcelot, Anthony, and Will, is as palpably alive as that of the Spectator Club.

Nowhere in *Salmagundi* is the joint nature and mildly Federalist bias of the series so evident as in the letters which Mustapha, at the moment a prisoner in New York, sends to

Asem Hacchem and other friends back in Tripoli. In addition to Goldsmith's *Citizen of the World*, which influenced all three authors but especially Paulding who initiated the Mustapha letters, there were also at hand recent American examples of the foreign visitor, notably Benjamin Silliman's *Letters of Shahcoolen* (1802) and, as we saw in the last chapter, Wirt's *Letters of the British Spy* (1803). Launcelot's introduction to the first letter establishes the familiar conventions:

> Among the few strangers whose acquaintance has entertained me, I particularly rank the magnanimous MUSTAPHA RUB-A-DUB KELI KHAN, a most illustrious Captain of a Ketch, who figured some time since, in our fashionable circles, at the head of a ragged regiment of tripolitan prisoners. His conversation was to me a perpetual feast. . . . he presented me with a bundle of papers, containing among other articles, several copies of letters, which he had written to his friends in Tripoli.— The following is a translation of one of them. The original is in arabic-greek, but by the assistance of Will Wizard, who understands all languages . . . I have been enabled to accomplish a tolerable translation. We should have found little difficulty in rendering it into english, had it not been for Mustapha's confounded pot-hooks and trammels. (90)

In creating this foreign-visitor series the *Salmagundi* authors exploited a recent episode. On February 25, 1805, seven Tripolitan prisoners, including one "Mustaffa, Captain of the Ketch, Abdullah," arrived in New York; a month later it was announced that "at the request of several Gentlemen, a Benefit will be given to the Turkish Captives, for the purpose of accommodating them with additional cloathes; they have at present no other apparel than what they had on at the time they were made prisoners of war."[24]

Mustapha dwells on both social and political topics: on the one hand, the annual Evacuation Day celebration at New York (November 25), American women, and the City Assembly; on the other, Jefferson's logocratic, economy-minded administration, patriotic dinners, and a city election. He expresses amusement at American women who, because they are accounted rational, are therefore allowed souls and "instead of being carefully shut up in harams and seraglioes, are abandoned to the direction of their own reason, and suffered to run about in perfect freedom, like other domestick animals." Since to be useful is to lose dignity, their labors "are directed not towards supplying their household but in decking their persons . . . not so much to please themselves, as to gratify others, particularly strangers." "Be not alarmed, I conjure thee, my dear Asem," says Mustapha reassuringly, "lest I should be tempted by these beautiful barbarians to break the faith I owe to the three-and-twenty wives from whom my unhappy destiny has perhaps severed me for ever. . . . not a single fat fair one could I behold . . . the females that passed in review before me, tripping sportively along, resembled a procession of shadows, returning to their graves at the crowing of the cock." Never "cease to watch over the prosperity of my house, and the welfare of my beloved wives. Let them want for nothing, my friend; but feed them plentifully on honey, boiled rice and water gruel, so that when I return to the blessed land of my fathers (if that can ever be!) I may find them improved in size and loveliness, and sleek as the graceful elephants that range the green valley of Abimar" (283-87).

In another social letter Mustapha explains that curiosity prompted him to accept an invitation to the City Assembly, "a numerous concourse of young people of both sexes, who, on certain occasions, gathered together to dance about a large room with violent gesticulation, and try to out-dress each other." This "dancing mania . . . prevails chiefly throughout the winter. . . . the patients seem infatuated with their malady, abandon themselves to its unbounded ravages, and expose their persons to wintry storms and midnight airs. . . . These fits continue at short intervals from four to five hours, till at last the lady is led off, faint, languid, exhausted, and panting, to her carriage— rattles home—passes a night of feverish restlessness, cold perspirations and troubled sleep—rises late next morning (if she rises at all) is nervous, petulant, or a prey to languid indifference all day . . . in the evening hurries to another dance . . . to go through exactly the same joyless routine" (288, 292-93).

Thomas Jefferson, who was midway through his second presidential term, is described thus by Mustapha: "This empire is governed by a grand and most puissant bashaw. . . . a very plain old gentleman [who] amuses himself with impaling butterflies and pickling tadpoles; he is rather declining in popularity, having given great offence by wearing red breeches, and tying his horse to a post" (92). "This vast empire," writes Mustapha in another letter, "may be compared to nothing more nor less than a mighty windmill, and the orators, and the chatterers, and the slang-whangers [i.e., editors], are the breezes that put it in motion; unluckily, however, they are apt to blow different ways. . . . the present bashaw, who is at the very top of the logocracy . . . is a man of superlative ventosity. . . . He *talks* of vanquishing all opposition by the force of reason and philosophy" (146-47). Although Mustapha was in want of breeches, it was impossible to furnish him a pair "until all the sages of the nation had been convened to *talk* over the matter, and debate upon the expediency of granting my request. . . . All the sages of an immense *logocracy* assembled together to talk about my breeches!" Farewell, Asem; "when thou numberest up the many blessings bestowed on thee by all bountiful Allah, pour forth thy gratitude that he has cast thy nativity in a land where there is no assembly of legislative chatterers . . . where the word *economy* is unknown—and where an unfortunate captive is not obliged to call upon the whole nation, to cut him out a pair of breeches" (171, 174). Mustapha's description of this windy, penny-pinching bashaw prefigures Irving's portrait in *A History of New York* of William the Testy, "a brisk, waspish, little old gentleman," his cheeks "scorched into a dusky red," who "was exceedingly fond of trying philosophical and political experiments" and who, being "a man of many words and great erudition," "was resolved to conquer the Yankees—by proclamation!" (IV, i). "Whatever precaution for public safety he adopted, he was so intent upon rendering it cheap, that he invariably rendered it ineffectual" (IV, iv).

Whereas all men desire to live in the memory of posterity, writes Mustapha, the Americans have originated the custom of holding a public dinner, at which they "offer up whole hecatombs of geese and calves, and oceans of wine in honour of the illustrious living. . . . it is ten chances to one that the great man does not taste a morsel from the table, and is, perhaps, five hundred miles distant . . . a patriot, under this *economick* government, may be often in want of a dinner, while dozens are devoured in his praise. . . . it is the rich only who indulge in the banquet." Americans honor "events as well as characters, and eat in triumph at the news of a treaty—at the anniversary of any grand national era, or at the gaining of that splendid victory of the tongue—an *election*. . . . Some, I have been told, actually fast for four and twenty hours preceding, that they may be enabled to do greater honour to the feast."

> Oh, Asem! couldst thou but witness one of these patriotick, these monumental dinners—how furiously the flame of patriotism blazes forth—how suddenly they vanquish armies, subjugate whole countries, and exterminate nations in a bumper, thou would more than ever admire the force of that omnipotent weapon the tongue. . . . But, alas, my friend, private resentment, individual hatred, and the illiberal *spirit of party*, are let loose on these festive occasions. . . . strange, that in the full flow of social enjoyment, these votaries of pleasure can turn aside to call down curses on the head of a fellow-creature. . . . what then can give rise to this uncharitable, this inhuman custom among the disciples of a master, so gentle and forgiving? It is that fiend POLITICKS. (262-65)

Mustapha is appalled by "that great political puppet-show— AN ELECTION," at which time the "ragged, dirty looking . . . representatives of the sovereign people, who come here to make governors, senators and members of assembly, and are the source of all power and authority in this nation," swagger about and imagine "themselves the bashaws of the land" (190, 193). "Once differ in *politicks*, in mere theories, visions and chimeras, the growth of interest, of folly, or madness," declares Mustapha, "and deadly warfare ensues; every eye flashes fire, every tongue is loaded with reproach, and every heart is filled with gall and bitterness. . . . *Politicks* pervade every city, every village, every temple, every porter-house. . . . the people appear to be in the unhappy state of a patient whose palate nauseates the medicine best calculated for the cure of his disease, and seem anxious to continue in the full enjoyment of their chattering epidemick." The evil "extends far deeper; it threatens to impair all social intercourse, and to sever the sacred union of family and kindred." "Equality, Asem, is one of the most consummate scoundrels that ever crept from the brain of a political juggler. . . . There will always be an inequality among mankind, so long as a portion of it is enlightened and industrious, and the rest idle and ignorant." In the election which Mustapha witnessed, "the people triumphed—and much good has it done them. . . . except a few noisy retainers who have crept into office, and a few noisy patriots on the other side, who have been kicked out, there is not the least difference" (233-36). Mustapha's account grew out of Irving's description of a New York city election in a letter of May 2, 1807, to Mary Fairlie: "I drank beer with the multitude, and I talked handbill fashion with the demagogues, and I shook hands with the mob—whom my heart abhorreth. . . . Such haranging & puffing & strutting among all the little great men of the day. . . . Every carriage that drove up disgorged a whole nursery of these pigmy wonders, who all seemed to put on the brow of thought, the air of bustle & business, and the big talk of general committee men."[25]

The Mustapha letters conform more closely to the convention of the foreign visitor than do other American examples like *Tomo Cheeki* and *The British Spy*. The emerging character of Mustapha imparts an exotic flavor to the series similar to Montesquieu's Usbek, Lyttelton's Selim, and Goldsmith's Lien Chi Altangi. Mustapha's letters would have sounded all the more plausible to New York readers because of the recently concluded war with Tripoli and the presence of prisoners in the city.

The *Salmagundi* authors broke off after the twentieth number, but not because their fund of information was exhausted. "It is not for want of subjects that we stop our career," declares Launcelot. "We are not in the situation of poor Alexander the Great, who wept, as well indeed he might, because there were no more worlds to conquer; for, to do justice to this queer, odd, rantipole city, and this whimsical country, there is matter enough in them, to keep our risible muscles, and our pens going until doomsday" (305-306). In fact, it had been Washington Irving's intention to extend "these papers by carrying out the invention and marrying Will Wizard to the eldest Miss Cockloft—with, of course, a grand wedding at Cockloft Hall."[26] The Irvings and Paulding were piqued with the publisher Longworth who, when they refused to follow his advice and take out a copyright, took it out himself, as was his right, and so ran off with the profit.

While it is evident that the *Salmagundi* authors, as they created their dramatis personae, were influenced by the example of

Sterne, what has been said of the characters in *Tristram Shandy* is more than can be claimed for those in *Salmagundi*: "their ruling passions are cunningly overlaid and softened by other and subtler qualities of mind and heart which transform them from mere eccentrics into human folk of flesh and blood."[27] The characters in *Salmagundi* resemble more nearly the only actual caricature in *Tristram Shandy*, the man-midwife Dr. Slop. Nevertheless, the fact that *Salmagundi* was kept in print throughout the nineteenth century, in spite of Washington Irving's low opinion of this early work, can be attributed in large part to the ongoing appeal of Launcelot Langstaff and his bachelor associates.

At the end of the series they remain united and bachelors still, unlike the members of the Spectator Club, of whom Addison writes: "Poor Sir *Roger* is dead, and the worthy Clergyman dying. Captain *Sentry* has taken Possession of a fair Estate, *Will Honeycomb* has married a Farmer's Daughter, and the *Templar* withdraws himself into the Business of his own Profession" (No. 542). Launcelot, having wished his subscribers a happy New Year, says in a final aside: "As little do they suspect that there is a knot of merry old bachelors seated snugly in the old-fashioned parlour of an old-fashioned dutch house . . . who amuse themselves of an evening by laughing at their neighbours, in an honest way, and who manage to jog on through the streets of our antient and venerable city, without elbowing or being elbowed by a living soul. . . . We hereby openly and seriously declare that we are not dead, but intend, if it please providence, to live for many years to come" (307). Will Wizard, reluctant to take leave of the public, has the last word: "I bid my readers an affectionate farewel; exhorting them to live honestly and soberly—paying their taxes and reverencing the state, the church and the corporation—reading diligently the bible, the almanack, the newspaper and Salmagundi—which is all the reading an honest citizen has occasion for—and eschewing all spirit of faction, discontent, irreligion and criticism" (315-16).

The *Oldstyle* letters and *Salmagundi* papers, together with *A History of New York* (1809), comprise the first stage in Washington Irving's career. What helps give coherence to these works is the evolving character of the Old Bachelor. Jonathan Oldstyle, who discourses on fashion and the theater, becomes split into several figures. From Oldstyle to Langstaff, Evergreen, and Wizard to Diedrich Knickerbocker, this persona grows more and more whimsical. In this first stage Irving's predilection for burlesque is everywhere present; for example, the description of Will Wizard's partner at a ball as "a young lady of most voluminous proportions, that quivered at every skip; and being braced up in the fashionable style, with whalebone, stay-tape and buckram, looked like an apple-pudding tied in the middle, or, taking her flaming dress into consideration, like a bed and bolsters rolled up in a suit of red curtains" (126). Only occasionally do these early works point clearly to the later, though in his *Salmagundi* writings (notably in the Will Wizard and Cockloft essays) Irving commingles the picturesque and the whimsical as he frequently does in *The Sketch Book* and succeeding books.

XI. CONCLUSION

⬚

ABOUT 1820 the familiar essay re-emerged after being hampered in its development for a century by the dominance of the periodical essay, but only after its practitioners had served an apprenticeship under the rule of the *Spectator*.[1] Leigh Hunt and Charles Lamb began their careers as essayists by contributing Addisonian papers to *The Reflector* (1810-11), a journal which "marked the fusion of the essay serial and the new type of review."[2] Within a decade Hunt, Lamb, William Hazlitt, and Thomas De Quincey, to name the most important English writers, were composing familiar essays for monthlies like *The London Magazine* and *The New Monthly Magazine and Literary Journal*. One critic, aware of the continuity of the essay tradition in England, draws a useful distinction between the familiar and the periodical essay: "Self-revelation is one of the distinguishing marks of the familiar essay in the seventeenth century, and it is to be found in some degree in the eighteenth century periodical essay, but it is not accompanied by impassioned recollection or other romantic sentiment." Addison and Steele "are not personal or intimate in the manner of the later familiar essayists, nor do they ever write of themselves with the passionate intensity which characterizes the self-revelation of Hazlitt, Lamb and Hunt." "Even though the essays of the latter part of the eighteenth century show some romantic feeling in the treatment of the picturesque in nature and in city life, they contain nothing comparable, in amount or kind, to the romantic treatment of nature in the work of Hunt, Lamb and Hazlitt."[3]

The career of Charles Brockden Brown dramatizes the fact that by the end of the eighteenth century the periodical essay in America was declining in vitality and beginning to lose its identity. He moved from the essay to prose fiction in less than a decade, much as Goldsmith had done in England a generation earlier. In fact his earliest prose work, *The Rhapsodist* (1789), foreshadows his novels; favoring Sterne over Addison, Brown modifies the spectator mask in the direction of the whimsical and dreamy, defining a rhapsodist as "one who delivers the sentiments suggested by the moment in artless and unpremeditated language,"[4] and does little more in this short serial than flesh out his persona. Nine years later, in *The Man at Home*,[5] an unnamed elderly man composes lucubrations at the home of a Philadelphia laundress where he secluded himself to avoid arrest for a debt he incurred on behalf of another man, and at the end of a fortnight surrenders to the sheriff and is led off to debtors' prison; significantly, this series, published only six months before Brown's first novel *Wieland*, is heavily narrative. Even before this serial had ended, Brown began publishing a fragmentary epistolary novel in which an indolent law student reveals to his sister the machinations of one Beddoes and the seeming immorality of Beddoes' sister Lucy.[6]

In actual fact, of course, the periodical essay survived into the early years of the nineteenth century. Even as the *Salmagundi* authors were preparing to parody the tradition a magazine critic advised, "As the cultivation of letters and science is mostly confined to a few professional individuals, it should be the aim of the periodical writer to introduce and diffuse a taste for useful and ornamental learning, in the engaging form of short and popular essays, which may be perused without much effort of intellect and without encroaching on the engagements of the high or stated employments of the middle classes of society."[7] One group of writers who took this advice to heart were the Anthology Society of Boston. In much the way the Royal Society of London in the 1660s had sought to purify and "fix" the English language, they exhibited in the pages of *The Monthly Anthology and Boston Review* (1803-11) the somewhat ludicrous spectacle of "Federalist men of letters [trying] to consolidate the invisible polity of letters for all time."[8] One literary consequence of this impossible dream was an attempt to prolong the life of the *Spectator* tradition, since among modern writers none was more highly revered by the Anthologists than Addison. Such veneration prompted J.S.J. Gardiner to compare Judith Murray unfavorably to her English predecessors, declaring that "justice would hardly allow us to exalt the *Gleaner* above the *Spectator* or *Rambler*."[9] Gardiner deplored the fact that American style lacks elegance and grace: "We appear to sit down to think what we shall write, not to write what we think. We are perpetually aiming at something sublime and original. . . . We substitute bombast for sublimity, and finery for elegance." Charging that Johnson, Gibbon, and Burke had corrupted American taste, Gardiner exhorted, "The repeated perusal of Addison might remedy the most striking defects of our compositions, by affording us a natural and easy flow of period with imagery, that has the glow of nature, not the glare of art."[10] Through at least the first third of the century lawyers, legislators, ministers, physicians, and teachers united in a critical effort to keep American literature on a neoclassical course. Four years after the *Monthly Anthology* ceased publication William Tudor, a former Anthologist and self-styled arbiter of literary taste, founded the influential and long-lived *North American Review* and became its first editor. "In no other period in American history," writes William Charvat of the years 1810-35, "has our culture been so completely and directly dominated by the professional classes; concomitantly, in no other period has the economically dominant class exhibited such an interest in the arts."[11] Although they failed to prevent the demise of the periodical essay, these conservative critics helped delay until the 1830s the movement toward literary independence and the flowering of romanticism.

"An era in essay writing was commenced by Steele and Addison, in their periodical papers suggested by the follies of contemporary society," declared a nineteenth-century editor. "This era closed with the production in America of the Salmagundi of Irving and Paulding, the Old Bachelor of Wirt and his associates, and the Lay Preacher of Dennie."[12] After the War of 1812, according to Harrison Meserole, there was "a slow turning away from the didacticism of the 'morals and manners' type of essay and a turning toward the kind of subjectivity which . . . we generally look for in the familiar essay."[13] Washington Irving, who as we have seen began his career as a periodical essayist, went abroad in 1815 to conduct the Liverpool branch of the family hardware business; when the Irving firm was forced into bankruptcy, he had to support himself by his pen. Three successful miscellanies that appeared shortly, beginning with *The Sketch Book* (1819-20), mark the emergence and maturation of Irving the familiar essayist. In 1822 a magazine critic, characterizing *The Sketch Book* as "the last link in the series of periodical essay writing," hastened to add that whereas periodical essays were written "with a direct moral tendency, to expose and to reform the ignorance and the follies of the age," Irving's work "has no direct moral purpose, but is founded on sentiment and deep feeling."[14] Meserole observes that like Lamb and Hazlitt, "Irving the familiar essayist knew that people are first of all interested in themselves and in other people and only secondarily in things"; he therefore used a wide variety of "devices—the personal anecdote, the biographical sketch, the character, the chance meeting, the vision or dream [i.e., daydream], the reminiscence, the observation, the tale of a traveler—to relate the what of an essay to the whom. . . . when interest in people and their ways is coupled with a keen eye for observation and an equally keen ear for language to communicate what is observed, an essayist of Irving's stature can emerge."[15] After the publication of *Tales of a Traveller* (1824), however, Irving all but abandoned the essay in favor of the tale, travel romance, history, and biography. James Kirke Paulding ranged even more widely than Irving. Although his son maintained that "he was by nature an essayist, and, of all men, wrote most directly out of his own experience, observation, or reflection,"[16] Paulding was also a novelist, critic, poet, writer of tales and sketches, letter writer, playwright, historian, and satirist. Most of the essays he wrote after *Salmagundi* appeared in *Letters from the South* (1817); "roughly speaking," says Meserole, "they are familiar essays, even though certain ones (I, II, III, XXXIII, XXXIX), because of their tone and subject matter, are poor examples."[17] In 1819 Paulding, acting without Irving, undertook a continuation of *Salmagundi*, but failed to recapture the sprightliness and spontaneity of the first series on which he and Irving had collaborated at the beginning of their careers.

Of the American serialists examined in this study the only ones whose present-day literary reputation rests chiefly on their accomplishment as essayists are Dennie and Murray, and possibly Hopkinson and Wirt. Franklin, Irving, and Paulding developed into wide-ranging prose writers, most of whose essays were written early and do not figure prominently in their careers. Whereas Trumbull and Freneau were recognized in their day as poets first and have been ever since, it is to be hoped that this book will convince readers of their impressive achievement as essayists. For Byles and Breintnall essay writing was secondary to their chosen vocations of minister and merchant, and it seems safe to conclude that the anonymous essayists, certainly those in the South, also regarded writing as an avocation. It is time, surely, to remember all these American descendants of Steele and Addison and to commemorate the tradition they kept popular throughout the eighteenth century.

CHECKLIST OF LITERARY SERIALS

📖

HAVING READ SELECTIVELY in American newspapers and magazines for the period 1722-1811, especially the post-Revolutionary years, I cannot claim to have located all literary serials; if Milton Ellis is accurate in his estimate that "between 1785 and 1800, perhaps a hundred short series of lighter periodical essays [were] contributed to various New England journals" (*Dennie*, p. 51), then the total number for the longer period runs in the hundreds. What follows is a list of the serials which were studied closely prior to writing this book; an asterisk identifies those that are discussed at length. The interested reader who wishes to examine individual serials in their entirety will find most of them available on microfilm and microcard and in facsimile and other editions as follows: *American Periodicals: 18th Century–1800-1850* (Ann Arbor: University Microfilms, 1956); *Early American Newspapers (1704-1820)* (New York: Readex Microprint Corporation, 1962-); *Early American Imprints* (Evans: 1639-1800; and Shaw-Shoemaker: 1801-1819) (New York: Readex Microprint Corporation, 1955-); microfilm of the *American Weekly Mercury, Maryland Gazette, Pennsylvania Gazette, South-Carolina Gazette,* and *Virginia Gazette;* and Scholars' Facsimiles & Reprints and other editions of Brown, Dennie, Franklin, Freneau, Irving, Silliman, and Wirt. Since all primary sources are cited in the checklist, they will not be listed in the bibliography.

*1. Silence Dogood, *New-England Courant* (Boston), April 2-October 8, 1722 (14 numbers; by Benjamin Franklin). Reprinted in *The Papers of Benjamin Franklin*, ed. Leonard W. Labaree and Others, I (New Haven: Yale Univ. Pr., 1959), 8-45.

*2. Proteus Echo, *New-England Weekly Journal* (Boston), April 10, 1727-April 1, 1728 (52 numbers; by Mather Byles,

Matthew Adams, and John Adams). Joseph T. Buckingham, *Specimens of Newspaper Literature* (Boston: Little, 1850), I, 91-100, reprints No. 1 and most of Nos. 2 and 3.

3. [Speculations], *New-England Weekly Journal*, January 6, 20, February 10, 17, 24, March 3, 10, 24, 1728/9, and March 30, April 7, 21, May 26, June 2, 9, 16, July 28, August 4, 18, 1729 (18 numbers; attributed to Governor William Burnet).

*4. The Plain-Dealer: Nos. 1-3, appearing in the fall of 1728 in issues of the *Maryland Gazette* (Annapolis) no longer extant, were reprinted in the *Pennsylvania Gazette* (Philadelphia), April 9, 23, 30, 1730; Nos. 4-10 appeared in the *Maryland Gazette*, December 10, 17, 24, 1728, and January 7, 14, 21, February 11, 1728/9 (10 numbers; first 2 numbers anonymous). Nos. 3-10 are reprinted from Ambrose Philips' *Free-Thinker* (1718-21), Nos. 48, 80, 50, 63, 34, 73, 53, 90, respectively.

*5. The Busy-Body, *American Weekly Mercury* (Philadelphia), February 4, 1728/9-September 18, 1729 (32 numbers; by Benjamin Franklin and Joseph Breintnall). Franklin wrote Nos. 1-4 and parts of Nos. 5 and 8; Breintnall, the rest. Nos. 1-5 and 8 are reprinted in *Papers of Franklin*, I, 113-39.

6. Untitled essays, *Weekly Rehearsal* (Boston), September 27, 1731-August 14, 1732 (48 numbers; a few by Jeremiah Gridley). The great majority of these essays were reprinted from British and Continental sources; the original ones were presumably written by the editor, Jeremiah Gridley. John K. Reeves, "Jeremy Gridley, Editor," *New England Quarterly*, 17 (1944), 265-81, conjectures that 5 of the essays may be by Gridley: the introductory editorial (Sept. 27, 1731) and the essays on lewd writers, scoffers at religion, and calumniators (Jan. 3, 1731/2), liberty (Jan. 24), truth (Feb. 28), and "On the Beauty of the Universe" (May 15, 1732). Buckingham, *Specimens*, I, 112-14, reprints the introductory editorial.

*7. The Meddlers Club, *South-Carolina Gazette* (Charleston), August 16-September 6, 1735 (4 numbers; anonymous). George F. Horner and Robert A. Bain, eds., *Colonial and Federalist American Writings* (New York: Odyssey, 1966), pp. 291-96, reprints the first, third, and fourth essays.

*8. The Monitor, *Virginia Gazette* (Williamsburg), September

10, 1736-February 22, 1736/7 (17 numbers; anonymous). Of the 22 numbers the first 5 are not extant. Nos. 6 and 9 are reprinted in Horner and Bain, pp. 296-300.

*9. Walter Dymocke Anonymous, *Virginia Gazette*, March 20-August 14, 1752 (14 numbers: 8 installments and 6 rejoinders; chiefly by John Robertson and Samuel Davies).

*10. The Humourist, *South-Carolina Gazette*, November 26, 1753-April 9, 1754 (18 numbers; anonymous).

11. The Hermit, *American Magazine, or Monthly Chronicle* (Philadelphia), October, 1757-October, 1758 (8 numbers; by William Smith). Reprinted with slight revisions in *The Works of William Smith, D.D., Late Provost of the College and Academy of Philadelphia*, ed. Horace Wemyss Smith (Philadelphia, 1803), I, 93-152. Nos. 1 and 3 are reprinted in Horner and Bain, pp. 307-12.

*12. The Prattler, *American Magazine, or Monthly Chronicle*, November, 1757-July, 1758 (7 numbers; anonymous).

13. The Visitant, *Pennsylvania Chronicle* (Philadelphia), February 1-May 16, 1768 (16 numbers; anonymous).

*14. The Meddler, *Boston Chronicle*, September 7, 1769-January 22, 1770 (10 numbers; by John Trumbull and possibly Timothy Dwight).

*15. The Correspondent: published in two series in the *Connecticut Journal* (New Haven), Nos. 1-8, February 23-July 6, 1770, and Nos. 9-38, February 12-September 3, 1773 (38 numbers; chiefly by John Trumbull). Trumbull probably wrote the first series alone; he was assisted in the second series by Timothy Dwight and David Humphreys. No. 8, on slavery, is reprinted in the *Journal of Negro History*, 14 (1929), 493-95.

*16. The Old Bachelor, *Pennsylvania Magazine* (Philadelphia), March, 1775-June, 1776 (12 numbers; by Francis Hopkinson and Thomas Paine). Nos. 2 and 4 are reprinted in *The Complete Writings of Thomas Paine*, ed. Philip S. Foner (New York: Citadel, 1945), II, 1091, 1118-20; "Consolation for the Old Bachelor" and Nos. 6 and 8, in *Comical Spirit of Seventy-Six: The Humor of Francis Hopkinson*, ed. Paul M. Zall (San Marino: Huntington Library, 1976), pp. 64-76.

17. Reflections on Marriage, *Pennsylvania Magazine*, Septem-

ber, December, 1775, and March, 1776 (3 numbers; by John Witherspoon). Reprinted in *The Works of the Rev. John Witherspoon* (Philadelphia, 1802), IV, 161-83.

*18. The Pilgrim, *Freeman's Journal* (Philadelphia), November 21, 1781-August 14, 1782 (19 numbers; by Philip Freneau). In *The Miscellaneous Works of Mr. Philip Freneau* (Philadelphia, 1788) there appeared 11 Philosopher of the Forest essays, 5 of which are new and the other 6, slightly revised Pilgrim essays. Reprinted in *The Prose of Philip Freneau*, ed. Philip M. Marsh (New Brunswick, N.J.: Scarecrow, 1955) are 8 Pilgrim essays (Nos. 6, 7, 9, 11, 12, 14, 15, 19), pp. 41-72, and 7 Philosopher of the Forest essays (Nos. 1, 2, 3, 5, 8, 10, 11), pp. 196-233.

19. Tom Taciturn, *Worcester Magazine*, April-September, 1786 (18 numbers; possibly by Edward Bangs).

20. The Trifler, *Columbian Magazine; or, a Monthly Miscellany* (Philadelphia), December, 1786, and June, July, September, November, 1787, and January, March, May, June, August, 1788 (10 numbers; anonymous).

21. The Friend, *New-Haven Gazette*, March 23-October 4, 1787 (15 numbers; by Timothy Dwight and possibly Josiah Meigs).

22. Tom Tinker, *Worcester Magazine*, March-April, 1787 (4 numbers; anonymous).

23. The Retailer, *Columbian Magazine; or, a Monthly Miscellany*, February-June, December, 1788, and February-April, July, September-November, 1789 (13 numbers; anonymous).

24. The Rhapsodist, *Columbian Magazine; or, a Monthly Miscellany*, August-November, 1789 (4 numbers; by Charles Brockden Brown). Reprinted in *The Rhapsodist and Other Uncollected Writings by Charles Brockden Brown*, ed. Harry R. Warfel (New York: Scholars' Facsimiles & Reprints, 1943), pp. 1-24.

25. The Reformer, *Massachusetts Magazine* (Boston), February, 1789-December, 1790 (14 numbers; variously attributed to Joseph Lathrop and William Hill Brown).

26. The Dreamer, *Massachusetts Magazine*, January, 1789-

November, 1790 (16 numbers; anonymous).

27. Philo, *Massachusetts Magazine*, September-December, 1789, and January-August, October-December, 1790 (15 numbers; anonymous).

28. The Rivulet, *Massachusetts Magazine*, April-December, 1790 (9 numbers; anonymous).

29. The Columbian Observer, *American Museum, or, Universal Magazine* (Philadelphia), February-August, October-December, 1791 (17 numbers; largely anonymous). Nos. 1, 2, and 4 are reprinted in Mathew Carey's *Miscellaneous Trifles in Prose* (Philadelphia, 1796), pp. 14-54.

30. The Repository, *Massachusetts Magazine*, September, 1792-November, 1794 (27 numbers; by Judith Sargent Murray).

31. The Essayist, *Massachusetts Magazine*, January, 1793-November, 1796 (22 numbers; anonymous).

32. The Investigator, *Massachusetts Magazine*, August-December, 1794, and January-August, 1795 (8 numbers; anonymous).

33. The Echo, *Massachusetts Magazine*, May-July, September-December, 1795 (7 numbers; anonymous).

*34. Tomo Cheeki: *Jersey Chronicle* (Mount Pleasant), May 23-October 31, 1795 (15 numbers; by Philip Freneau); when Freneau reissued these essays in the *Time-Piece* (New York), he composed 2 new ones which appeared May 22 and June 16, 1797. Eleven of these essays are reprinted in *The Prose of Philip Freneau*, pp 331-46, 351-53, 357-62.

35. The Dead and the Living Languages, *Massachusetts Magazine*, August-December, 1796 (6 numbers; anonymous).

*36. The Farrago: published between February 14, 1792, and July 24, 1802, in the *Morning Ray* (Windsor, Vt.), *Eagle or Dartmouth Centinel* (Hanover, N.H.), *Tablet* (Boston), and *Port Folio* (Philadelphia) (26 numbers; by Joseph Dennie). Nos. 1 and 3 are reprinted in Harold Milton Ellis, *Joseph Dennie and His Circle: A Study in American Literature from 1792 to 1812*, Bulletin of the Univ. of Texas, No. 3 (Austin, 1915), pp. 228-35.

*37. The Lay Preacher: published between 1795 and 1818 in the

New Hampshire Journal: Or *The Farmer's Weekly Museum* (Walpole) (90 numbers), *Eagle* or *Dartmouth Centinel* (1 number), *Gazette of the United States* (Philadelphia) (13 numbers), *Port Folio* (11 numbers), *New England Galaxy* (Boston) (1 number), and 1 number as a separate leaflet in Philadelphia in 1818 (117 numbers in all; by Joseph Dennie). Book editions of these essays, representing half the total, appeared in 1796 and 1817; under the title *The Lay Preacher by Joseph Dennie* these two collections were reprinted in a single volume by Milton Ellis (New York: Scholars' Facsimiles & Reprints, 1943).

*38. Hezekiah Salem, *Time-Piece*, October 23-November 17, 1796 (7 numbers; by Philip Freneau). Four of these essays are reprinted in *The Prose of Philip Freneau*, pp. 378-80, 381-86.

39. The Observer, *South Carolina Weekly Museum* (Charleston), January 1, 21, February 18, March 4, 1797 (4 numbers; anonymous).

40. The Schemer, *Weekly Magazine of Original Essays* (Philadelphia), March 10-July 7, 1798 (14 numbers; anonymous).

41. The Ubiquitarian, *Weekly Magazine of Original Essays*, February-June, 1798 (17 numbers; anonymous).

*42. The Gleaner: Judith Sargent Murray's *The Gleaner. A Miscellaneous Production. In Three Volumes. By Constantia* (Boston, 1798) runs to 100 numbers, of which the first 31 (expanded to 34 in the first volume of the book edition) originally appeared in the *Massachusetts Magazine*, February, 1792-December, 1794.

*43. Robert Slender, *Aurora* (Philadelphia), March 25, 1799-February 19, 1801 (37 numbers; by Philip Freneau). The first 24 of these letters with a dedication appeared in book form, *Letters on Various interesting and important Subjects* (Philadelphia, 1799), which was reprinted by Harry Hayden Clark (New York: Scholars' Facsimiles & Reprints, 1943). The dedication and 14 letters are reprinted in *The Prose of Philip Freneau*, pp. 395-440.

44. The Moral Monitor: Nathan Fiske's *The Moral Monitor: or, A Collection of Essays on Various Subjects* (2 vols., Worcester, 1801) runs to 150 numbers, most of which originally ap-

peared in Massachusetts serials: "The Neighbour," *Massachusetts Spy* (Worcester), April 14, 1791-December 4, 1799 (74 numbers); "The Worcester Speculator," *Massachusetts Spy*, April 10, 1788-June 30, 1791 (17 numbers); "The General Observer," *Massachusetts Magazine*, January, 1789-November, 1794 (19 numbers); "The Philanthropist," *Massachusetts Magazine*, January, 1789-December, 1790 (23 numbers).

45. Shahcoolen, *Commercial Advertiser* (New York), October 5, 7, 9, 12, 14, 20, 27, 29, November 7, 9, 12, 16, 25, December 21, 1801 (14 numbers; by Benjamin Silliman). Issued in book form as *Letters of Shahcoolen, a Hindu Residing in Philadelphia* (Boston, 1802); under the title *Letters of Shahcoolen (1802) by Benjamin Silliman*, this volume was reprinted by Ben Harris McClary (Gainesville, Fla.: Scholars' Facsimiles & Reprints, 1962).

*46. Jonathan Oldstyle, *Morning Chronicle* (New York), November 15, 1802-April 23, 1803 (9 numbers; by Washington Irving). Reprinted in *Letters of Jonathan Oldstyle, Gent. and Salmagundi; or, the Whim-Whams and Opinions of Launcelot Langstaff, Esq. and Others*, eds. Bruce I. Granger and Martha Hartzog (Boston: Twayne, 1977), pp. 3-35.

*47. The British Spy, *Virginia Argus* (Richmond), August 20-September 24, 1803 (10 numbers; by William Wirt). Issued in book form as *The Letters of the British Spy* (Richmond, 1803); Richard Beale Davis has edited a facsimile reprint of the 1832 New York (10th) edition (Chapel Hill: Univ. of North Carolina Pr., 1970).

48. From a Student's Diary, *Literary Magazine and American Register* (Philadelphia), October, 1803-May, 1804 (7 numbers; anonymous).

49. The Remarker, *Monthly Anthology and Boston Review*, September, 1805-August, 1809 (45 numbers). The following members of the Anthology Society of Boston contributed to the series: Paul Allen (No. 37), Joseph Buckminster (Nos. 5, 34), Edmund Trowbridge Dana (Nos. 6, 18), William Emerson (Nos. 3, 8 [?], 19, 41), Alexander Hill Everett (No. 43), Robert Field (Nos. 8 [?], 16, 22-23), Robert Hallowell Gardiner (Nos. 9, 20, 40), John Sylvester John Gardiner (Nos. 2,

4, 17, 24, 35, 38, 44), John Thornton Kirkland (Nos. 29-32, 45), John Lowell (No. 26), Andrews Norton (No. 14), R.W. Francis Parkman (No. 42), James Savage (Nos. 15, 21, 27), William Smith Shaw (No. 12), John Stickney (No. 39), Peter Oxenbridge Thacher (No. 13), Samuel Cooper Thacher (Nos. 7, 28), William Tudor (No. 11), Arthur Maynard Walter (Nos. 1, 25), Benjamin Welles (No. 10), and Sidney Willard (Nos. 33, 36). Nos. 4-5, 10, 12, 21, 34-35 are reprinted in whole or part in *The Federalist Literary Mind: Selections from the Monthly Anthology and Boston Review, 1803-1811*, ed. Lewis P. Simpson (Baton Rouge: Louisiana State Univ. Pr., 1962), pp. 148-51, 178-84, 212-16, 160-63, 72-74, 196-202, 203-207.

*50. Salmagundi: published irregularly in wrappers, January 24, 1807-January 25, 1808; then gathered and bound in two-volume sets by David Longworth of New York in 1807 and 1808 (20 numbers; by Washington and William Irving and James Kirke Paulding). Reprinted in *Salmagundi*, eds. Granger and Hartzog, pp. 67-316.

*51. The Old Bachelor: *Enquirer* (Richmond), December 22, 1810-December 24, 1811 (28 numbers; principally by William Wirt); for the first book edition, published at Richmond in 1814, Wirt and his collaborators wrote 5 new essays. The second half of No. 31 is reprinted in *Cyclopaedia of American Literature*, eds. Evert A. and George L. Duyckinck (New York: Scribner, 1855), I, 621-23.

NOTES

$\square$

Notes to Chapter One *(pages 3-8)*

1. Anthony Ashley Cooper, third earl of Shaftesbury, *Characteristics of Men, Manners, Opinions, Times*, ed. John M. Robertson (Indianapolis: Bobbs-Merrill, 1964), pp. 109, 108.
2. Melvin R. Watson, *Magazine Serials and the Essay Tradition, 1746-1820* (Baton Rouge: Louisiana State Univ. Pr., 1956), p. 69.
3. Walter Graham, *The Beginnings of English Literary Periodicals* (New York: Oxford Univ. Pr., 1926), p. 2.
4. Graham, p. 45.
5. Graham, p. 62.
6. George S. Marr, *The Periodical Essayists of the Eighteenth Century* (London: J. Clarke, 1924,) p. 32.
7. *History of the Royal Society* (London, 1667), pp. 112, 113.
8. George Williamson, *The Senecan Amble: Prose Form from Bacon to Collier* (Chicago: Univ. of Chicago Pr., 1951), ch. 11.
9. *The Lives of the Most Eminent English Poets* (London: Methuen, 1896), II, 103-104.
10. Huntington Brown, *Prose Styles: Five Primary Types* (Minneapolis: Univ. of Minnesota Pr., 1966), p. 84. "Good expository prose is coherent," writes Brown; "sentence members of like grammatical order, and groups of sentences, are often linked together by similarities of form, repeated key words, and the like, but, except where concerned to present a tightly reasoned argument (e.g., a theorem in plane geometry), commonly diffusive rather than closely unified" (p. 40).
11. Ernest Claude Coleman, "The Influence of the Addisonian Essay in America Before 1810," diss., Univ. of Illinois, 1936, p. 16.
12. *The Spectator*, ed. Donald F. Bond (Oxford: Clarendon, 1965), I, lxiii-lxiv.
13. *The Spectator*, I, lxiii.
14. William Henry Irving, *The Providence of Wit in the English Letter Writers* (Durham: Duke Univ. Pr., 1955), esp. chs. 3, 5-7, 11; Chauncey Brewster Tinker, *The Salon and English Letters* (New York: Macmillan, 1915), ch. 13.
15. Quoted in Irving, p. 120.
16. *The Spectator*, I, xxxix, xlii. Irving maintains that "the style of the letters used in the *Tatler* and *Spectator* is toned down to the usual

informal plain style of the other material in these journals" (p. 169).

17. *The Spectator*, I, xl. See also *New Letters to the Tatler and Spectator*, ed. Richmond P. Bond (Austin: Univ. of Texas Pr., 1959).

18. Watson, *Magazine Serials*, p. 12.

19. Martha Pike Conant, *The Oriental Tale in England in the Eighteenth Century* (1908; rpt. New York: Octagon, 1966), p. xvii.

20. Watson, *Magazine Serials*, pp. 12, 13.

21. *The New Cambridge Bibliography of English Literature*, ed. George Watson (Cambridge: Cambridge Univ. Pr., 1971), II, 1269-90.

22. Marr, p. 114.

23. Marr, p. 131.

24. Melvin R. Watson, "The *Spectator* Tradition and the Development of the Familiar Essay," *ELH*, 13 (1946), 193-98.

25. Thomas Goddard Wright, *Literary Culture in Early New England, 1620-1730* (New Haven: Yale Univ. Pr., 1920), p. 184.

26. *Diary of Cotton Mather*, ed. W.C. Ford (1911-12; rpt. New York: Ungar, 1957), II, 227.

27. William C. Lane, "The Telltale, 1721," *Publications of the Colonial Society of Massachusetts*, 12 (1909), 220-27.

28. *The Moral Monitor* (Worcester: Isaiah Thomas, 1801), I, 13-14.

NOTES TO CHAPTER TWO

1. *New-England Courant*, Sept. 4, 1721.

2. *Journals of the House of Representatives of Massachusetts* (Boston: Massachusetts Historical Society, 1923), IV, 72.

3. *Journals*, IV, 208.

4. *The Autobiography of Benjamin Franklin*, ed. Leonard W. Labaree and Others (New Haven: Yale Univ. Pr., 1964), p. 69.

5. *The Papers of Benjamin Franklin*, ed. Leonard W. Labaree and Others, I (New Haven: Yale Univ. Pr., 1959), 49.

6. *Autobiography*, p. 67.

7. *New-England Courant*, Sept. 4, 1721.

8. See W.C. Ford, "Franklin's New England Courant," *Proceedings of the Massachusetts Historical Society*, 57 (1924), 336-53, wherein these Couranteers and eleven others are identified by name in Benjamin Franklin's marked file of the first 43 numbers of the *Courant*.

9. *New-England Courant*, Nov. 20, 1721.

10. *Boston Gazette*, Jan. 15, 1721/2.

11. *Boston News Letter*, Aug. 28, 1721. See George F. Horner, "Franklin's *Dogood Papers* Re-examined," *Studies in Philology*, 37 (1940), 508-509.

12. John Checkley, Preface to *Choice Dialogues* (Boston, 1720), p. i; *Boston Gazette*, Feb. 5, 1721/2. Both sources are quoted in Horner, p. 508.

13. Harold Lester Dean, "The *New-England Courant*, 1721-1726: A

Chapter in the History of American Culture," diss., Brown Univ., 1943, p. 300.

14. *Lectures on Rhetoric and Belles Lettres* (Edinburgh, 1783), Lecture 19.

15. *Autobiography*, pp. 62, 67-68.

16. *New-England Courant*, Apr. 2, 16, 30, May 14, 28, June 11, 25, July 9, 23, Aug. 13, 20, Sept. 10, 24, Oct. 8, 1722. Reprinted in *Papers of Franklin*, I, 8-45. Quotations from the *Dogood* papers will be identified by number and date in the body of the text.

17. *Dogood* No. 10 quotes Defoe's *Essay on Projects* on insurance for widows; *Dogood* No. 8 reprints most of *Cato's Letter* No. 15 on freedom of speech, and *Dogood* No. 9 on public hypocrisy quotes the end of *Cato's Letter* No. 31; and *Dogood* No. 14 on religious zeal excerpts Addison's *Spectator* No. 185 and *Guardian* No. 80.

18. James Parton observes that had Josiah Franklin carried out his intention of seeing his son Benjamin trained for the ministry, "the Harvard of that day would have choked or expelled him" (*Life and Times of Benjamin Franklin* [Boston: Houghton, 1864], II, 641).

19. *Boston Gazette*, May 28, 1722. The author, who signed himself "John Harvard," was probably Samuel Mather.

20. *New-England Courant*, June 4, 1722.

21. *Colonial American Poetry*, ed. Kenneth Silverman (New York: Hafner, 1968), p. 130.

22. *Pennsylvania Gazette*, Jan. 13, 1737; reprinted in *Papers of Franklin*, II, 173-78.

23. *New-England Courant*, Dec. 3, 1722.

24. *Autobiography*, p. 68.

25. *Autobiography*, p. 70.

26. Clifford K. Shipton, *New England Life in the 18th Century* (Cambridge, Mass.: Harvard Univ. Pr., 1963), pp. 229, 230-31.

27. Shipton, p. 228. Arthur Bernon Tourtellot, going counter to general scholarly opinion, argues that it was Byles, not Samuel Mather, who dubbed the Couranteers "the *Hell-Fire Club of Boston*" (*Benjamin Franklin: The Shaping of Genius: The Boston Years* [Garden City, N.Y.: Doubleday, 1977], p. 352).

28. Franklin to Byles, June 1, 1788, *The Writings of Benjamin Franklin*, ed. Albert Henry Smyth (New York: Macmillan, 1906), IX, 655-56.

29. Fifty-two numbers of *Proteus Echo* appeared in the *New-England Weekly Journal* between Apr. 10, 1727, and Apr. 1, 1728. C. Lennart Carlson, solving a cryptic reference in the final number to the authors' use of initials as signatures, states that of the 52 essays (and poems) "at least nineteen were by John Adams, fourteen by Matthew Adams, and fourteen by Mather Byles" (*American Literature*, 12 [1940], 348). John Adams wrote Nos. 5, 7, 10, 12, 15, 16, 18, 21, 23, 25, 27, 29, 31, 33, 35, 38, 40, 43, 46, 49; Matthew Adams, Nos. 2, 4, 8, 13, 19, 26, 32, 36, 39, 42, 45, 50, 51; and Mather Byles, Nos. 1, 3, 6, 9, 11, 14, 17, 20, 22, 24, 30, 34,

37, 52. The authorship of the remaining 5 numbers (28, 41, 44, 47, 48) cannot be determined. Six of the poems reappeared in Byles's *Poems on Several Occasions* (Boston, 1744), and 1 ("The Hundred and Fourth Psalm, Paraphrased") in John Adams's posthumous *Poems on Several Occasions* (Boston, 1745). Quotations from this serial will be identified by number and date in the body of the text.

30. Shipton, p. 229, presumably referring to "The Telltale."

31. An excerpt from this oriental tale appears in *Cyclopaedia of American Literature*, eds. Evert A. and George L. Duyckinck (New York: Scribner, 1855), I, 120, where it is attributed to Byles.

32. No. 8, May 29, 1727.

33. No. 12, June 26, 1727.

34. Nos. 18, 23, 40, Aug. 7, Sept. 11, 1727, and Jan. 8, 1727/8.

35. No. 25, Sept. 25, 1727.

36. No. 21, Aug. 28, 1727.

37. No. 34, Nov. 27, 1727.

38. No. 37, Dec. 18, 1727.

39. No. 7, May 22, 1727.

40. No. 11, June 19, 1727.

41. No. 16, July 24, 1727.

42. No. 17, July 31, 1727.

43. No. 39, Jan. 1, 1727/8.

44. No. 49, Mar. 11, 1727/8.

45. No. 50, Mar. 18, 1727/8.

46. No. 26, Oct. 2, 1727.

47. No. 29, Oct. 23, 1727.

48. No. 30, Oct. 30, 1727.

49. No. 35, Dec. 4, 1727.

50. No. 41, Jan. 15, 1727/8.

51. No. 43, Jan. 29, 1727/8.

52. No. 51, Mar. 25, 1727/8.

53. It is testimony to the popularity of this early example of American literary criticism that it was reprinted in the *American Magazine and Historical Chronicle*, 2 (Jan., 1745), 1-4, where the name is changed from "George Brimstone" to "Richard Stentor," and again in the *Boston Magazine*, 1 (Nov., Dec., 1783), 8, 49-51.

54. Perry Miller, *The New England Mind: From Colony to Province* (Cambridge, Mass.: Harvard Univ. Pr., 1953), p. 395.

55. "Of Style" (1698), in *Critical Essays of the Eighteenth Century*, ed. W.H. Durham (New Haven: Yale Univ. Pr., 1915), p. 80.

56. Shipton, pp. 229, 234.

NOTES TO CHAPTER THREE

1. Quoted in James Truslow Adams, *Provincial Society, 1690-1763* (New York: Macmillan, 1927), p. 114.

2. Franklin characterized Breintnall (d. 1746), who was a Quaker

merchant, as "a great Lover of Poetry, reading all he could meet with, writing some that was tolerable; very ingenious in many little Nicknackeries, and of sensible Conversation" (*Autobiography*, p. 117). See Stephen Bloore, "Joseph Breintnall: First Secretary of the Library Company," *Pennsylvania Magazine of History and Biography*, 59 (1935), 42-56.

3. The 32 *Busy-Body* papers appeared in the *American Weekly Mercury*, Feb. 4, 11, 18, 25, Mar. 4, 13, 20, 1728/9, and Mar. 27, Apr. 10, 17, May 1, 8, 15, 22, 29, June 5, 11, 19, 26, July 3, 10, 17, 24, 31, Aug. 7, 14, 21, 28, Sept. 4, 11, 17, 25, 1729. There seems no reason to doubt what someone, probably Franklin himself, wrote in the margin of the issue of Feb. 18, 1728/9: "The Busy Body was begun by B.F. who wrote the first four Numbers, part of No. 5, part of No. 8, the rest by J. Brintnal." After *Busy-Body* Nos. 1-5 and 8 were reprinted in *Papers of Franklin*, I, 113-39, J.A. Leo Lemay, in *American Literature*, 37 (1965), 307-11, demonstrated that of 2 editions of the Mar. 27, 1729, issue of the *Mercury*, the first, which was suppressed before distribution, "contains a hitherto unnoticed addition to Franklin's 'Busy-Body No. 8,' " a letter favoring paper currency. Quotations from *The Busy-Body* will be identified by number and date in the body of the text.

4. Anna J. De Armond, *Andrew Bradford: Colonial Journalist* (Newark, Del., 1949), p. 45.

5. *American Weekly Mercury*, Jan. 28, 1728/9. This essay is reprinted in *Papers of Franklin*, I, 112-13, and there assigned to Franklin.

6. *Universal Instructor*, Feb. 25, 1728/9.

7. *Universal Instructor*, Mar. 13, 1728/9.

8. *Universal Instructor*, Apr. 10, 1729.

9. Mock-advertisement is a convention associated with the periodical essay from an early date. In the *Spectator*, for example, appear Steele's advertisements for the Italian surgeon (No. 22), the widow who teaches birds to imitate human voices (No. 36), and the exercise of the snuff-box (No. 138).

10. No. 4, *American Weekly Mercury*, Feb. 25, 1728/9. In subsequent citations the name of this newspaper will be omitted.

11. No. 20, July 3, 1729.

12. No. 29, Sept. 4, 1729.

13. No. 3, Feb. 18, 1728/9.

14. No. 15, May 29, 1729.

15. No. 23, July 24, 1729.

16. No. 31, Sept. 18, 1729.

17. No. 12, May 8, 1729.

18. No. 13, May 15, 1729.

19. No. 25, Aug. 7, 1729.

20. No. 30, Sept. 11, 1729.

21. *Autobiography*, p. 120.

22. *Busy-Body* No. 7 reprints *Cato's Letter* No. 100 on libel; *Busy-Body* No. 10 carries an extract from *Cato's Letter* No. 102 on the

contemptibleness of grandeur without virtue; and *Busy-Body* No. 11 reprints *Cato's Letter* No. 106 on colonies and plantations. When charged with "palming your *Cato's*, and the rest of your musty Philosophers upon us" (No. 14, May 22, 1729), Breintnall's Busy-Body asks, "Of what Worth is a Mine to any Man who having it in Possession knows not how to get the Ore out of the Earth, or, if hove up, to refine it?" (No. 26, Aug. 14, 1729).

23. *Autobiography*, p. 165.

24. *Pennsylvania Gazette*, July 10, 24, Sept. 12, 1732; reprinted in *Papers of Franklin*, I, 237-48.

25. *Papers of Franklin*, II, 405.

26. *Observations on a Variety of Subjects* . . . (Philadelphia, 1774), pp. 29, 30, quoted in Daniel J. Boorstin, *The Americans: The Colonial Experience* (New York: Random House, 1958), p. 316.

27. Carl and Jessica Bridenbaugh, *Rebels and Gentlemen: Philadelphia in the Age of Franklin* (New York: Reynal & Hitchcock, 1942), p. 134.

28. Bridenbaugh, p. 104.

29. *American Magazine*, 1 (Oct. 1757), 6.

30. *American Magazine*, Oct., Dec. 1757, and Jan., Mar., Apr., July, Sept., Oct. 1758, pp. 37-43, 123-25, 181-84, 290-94, 330-31, 505-507, 600-602, 623-27.

31. For a discussion of these serials, see Lyon N. Richardson, *A History of Early American Magazines, 1741-1789* (1931; rpt. New York: Octagon, 1966), pp. 109-10.

32. This serial in 7 parts, 5 of them numbered, appeared in the *American Magazine*, Nov., Dec. 1757, and Jan., Mar., Apr., June, July, 1758, pp. 76-78, 125-28, 169-73, 255-56, 328-29, 431-33, 497-99. Quotations from *The Prattler* will be identified by number or title and date in the body of the text.

33. Richardson, p. 112.

34. Compare *Spectator* No. 320 on female inquisitors.

35. *Pennsylvania Packet*, Nov. 21, 1774.

36. *Pennsylvania Magazine*, 1 (Jan., 1775), 10-11.

37. *The Complete Writings of Thomas Paine*, ed. Philip S. Foner (New York: Citadel, 1945), II, 1131.

38. David Freeman Hawke, *Paine* (New York: Harper & Row, 1974), pp. 34-35.

39. *Pennsylvania Magazine*, No. 1, Mar. 1775, pp. 111-13; No. 2, Apr. 1775, p. 168 (Paine); No. 3, May 1775, pp. 213-15; No. 4, June 1775, pp. 263-65 (Paine?); "Consolation for the Old Bachelor," June 1775, pp. 254-57 (Hopkinson); No. 5, July 1775, pp. 311-12; No. 6, Oct. 1775, pp. 455-57 (Hopkinson); No. 7, Nov. 1775, pp. 511-13; No. 8, Dec. 1775, pp. 551-54 (Hopkinson); "To the Old Bachelor," Jan. 1776, pp. 267-68. For a discussion of these attributions, see George E. Hastings, *The Life and Works of Francis Hopkinson* (Chicago: Univ. of Chicago Pr., 1926), pp. 186-91, and Frank Smith, "New Light on Thomas Paine's First Year

in America," *American Literature*, 1 (1930), 347-71. Quotations from *The Old Bachelor* will be identified by number or title and date in the body of the text.

40. *Pennsylvania Magazine*, 2 (Apr., 1776), 186.

41. See Richardson, p. 188; Bridenbaugh, p. 106.

42. John F. Watson, *Annals of Philadelphia and Pennsylvania in the Olden Times* (Philadelphia: Carey and Hart, 1845), I, 432-33, describes a Bachelors' Hall which burned down before the Revolution.

43. Distressed by the satirical treatment of marriage in *The Old Bachelor*, John Witherspoon over the signature "Epaminondas" set down his reflections on marriage in the *Pennsylvania Magazine*, Sept., Dec. 1775, and Mar. 1776: "1. Nothing can be more contrary to reason or public utility, than the conversation and writings of those who turn matrimony into ridicule" (I, 409); "2. In the married state in general there is not so much happiness as young lovers dream of, nor is there by far so much happiness, as loose authors universally suppose" (I, 410); "3. It is by far the safest and most promising way to marry with one nearly equal in rank, and perhaps image; but if there is to be a difference, the risk is much greater when a man marries below his rank, than when a woman descends from hers" (I, 543); "4. That it is not by far of so much consequence what are the talents, temper, turn of mind, character, or circumstances of both or either of the parties, as that there be a certain suitableness or correspondence of those of the one to those of the other" (II, 109).

NOTES TO CHAPTER FOUR

1. *A Southern Reader* (New York: Knopf, 1955), p. 645.

2. "Plain-Dealer No. 2," *Pennsylvania Gazette*, Apr. 16, 1730 (from a 1728 issue of the *Maryland Gazette* no longer extant).

3. *Intellectual Life in Jefferson's Virginia, 1790-1830* (Chapel Hill: Univ. of North Carolina Pr., 1964), p. 279.

4. See *Another Secret Diary of William Byrd of Westover, 1739-1741*, ed. Maude H. Woodfin (Richmond: Dietz, 1942), pp. 187-387.

5. *DAB*, VII, 250.

6. Lawrence C. Wroth, *William Parks: Printer and Journalist of England and America* (Richmond: William Parks Club, 1926), p. 40, conjectures that the first issue appeared on Sept. 12; Clarence S. Brigham, *History and Bibliography of American Newspapers, 1690-1820* (Worcester: American Antiquarian Society, 1947), I, 218, on Sept. 16.

7. Nos. 1-3 appeared originally in the fall of 1728 in issues of the *Maryland Gazette* no longer extant, and were reprinted in the *Pennsylvania Gazette*, Apr. 9, 23, 30, 1730; Nos. 4-10 appeared in the *Maryland Gazette*, Dec. 10, 17, 24, 1728, and Jan. 7, 14, 21, Feb. 11, 1728/9. *Plain-Dealer* Nos. 3-10 are reprinted from Ambrose Philips' *Free-Thinker* (1718-21), Nos. 48, 80, 50, 63, 34, 73, 53, 90, respectively.

See Alfred Owen Aldridge, "Benjamin Franklin and the Maryland Gazette," *Maryland Historical Magazine*, 44 (1949), 177-89, and Nicholas Joost, " 'Plain-Dealer' and *Free-Thinker*: A Revaluation," *American Literature*, 23 (1951), 31-37.

8. No. 1, *Pennsylvania Gazette*, Apr. 9, 1730.

9. No. 2, *Pennsylvania Gazette*, Apr. 16, 1730.

10. Elizabeth Christine Cook, *Literary Influences in Colonial Newspapers, 1704-1750* (1912; rpt. Port Washington, N.Y.: Kennikat, 1966), p. 155.

11. Although this issue is no longer extant, Parks's editorial from which this quotation is taken can be found in the *Virginia Historical and Literary Companion*, 6 (1853), 20-22.

12. William Henry Castles, Jr., "*The Virginia Gazette*, 1736-1766: Its Editors, Editorial Policies, and Literary Content," diss., Univ. of Tennessee, 1962, estimates that "112 of the available 210 essays appear to have been composed by readers" (pp. 323-24).

13. *Collected Poems of Samuel Davies, 1723-1761*, ed. Richard Beale Davis (Gainesville: Scholars' Facsimiles & Reprints, 1968), p. xii. "That Davies was the principal figure of the new evangelism in Virginia," writes Davis, "undoubtedly was a major reason for attempting to make him ridiculous through his verse, which was almost entirely religiously meditative and evangelical in character." His poetry was "sublime in aim and imagery and theme. Its form is derived from the hymns of Watts and Doddridge, from Milton, Pope, the Bible, the classics, and what his age called the Pindaric ode" (pp. xii, xix).

14. Robert M. Myers, "The Old Dominion Looks to London: A Study of English Literary Influences upon *The Virginia Gazette* (1736-1766)," *Virginia Magazine of History and Biography*, 54 (1946), 197-200, discusses the series succinctly and effectively. See also Jack D. Wages, "Elegy and Mock Elegy in Colonial Virginia," *Studies in the Literary Imagination*, 9 (1976), 77-93.

15. *Virginia Gazette*, Sept. 10, 17, Oct. 1, 15, 22, 29, Nov. 5, 12, 19, 26, Dec. 10, 31, 1736, and Jan. 21, 28, Feb. 4, 11, 25, 1736/7. Interspersed with the later numbers of *The Monitor* are three replies by "Zoilus," which appeared Jan. 21, Feb. 4, Mar. 18, 1736/7. Quotations from *The Monitor* and Zoilus' replies will be identified by number and date in the body of the text.

16. Robert D. Arner, "The Short, Happy Life of the Virginia 'Monitor,' " *Early American Literature*, 7 (1972), suggests that stylistic differences within the series "reinforce the argument for dual authorship" (p. 139), but thinks that the *Monitor* essays "do not seem sophisticated enough to be the work of a thoroughly trained faculty member" (p. 147). Among students who may possibly have had a hand in the work, according to Arner, are Philip Ludwell, Thomas Dawson, and John Page.

17. Cook, p. 179.

18. Cook suggests that the Monitor's club may have been modeled

upon the Fiddle-faddle Club (*Grubstreet Journal* No. 176, May 10, 1733), which is composed of Lady Tiptoe, Lady Fancyfull, Lady Lazy, Caecilia Thoughtless, Miss Love-Mode, Miss At-all, and Coquetilla (p. 189).

19. No. 6, Sept. 10, 1736.

20. No. 13, Nov. 12, 1736.

21. No. 16, Dec. 10, 1736.

22. No. 18, Jan. 21, 1736/7.

23. No. 20, Feb. 4, 1736/7.

24. *Another Secret Diary of William Byrd of Westover, 1739-1741*, pp. 288-90.

25. Hennig Cohen, *The South Carolina Gazette, 1732-1775* (Columbia: Univ. of South Carolina Pr., 1953), p. 13.

26. *South-Carolina Gazette*, Jan. 8, 1731/2. Hereafter all quotations from this newspaper will be identified by date in the body of the text.

27. Cook, p. 258.

28. Cohen, p. 213.

29. *South-Carolina Gazette*, Nov. 26, 1753-Apr. 9, 1754. Of the 18 essays those which appeared weekly between Jan. 1 and Apr. 2 are numbered I to XIV. At this distance it is impossible to identify the author, or what is more likely authors, of this series. On Jan. 22, 1731/2, Thomas Whitmarsh had promised to conceal the names of his contributors, a practice observed by subsequent editors.

30. Pasquier Quesnell, *Le Nouveau Testament en Français, avec des Reflexions morales sur chaque verset* (1693).

31. Thomas Percy, *Reliques of Ancient English Poetry* (Edinburgh, 1858), III, 246-51. The burlesque criticism of this ballad, here truncated and modified, first appeared in *Mist's Weekly Journal*, Sept. 2, 1721, and was reprinted in the *New-England Courant*, Dec. 16, 1723; it is reproduced by Roger P. McCutcheon, "Another Burlesque of Addison's Ballad Criticism," *Studies in Philology*, 23 (1926), 452-56.

32. In *Spectator* No. 13 Addison tells of a tame lion, sent from the Tower of London on opera night, who roared "twice or thrice in a Thorough Base, before he fell at the Feet of *Hydaspes*."

33. Samuel Johnson, *Essays from the* Rambler, Adventurer, *and* Idler, ed. W.J. Bate (New Haven: Yale Univ. Pr., 1968), p. xiv; Cook, p. 263.

NOTES TO CHAPTER FIVE

1. "Memoir of the Life and Writings of John Trumbull, LL.D.," in *The Poetical Works of John Trumbull* (Hartford, 1820), I, 10, 12.

2. The 10 *Meddler* essays were published in the *Boston Chronicle* between Sept. 7, 1769, and Jan. 22, 1770; located among the Tyler Papers in the Cornell University Library (hereinafter: Cornell MSS) are manuscript versions in Trumbull's hand of Nos. 1, 2, 5, 7, 8, and 10. Trumbull may have been assisted by his younger college friend,

Timothy Dwight; see Victor E. Gimmestad, *John Trumbull* (New York: Twayne, 1974), pp. 31, 33-34. The 38 *Correspondent* essays were published in two series in the *Connecticut Journal*: Nos. 1-8 between Feb. 23 and July 6, 1770, and Nos. 9-38 between Feb. 12 and Sept. 3, 1773; manuscript versions in Trumbull's hand of Nos. 1-8 (except No. 3) are among the Cornell Mss. "Nearly two thirds were of my own Composition," writes Trumbull, "the rest by Others" (Cornell Mss). He probably wrote the first series alone; those who assisted him in the second series included Timothy Dwight and David Humphreys, another of his younger friends at Yale (Alexander Cowie, *John Trumbull, Connecticut Wit* [Chapel Hill: Univ. of North Carolina Pr., 1936], p. 83).

3. Cowie, *Trumbull*, pp. 57-58.

4. *The Satiric Poems of John Trumbull*, ed. Edwin T. Bowden (Austin: Univ. of Texas Pr., 1962), p. 49.

5. No. 9, *Connecticut Journal*, Feb. 12, 1773. I have examined these theological and philosophical attacks in "John Trumbull and Religion," *American Literature*, 23 (1951), 57-79.

6. No. 1, *Boston Chronicle*, Sept. 7, 1769. Hereafter quotations from *The Meddler* will be identified by number and date in the body of the text.

7. *Satiric Poems of Trumbull*, pp. 81, 90.

8. *Satiric Poems of Trumbull*, p. 68.

9. Quoted in Leon Howard, *The Connecticut Wits* (Chicago: Univ. of Chicago Pr., 1943), p. 27.

10. *The Works of John Dryden*, ed. Sir Walter Scott and George Saintsbury (Edinburgh, 1883), V, 124.

11. Alexander Cowie, "John Trumbull as a Critic of Poetry," *New England Quarterly*, 11 (1938), 789, identifies the "late Poet" as Timothy Dwight, whose *Conquest of Canaan* Trumbull "read and criticized in progress."

12. No. 1, *Connecticut Journal*, Feb. 23, 1770. Hereafter quotations from *The Correspondent* will be identified by number and date in the body of the text.

13. Cornell Mss. After receiving his Master's degree he went to Wethersfield, where he seems to have taught school.

14. No. 17, *Connecticut Journal*, Apr. 9, 1773. In subsequent citations the name of this newspaper will be omitted.

15. No. 31, July 16, 1773.

16. No. 21, May 7, 1773.

17. Cowie, *Trumbull*, p. 89, attributes these lines to Humphreys.

18. *Satiric Poems of Trumbull*, pp. 49, 65.

19. No. 10, Feb. 19, 1773.

20. No. 12, Mar. 5, 1773.

21. No. 18, Apr. 16, 1773.

22. No. 24, May 28, 1773.

23. This essay has been reprinted in the *Journal of Negro History*, 14

(1929), 493-95.

24. *Federal Gazette*, Mar. 23, 1790; reprinted in *Writings of Franklin*, X, 86-91.

25. No. 3, Mar. 9, 1770.

26. No. 13, Mar. 12, 1773.

27. No. 16, Apr. 2, 1773.

28. No. 2, Mar. 2, 1770.

29. No. 3, Mar. 9, 1770.

30. No. 24, May 28, 1773.

31. A week earlier the *Connecticut Journal* carried an epitaph on the Correspondent, inserted by one of Trumbull's enemies; see Cowie, *Trumbull*, p. 91, for the text.

32. Trumbull briefly considered reviving the series. In an undated essay that reads like a self-portrait, a man "about five feet, & four inches high, of a youthful Countenance, which tho' now somewhat pale & ghastly, shewed no small remains of vivacity & spirit," suddenly stands before the editor and declares: "I am the Correspondent, returned again to scourge [the] vices of the times. Publish this essay & from time to time I shall fur[nish] thee with others. So saying he delivered me a Paper & immediately disa[ppeared] from my sight" (Cornell Mss). Nothing came of this plan, however.

33. *An Essay on the Use and Advantages of the Fine Arts. Delivered at the Public Commencement, in New-Haven, September 12th, 1770* (New Haven, [1770]), p. 15.

Notes to Chapter Six

1. Harry Hayden Clark, "What Made Freneau the Father of American Prose?" *Transactions of the Wisconsin Academy of Sciences, Arts and Letters*, 25 (1930), 39-50.

2. Martin Christadler, *Der amerikanische Essay, 1720-1820* (Heidelberg: Carl Winter, 1968), p. 184.

3. I am indebted to Mary Witherspoon Bowden for this estimate. Although Philip Marsh, *Freneau's Published Prose: A Bibliography* (Metuchen, N.J.: Scarecrow, 1970), lists over one thousand items, more than half of these are suspect.

4. Another serial, not included because too immediate in purpose, should be mentioned. Between Aug. 25 and Oct. 5, 1804, 20 letters signed by members of the Bunker family appeared in Duane's *Aurora*; these letters center on a congressional contest in Philadelphia involving two Republican candidates, Dr. Michael Leib (supported by the *Aurora*) and William Penrose. It seems certain that Freneau authored the letters from Polly Bunker and her nephew Jonathan, the most vividly drawn personae in the series.

5. *The American Village* (New York, 1772), p. 18.

6. Lewis Leary, *That Rascal Freneau: A Study in Literary Failure* (1941; rpt. New York: Octagon, 1971), p. 21.

7. Leary, *Freneau*, p. 26.

8. Nineteen essays appeared in the *Freeman's Journal*, Nov. 21, 1781-Aug. 14, 1782. Six years later, in *The Miscellaneous Works of Mr. Philip Freneau* (Philadelphia, 1788), pp. 281-380, the series was extended and renamed *The Philosopher of the Forest;* of the 11 *Philosopher* essays 6 were slightly revised *Pilgrim* essays: No. 1 (*Pilgrim* No. 1), No. 4 (*Pilgrim* No. 3), No. 5 (*Pilgrim* No. 2), No. 6 (*Pilgrim* No. 4), No. 10 (*Pilgrim* No. 8), and No. 11 (*Pilgrim* No. 16). Judging by the Pilgrim's statement at the end of No. 19 (Aug. 14, 1782), that he is composing thoughts on treating brute animals tenderly "which shall appear in some future paper," it would seem that Freneau did not then intend to break off the series. The only clue as to when he began the *Philosopher* series is a note at the end of No. 7: "Written 1783." The discussion which follows is based on the newspaper text of the 19 *Pilgrim* essays and the book edition of the 5 new *Philosopher* essays, Nos. 2-3, 7-9.

9. No. 1, *Freeman's Journal*, Nov. 21, 1781. Hereafter quotations from *The Pilgrim* will be identified by number and date in the body of the text.

10. In *Philosopher* No. 5, the revision of this *Pilgrim* essay, Freneau renamed England the island of "Snatchaway."

11. Apparently, Freneau's animus against Tories softened after the Revolution, judging by the omission of these 2 essays from *The Philosopher of the Forest*.

12. In "The Political Balance," a Hudibrastic poem published in the *Freeman's Journal*, Apr. 3, 1782, Freneau, weighing the military and political fortunes of England and America, writes, "Britannia so small, and Columbia so large— / A ship of first rate, and a ferryman's barge."

13. Nos. 3, 12, 18, *Freeman's Journal*, Dec. 5, 1781, and Feb. 13, July 24, 1782. In subsequent citations the name of this newspaper will be omitted.

14. No. 6, Dec. 26, 1781.

15. No. 9, Jan. 16, 1782; No. 19, Aug. 14, 1782.

16. No. 7, Jan. 2, 1782.

17. No. 8, *Miscellaneous Works*, p. 343. In the other dream vision the Philosopher reflects on the creation of man and beasts (Nos. 2-3, *Miscellaneous Works*, pp. 290-305). These 2 dream visions are examined by Lewis Leary, "The Dream Visions of Philip Freneau," *Early American Literature*, 11 (1976), 167-71.

18. Fifteen essays, entitled "Tomo Cheeki, The Creek Indian in Philadelphia," appeared in the *Jersey Chronicle*, May 23-Oct. 31, 1795; when Freneau reprinted these essays two years later in the *Time-Piece*, he composed 2 new ones which appeared May 22 and June 16, 1797.

19. Leary, *Freneau*, p. 261.

20. *Miscellaneous Essays*, pp. 122-28. In 1784 Freneau had written a poem entitled "The Dying Indian: Tomo Chequi."

21. *Daily Advertiser*, Sept. 1, 8, 17, 1790.

22. *Jersey Chronicle*, May 23, 1795. Hereafter quotations from the *Jersey Chronicle* text of *Tomo Cheeki* will be identified by date in the body of the text.

23. *Time-Piece*, June 16, 1797.

24. Originally published as the first of the Opay Mico essays under the title "A Short Discourse upon Drunkenness," *Daily Advertiser*, Sept. 1, 1790.

25. Originally published as the third of the Opay Mico essays under the title "A Discourse upon Horse Shoes," *Daily Advertiser*, Sept. 17, 1790.

26. See also *Jersey Chronicle*, July 4, Aug. 8, 1795.

27. First published in the *National Gazette*, Jan. 12, 1792.

28. Harry Hayden Clark, "The Literary Influences on Philip Freneau," *Studies in Philology*, 22 (1925), 26.

29. The seven titled essays in this series appeared in the *Time-Piece* in 1797: "On the Culture of Pumpkins," Oct. 23; "A Sketch of Biography," Oct. 25; "Rules how to get through a crowd," Oct. 31; "From Hezekiah Salem's Last Basket," Nov. 1; "A few Words on Duelling," Nov. 10; "The Howling House," Nov. 13; and "A Scrap, from a Keg, of Hezekiah Salem's Sermons," Nov. 17. The Salem name reappeared in the 1809 edition of Freneau's poems; see Philip Marsh, "Freneau's 'Hezekiah Salem,' " *New England Quarterly*, 18, (1945), 256-59. Quotations will be identified by date in the body of the text.

30. *The Prose of Philip Freneau*, ed. Philip M. Marsh (New Brunswick, N.J.: Scarecrow, 1955), p. 564.

31. Thirty-seven *Slender* letters were published during these two years. Between Mar. 25 and Oct. 2, 1799, the first 23 of these letters, all but one signed "Robert Slender," appeared in the *Aurora*: Mar. 25, 29, Apr. 23, May 3, 7, 16, 20, June 11, 18 (signed "Simon Simple"), 19, July 6, Aug. 1, 8, 9, 16, 17, 20, 23, 24, Sept. 3, 11, 27, Oct. 2. For the book edition, *Letters on Various interesting and important Subjects*, published at Philadelphia on Dec. 30, 1799, Freneau reprinted these letters, adding a dedication and a new letter (No. 21). Although he promised at the end of this book to publish a second volume, "should these Letters meet with a favourable reception in their present form," no such volume was forthcoming even though he wrote an additional 13 *Slender* letters for the *Aurora*: Aug. 6 (signed "Slender Thomas"), Nov. 6, 9, 23, 30, Dec. 4, 1799; Aug. 5, Sept. 10, Oct. 2, 9, Nov. 17, 18, 1800; Feb. 19, 1801.

32. *A Journey from Philadelphia to New-York* (Philadelphia, 1787).

33. *Letters on Various interesting and important Subjects*, pp. iv-v, 19. Hereafter quotations from the Scholars' Facsimiles & Reprints edition of this book, edited by Harry Hayden Clark (New York, 1943), will be identified by page in the body of the text.

34. *Letters*, pp. 72-78; *Aurora*, Nov. 9, 1799, Sept. 10, Oct. 9, 1800.

35. *Letters*, pp. 107-27. For background see Donald H. Stewart, *The Opposition Press of the Federalist Period* (Albany: State University of

New York, 1969), pp. 242-45.
36. *Letters*, pp. 138-42; *Aurora*, Feb. 19, 1801.
37. *Aurora*, Nov. 9, 1799.
38. *Aurora*, Oct. 9, 1800.
39. "Advice to Authors," *Miscellaneous Works*, pp. 42-48.

NOTES TO CHAPTER SEVEN

1. *Port Folio*, Dec. 24, 1803, p. 410.
2. Quoted in Harold Milton Ellis, *Joseph Dennie and His Circle: A Study in American Literature from 1792 to 1812*, Bulletin of the Univ. of Texas, No. 3 (Austin, 1915), p. 31.
3. *The Lay Preacher by Joseph Dennie*, ed. Milton Ellis (New York: Scholars' Facsimiles & Reprints, 1943), p. 162. Hereafter referred to as *The Lay Preacher*.
4. *Specimens of Newspaper Literature* (Boston: Little, 1850), II, 196.
5. *Farmer's Weekly Museum*, Apr. 5, 1796.
6. Laura Green Pedder, *The Letters of Joseph Dennie, 1768-1812*, Univ. of Maine Studies, 2d series, No. 36 (Orono, 1936), p. 183.
7. As editor of the *Port Folio* Dennie collaborated in other serials which will not be considered: with Royall Tyler in *Colon and Spondee* (Dennie was Colon); also with Tyler in *An Author's Evening*; with many others, including Charles Brockden Brown, in *The American Lounger*. See Randolph C. Randall, "Authors of the *Port Folio*, Revealed by the Hall Files," *American Literature*, 11 (1940), 379-416.
8. Ellis, *Dennie*, pp. 238-39, lists 26 *Farrago* essays, numbering them chronologically: Nos. 1-4, *Morning Ray* (Windsor, Vt.), Feb. 14, 21, Mar. 6, 20, 1792; Nos. 8-22, *Eagle or Dartmouth Centinel* (Hanover, N.H.), Aug. 17, 26, Sept. 9, 16, Oct. 21, 28, 1793, and Jan. 27, Feb. 10, Mar. 3, 10, July 14, 21, 28, Aug, 4, 18, 1794; Nos. 23-28, *Tablet* (Boston), May 19, June 9, 16, 23, July 21, Aug. 4, 1795; No. 29, *Port Folio*, July 24, 1802. A note to No. 29, "written originally in the country, but never before published," makes it clear that this essay was composed at the same time as the others in the series. No trace of Nos. 5-7 has been found. Quotations from *The Farrago* will be identified by number and date in the body of the text.
9. *Letters of Dennie*, pp. 138-39.
10. See *Letters of Dennie*, p. 148; *Port Folio*, Jan. 3, 1801, p. 3.
11. No. 9 discusses indolence and No. 19, speculators.
12. *Letters of Dennie*, p. xiv. Dennie called Harvard "that rubbish of a school," that "sink of vice, that temple of dulness, that roost of owls" (*Letters of Dennie*, p. 15).
13. *Letters of Dennie*, pp. 133, 141.
14. A total of 117 *Lay Preacher* essays appeared between 1795 and 1818: *New Hampshire Journal: Or The Farmer's Weekly Museum* (hereafter: *Farmer's Museum*), Oct. 13, 1795-Aug. 26, 1799 (90 essays); *Eagle or Dartmouth Centinel*, Apr. 4, 1796 (1 essay); *Gazette of the*

United States (Philadelphia), Nov. 8, 1799-Mar. 15, 1800 (13 essays); *Port Folio*, Jan. 17, 1801-Feb. 13, 1808 (11 essays); *New England Galaxy* (Boston), July 10, 1818 (1 essay); and one essay as a separate leaflet in Philadelphia, in 1818. Book editions of these essays, representing half the total number, appeared in 1796 and 1817; Milton Ellis reissued these two collections in a single volume in 1943. I have adopted the chronological numbering devised by Ellis, *Dennie*, pp. 240-44.

15. *Letters of Dennie*, p. 158.

16. *The Lay Preacher*, p. vi.

17. *The Lay Preacher*, p. 3. Benefiting from the aphoristic style of Noah Webster's *Prompter* (1790), Dennie wrote him on Sept. 8, 1796, "The simplicity and ease of that little volume taught me the value of the Franklin Style" (*Letters of Dennie*, p. 155). A few years later, however, Dennie advised readers of the *Port Folio* that "ever since the era of Dr. Franklin, the love of proverbs has waxed exceedingly fervent, among our countrymen," with a resulting "debasement of the dignity and elegance of diction" and an increase in "the woeful insipidity of the simple style" (Mar. 12, 1803, p. 87). See Lewis Leary, "Joseph Dennie on Benjamin Franklin," *Pennsylvania Magazine of History and Biography*, 72 (1948), 240-46.

18. *Port Folio*, Jan. 3, 1801, p. 3.

19. No. 113, *Port Folio*, Jan. 23, 1808, p. 50; reprinted in *The Lay Preacher*, pp. 100-101.

20. No. 77, *Farmer's Museum*, Aug. 20, 1798; reprinted in *The Lay Preacher*, p. 124.

21. No. 69, *Farmer's Museum*, June 26, 1798.

22. No. 11, *Farmer's Museum*, Dec. 22, 1795; reprinted in *The Lay Preacher*, p. 54. "Clumsy College" is an allusion to Harvard where Dennie spent three years (1787-90).

23. No. 13, *Farmer's Museum*, Jan. 5, 1796; reprinted in *The Lay Preacher*, pp. 62-63.

24. No. 106, *Port Folio*, Jan. 17, 1801, p. 21; reprinted in *The Lay Preacher*, p. 97.

25. No. 52, *Farmer's Museum*, Jan. 17, 1797; reprinted in *The Lay Preacher*, p. 147.

26. No. 73, *Farmer's Museum*, July 24, 1798; reprinted in *The Lay Preacher*, p. 149.

27. No. 19, *Farmer's Museum*, Feb. 16, 1796; reprinted in *The Lay Preacher*, p. 15.

28. No. 10, *Farmer's Museum*, Dec. 15, 1795; reprinted in *The Lay Preacher*, p. 17.

29. No. 57, *Farmer's Museum*, Apr. 4, 1797.

30. No. 47, *Farmer's Museum*, Sept. 13, 1796.

31. No. 29, *Farmer's Museum*, Apr. 26, 1796; reprinted in *The Lay Preacher*, p. 48.

32. No. 8, *Farmer's Museum*, Dec. 1, 1795; reprinted in *The Lay Preacher*, p. 18.

33. No. 89, *Farmer's Museum*, July 29, 1799.

34. No. 78, *Farmer's Museum*, Aug. 27, 1798.

35. Rebecca (No. 36), Ruth (No. 51), Samson (No. 61), Hagar and Ishmael (No. 76), Moses and the Daughters of Midian (No. 77), Jacob and Leah (No. 85), the Youth of David (No. 99), the Prodigal's Return (No. 103), Samuel (No. 107), Esther (No. 111), Job (No. 115), and David and Michal (No. 117).

36. No. 28, *Farmer's Museum*, Apr. 19, 1796; reprinted in *The Lay Preacher*, pp. 43, 44.

37. No. 105, *Gazette of the United States*, Mar. 15, 1800.

38. No. 73, *Farmer's Museum*, July 24, 1798; reprinted in *The Lay Preacher*, pp. 150-51.

39. No. 30, *Farmer's Museum*, May 3, 1796; reprinted in *The Lay Preacher*, pp. 88, 89.

40. No. 8, *Farmer's Museum*, Dec. 1, 1795; reprinted in *The Lay Preacher*, pp. 18-20.

41. No. 39, *Farmer's Museum*, July 19, 1796; reprinted in *The Lay Preacher*, pp. 143-44.

42. No. 43, *Farmer's Museum*, Aug. 16, 1796.

43. No. 44, *Farmer's Museum*, Aug. 23, 1796.

44. No. 46, *Farmer's Museum*, Sept. 6, 1796; reprinted in *The Lay Preacher*, pp. 169-70.

45. No. 94, *Gazette of the United States*, Nov. 23, 1799.

46. No. 95, *Gazette of the United States*, Nov. 30, 1799.

47. No. 11, *Farmer's Museum*, Dec. 22, 1795; reprinted in *The Lay Preacher*, pp. 53-54.

48. No. 118, *New England Galaxy*, July 10, 1818.

49. Most of the criticism appeared in *An Author's Evening* and *The American Lounger*. Lewis Leary has examined this criticism in several places, notably in *Soundings: Some Early American Writers* (Athens: Univ. of Georgia Pr., 1975), pp. 253-70.

50. No. 78, *Farmer's Museum*, Aug. 27, 1798.

51. No. 79, *Farmer's Museum*, Sept. 3, 1798.

52. No. 80, *Farmer's Museum*, Sept. 10, 1798.

53. No. 81, *Farmer's Museum*, Oct. 1, 1798.

54. No. 82, *Farmer's Museum*, Dec. 10, 1798.

55. No. 74, *Farmer's Museum*, July 31, 1798.

56. No. 48, *Farmer's Museum*, Oct. 25, 1796.

57. No. 56, *Farmer's Museum*, Mar. 7, 1797.

58. No. 13, *Farmer's Museum*, Jan. 5, 1796; reprinted in *The Lay Preacher*, p. 63.

59. No. 72, *Farmer's Museum*, July 17, 1798; reprinted in *The Lay Preacher*, pp. 172, 174.

60. No. 3, *Farmer's Museum*, Oct. 27, 1795; reprinted in *The Lay Preacher*, p. 13.

61. No. 53, *Farmer's Museum*, Jan. 24, 1797.

62. No. 98, *Gazette of the United States*, Dec. 21, 1799.

63. No. 40, *Farmer's Museum*, July 26, 1796; reprinted in *The Lay Preacher*, p. 77.

64. Ellis, *Dennie*, p. 219. Ellis continues: "His was the rapid flow of ideas of an eloquent conversationalist, rather than the polished, orderly prose of a thoughtful and painstaking writer. His imagination was active, and his range of interest wide. A natural result is that frequently his essays are rambling and discursive, bringing in irrelevant ideas as they occurred to his vagrant fancy, and ending apparently at the bottom of the page, rather than at any logical conclusion" (p. 220).

65. *Letters of Dennie*, pp. 171-72.

66. *Port Folio*, Feb., 1812, p. 188.

67. Rufus W. Griswold, *Curiosities of American Literature* (New York: World, 1876), p. 51.

Notes to Chapter Eight

1. *Massachusetts Magazine*, 1 (1789), Preface.

2. *Massachusetts Magazine*, 2 (Jan., 1790), "To our Patrons and Correspondents," 1.

3. *Massachusetts Magazine*, 2 (Dec., 1790), "Acknowledgments to Correspondents," 706.

4. *The Gleaner. A Miscellaneous Production. In Three Volumes. By Constantia* (Boston, 1798), III, 315, 316.

5. Universalism "has to do with the theological question of the extent of the benefit wrought by the atoning death of Christ, and with the relation of the Calvinian doctrines of election and predestination to the expressed purpose of the gospel, that all men might be saved" (*Encyclopaedia of Religion and Ethics*, ed. James Hastings [Edinburgh: T. & T. Clark, 1908-21], XII, 529).

6. *DAB*, VII, 364.

7. *Massachusetts Magazine*, 4 (Sept., 1793), 522, 523.

8. *Massachusetts Magazine*, 6 (Aug., 1794), 461.

9. Vena Bernadette Field, *Constantia: A Study of the Life and Works of Judith Sargent Murray, 1751-1820*, Univ. of Maine Studies, 2d series, No. 17 (Orono, 1931), p. 32.

10. *The Gleaner* runs to 100 numbers. The first 31 numbers, expanded to 34 in the first volume of the book edition, originally appeared in the *Massachusetts Magazine* between Feb. 1792 and Dec. 1794 and tell most of the Story of Margaretta. The book edition is accurate in stating that the essays in the first volume "now stand precisely in the order, and nearly in the manner, in which they were first presented" (I, 13) in the magazine. The second and third volumes are so miscellaneous and advance so little the story as to merit only incidental attention. All quotations are from the book edition rather than the magazine version and will be identified by volume, number, and page in the body of the text thus: I, i, 1.

11. Roger B. Stein, "Royall Tyler and the Question of Our Speech,"

New England Quarterly, 38 (1965), maintains that Tyler searched "amid the babble of his characters' speeches for a native voice" (p. 463) and was unable finally to choose between "Jonathan's dialect" and "Manly's sententious oratory" (p. 472).

12. Tremaine McDowell, "Sensibility in the Eighteenth-Century American Novel," *Studies in Philology*, 24 (1927), 383.

13. Herbert Ross Brown, *The Sentimental Novel in America, 1789-1850* (Durham: Duke Univ. Pr., 1940), p. 8.

14. Brown, p. 13.

15. Brown, p. 9.

16. Sarah Sayward Wood, *Julia, and the Illuminated Baron* (Portsmouth, N.H., 1800), p. 82.

17. Henry Sherburne, *The Oriental Philanthropist* (Portsmouth, N.H., 1800), p. 5.

Notes to Chapter Nine

1. Richard Beale Davis, *Francis Walker Gilmer: Life and Learning in Jefferson's Virginia* (Richmond: Dietz, 1939), pp. xii-xiii.

2. John Pendleton Kennedy, *Memoirs of the Life of William Wirt* (Philadelphia: Lea and Blanchard, 1849), I, 277. Referred to hereafter as *Memoirs*.

3. *Memoirs*, I, 57.

4. Joseph C. Robert, "William Wirt, Virginian," *Virginia Magazine of History and Biography*, 80 (1972), 392.

5. *The Letters of the British Spy* (10th ed., New York, 1832), ed. Richard Beale Davis (Chapel Hill: Univ. of North Carolina Pr., 1970), p. 242. All quotations are from this reprint edition and will be identified hereafter by page in the body of the text.

6. Jay B. Hubbell, *The South in American Literature, 1607-1900* (Durham: Duke Univ. Pr., 1954), p. 236.

7. Richard Beale Davis maintains, "Wirt never outgrew his love for *Tristram Shandy*, and the whim-whams of Uncle Toby and Brother Shandy are behind the strong sensibility in all his communications with his friends" (*Intellectual Life in Jefferson's Virginia*, p. 294).

8. Davis, *Gilmer*, p. 273.

9. This series of 26 essays, which appeared in the Richmond *Enquirer* between Aug. 11, 1804, and Apr. 19, 1805, was initiated by James Ogilvie of the Rainbow Association, who enlisted the services of the other members. It will not be considered here because Wirt contributed only 2 numbers, "On the Conditions of Women," Aug. 18, and "On Forensic Eloquence," Nov. 10. See Jay B. Hubbell, "William Wirt and the Familiar Essay," *William and Mary Quarterly*, 2d series, 23 (1943), 139-44, and Robert, pp. 408-409, for further information about the series.

10. Quoted in Hubbell, *William and Mary Quarterly*, 2d series, 23 (1943), 137.

11. These first appeared in the *Virginia Argus*, Aug. 20, 24, 27, 31, Sept. 3, 7, 10, 14, 21, 24, 1803; the first book edition, entitled *The Letters of the British Spy*, was published at Richmond in October or November, 1803.

12. *Letters of the British Spy*, pp. 176, 183, 194, 216.

13. Wirt to Dabney Carr, Jan. 16, 1803, *Memoirs*, I, 113.

14. *Memoirs*, I, 297.

15. Davis, *Intellectual Life in Jefferson's Virginia*, pp. 260-61; Wilbur Samuel Howell, *Eighteenth-Century British Logic and Rhetoric* (Princeton: Princeton Univ. Pr., 1971), pp. 653-54.

16. After the first book edition Wirt softened the portrait of Wickham.

17. Actually Waddell was well known in his day.

18. *Letters of the British Spy*, pp. xviii-xix. In truth, writes Jay Hubbell, "the *Spy* reflects the contradictions of a transition period. It is a mixture of early Romanticism and of Neoclassicism, of sensibility, sentiment, and piety" (*The South in American Literature*, p. 237).

19. Wirt to Carr, Jan. 16, June 8, 1804, *Memoirs*, I, 116-17, 121, 122.

20. *Monthly Review*, 2d series, 71 (May, 1813), 109, quoted in William B. Cairns, *British Criticism of American Writings, 1783-1815* (Madison: Univ. of Wisconsin Pr., 1918), p. 86.

21. B. Randolph Wellford, "Check-List of William Wirt's *The Letters of the British Spy*," *Sec. News Sheet* (Bibliog. Soc. Univ. Va.), 31 (1954), 10-16. Wellford says that the tenth New York edition (1832) went through many printings.

22. *Memoirs*, I, 292-93. Although Kennedy says that *The Sylph* was an abortive essay serial begun by Wirt in the *Enquirer* in the fall of 1810 and quickly dropped because he thought it displayed "too palpable fiction, want of community of character and interests, and un-manageability" (*Memoirs*, I, 263), no such serial was ever published; if it exists, it would be in an as yet undiscovered manuscript.

23. Of the 33 numbers comprising *The Old Bachelor* the first 28 were published originally in the *Enquirer*, Dec. 22, 25, 29, 1810, and Jan. 1, 5, 10, 12, 15, 19, 22, 26, Feb. 2, 7, 26, Mar. 5, 8, 12, 15, 26, 29, Apr. 5, July 5, Aug. 6, 13, 20, Dec. 12, 17, 24, 1811. For the first book edition, published at Richmond in 1814, Wirt and his collaborators turned "the spit for five or six revolutions more" (*Memoirs*, I, 350) and wrote 5 new numbers. St. George Tucker, who contributed slightly if at all to this series of published essays, produced 22 essays "For the old Batchellor," written mainly in August and September, 1811; Carl Dolmetsch is preparing an edition of these unpublished essays.

24. Nos. 1-3, 5, 9-12, 15, 17-19, 23, 30-32. These attributions are based on information to be found in *Memoirs*, I, 293, 296, 312; Hubbell, *William and Mary Quarterly*, 2d series, 23 (1943), 147-48; Davis, *Intellectual Life in Jefferson's Virginia*, pp. 283-84. The following pseudonyms in the *Old Bachelor* series have been identified by

Kennedy, Hubbell, or Davis: "Arthur O'Flannegan" (Wirt), "Galen" (Frank Carr), "Alfred" (Parker), "Obadiah Squaretoes" (Dabney Carr), "Edward Melmoth" and "Tim Lovetruth" (Girardin), "John Truename" (Watson), "Richard Vamper" and "Peter Schryphel" (George Tucker), "Diogenes" and "Susannah Thankful" (St. George Tucker?).

25. *Letters of the British Spy*, p. 63. See *Edinburgh Review*, 30 (Jan., 1810), 442-53. In *Old Bachelor* Nos. 2 and 17 such misrepresentation, especially of Virginia, is refuted. Hubbell, *The South in American Literature*, p. 17, says that "the motive behind much Colonial Writing, particularly in the South, was a desire to correct British misconceptions of American life."

26. Nos. 11, 7, *Enquirer*, Jan. 26, 12, 1811. The newspaper version of the first 28 numbers of *The Old Bachelor* has been followed rather than the book edition in which the expression is frequently more euphemistic and less vivid; quotations are identified by number and date in the body of the text.

27. No. 29, *The Old Bachelor* (Baltimore, 1818), II, 126, 132, 133.

28. No. 33, *The Old Bachelor*, II, 191-215.

29. No. 30, *The Old Bachelor*, II, 141-46.

30. No. 31, *The Old Bachelor*, II, 150-63. The Englishman Thomas Abthorpe Cooper (1776-1849) was the leading actor and manager at the Park Theater in New York City.

31. *Memoirs*, I, 313.

32. *Memoirs*, I, 350.

33. *Memoirs*, I, 308.

34. *Analectic Magazine*, 12 (Oct., 1818), 268.

35. Kennedy, *Memoirs*, I, 296.

36. *Memoirs*, I, 370.

NOTES TO CHAPTER TEN

1. Eleanor Scott, "Early Literary Clubs in New York City," *American Literature*, 5 (1933), 16.

2. William I. Paulding, *Literary Life of James K. Paulding* (New York: Scribner, 1867), p. 29.

3. William Dunlap, *History of the American Theatre* (1832; rpt. New York: Burt Franklin, 1963), I, 373.

4. Paulding, *Literary Life*, p. 26.

5. *The Letters of James Kirke Paulding*, ed. Ralph M. Aderman (Madison: Univ. of Wisconsin Pr., 1962), p. 17.

6. Among the pieces that can possibly be attributed to Paulding are "The Eccentric Man," Oct. 22, 1802; "Woman:—An Apologue," Oct. 28, 1802; and "The Stroke of Death," Nov. 9, 1802.

7. Washington Irving, *Journals and Notebooks, Volume I, 1803-1806*, ed. Nathalia Wright (Madison: Univ. of Wisconsin Pr., 1969), p. 433.

8. *Journals and Notebooks*, I, xxviii, xxiv, xxxv.

9. *Washington Irving's Contributions to* The Corrector, ed. Martin Roth (Minneapolis: Univ. of Minnesota Pr., 1968). The contributions attributed with certainty to Washington Irving are Nos. 6, 8, 14, 15, 16, 19, 23, 25, 28, 30, 32, 34.

10. Pierre M. Irving, *The Life and Letters of Washington Irving* (New York: Putnam, 1862-64), I, 175.

11. *Letters of Washington Irving to Henry Brevoort*, ed. George S. Hellman (New York: Putnam, 1918), p. 396.

12. *Letters of Irving to Brevoort*, p. 207.

13. The 9 letters of Jonathan Oldstyle appeared in the *Morning Chronicle*, Nov. 15, 20, Dec. 1, 4, 11, 1802, and Jan. 17, 22, Feb. 8, Apr. 23, 1803. The New York publisher William Clayton, in his book edition of 1824, was the first to give the letters the now familiar title, *Letters of Jonathan Oldstyle, Gent.* Quotations from the *Oldstyle* letters will be drawn from *Letters of Jonathan Oldstyle, Gent.* and *Salmagundi; or, the Whim-Whams and Opinions of Launcelot Langstaff, Esq. and Others*, eds. Bruce I. Granger and Martha Hartzog (Boston: Twayne, 1977), and will be identified by page in the body of the text.

14. Stanley T. Williams, *The Life of Washington Irving* (New York: Oxford Univ. Pr., 1935), I, 37.

15. *New-York Mirror*, Feb. 2, 1833.

16. *American Citizen*, Feb. 3, 1803.

17. *Evening Post*, Feb. 7, 1803.

18. *Blackwood's Edinburgh Magazine*, 18 (Jan., 1825), 60-61.

19. *Salmagundi; or, the Whim-Whams and Opinions of Launcelot Langstaff, Esq. and Others*, eds. Granger and Hartzog, p. 99. Hereafter quotations from this edition will be identified by page in the body of the text.

20. *Tristram Shandy*, Vol. II, Ch. 5.

21. See Assignments of Authorship discussion in the Historical Note to *Salmagundi*, eds. Granger and Hartzog, pp. 327-36.

22. *Tristram Shandy*, Vol. V, Ch. 17.

23. Joseph Dennie, whom Washington Irving met while on a visit to Philadelphia in March 1807, recognized this characterization of Langstaff as a sketch of himself. See Ellis, *Dennie*, pp. 197-98.

24. *Evening Post*, Mar. 29, 1805.

25. Holograph, Yale Univ.

26. *Cyclopaedia of American Literature*, ed. Duyckinck, II, 47. At the end of *Salmagundi. Second Series* No. 13 (Aug. 19, 1820) Paulding announces the marriage of Barbara Cockloft and Will Wizard.

27. *Tristram Shandy*, ed. James A. Work (New York: Odyssey, 1940), p. lii.

NOTES TO CHAPTER ELEVEN

1. Watson, "The *Spectator* Tradition and the Development of the Familiar Essay," *ELH*, 13 (1946), 215.

2. Marie Hamilton Law, *The English Familiar Essay in the Early Nineteenth Century* (1934; rpt. New York: Russell & Russell, 1965), p. 38.

3. Law, pp. 185, 219, 230.

4. "The Rhapsodist No. 1," *Columbian Magazine; or, Monthly Miscellany*, 3 (Aug., 1789), 467; reprinted in *The Rhapsodist and Other Uncollected Writings by Charles Brockden Brown*, ed. Harry R. Warfel (New York: Scholars' Facsimiles & Reprints, 1943), p. 5.

5. *Weekly Magazine of Original Essays*, Feb. 3-Apr. 28, 1798 (13 numbers); reprinted in *The Rhapsodist and Other Uncollected Writings*, pp. 27-98.

6. "A Series of Original Letters," *Weekly Magazine of Original Essays*, Apr. 21-June 2, 1798 (9 numbers); reprinted in *The Rhapsodist and Other Uncollected Writings*, pp. 101-31.

7. "Duty of Periodical Essayists," *Literary Magazine and American Register*, 6 (Oct., 1806), 265; quoted in Fred Lewis Pattee, *The First Century of American Literature, 1770-1870* (New York: Appleton, 1935), p. 207.

8. Lewis P. Simpson, "Federalism and the Crisis of Literary Order," *American Literature*, 32 (1960), 266.

9. "The Remarker No. 4," *Monthly Anthology and Boston Review*, 2 (Dec., 1805), 631; reprinted in *The Federalist Literary Mind: Selections from the Monthly Anthology and Boston Review, 1803-1811*, ed. Lewis P. Simpson (Baton Rouge: Louisiana State Univ. Pr., 1962), p. 148.

10. "The Remarker No. 38," *Monthly Anthology and Boston Review*, 5 (Nov., 1808), 599, 600.

11. *The Origins of American Critical Thought, 1810-1835* (Philadelphia: Univ. of Pennsylvania Pr., 1936), p. 5.

12. *The Prose Writers of America*, ed. Rufus W. Griswold (Philadelphia: Carey and Hart, 1849), p. 38.

13. "The American Familiar Essay, 1815-1835," diss., Univ. of Maryland, 1960, p. 196.

14. "Essay Writing," *North American Review*, 14 (Apr., 1822), 332, 333.

15. "The American Familiar Essay," pp. 204, 205, 213.

16. William I. Paulding, *Literary Life of James K. Paulding*, p. v.

17. "The American Familiar Essay," pp. 247-48.

BIBLIOGRAPHY

◫

Adams, James Truslow. *Provincial Society, 1690-1763*. New York: Macmillan, 1927.

Aldridge, Alfred Owen. "Benjamin Franklin and the Maryland Gazette." *Maryland Historical Magazine*, 44 (1949), 177-89.

American Bibliography: A Preliminary Checklist for 1801-1819. Comps. Ralph R. Shaw and Richard H. Shoemaker. 19 vols. New York: Scarecrow, 1958-63.

Another Secret Diary of William Byrd of Westover, 1739-1741. Ed. Maude H. Woodfin. Richmond: Dietz, 1942.

Arner, Robert D. "The Short, Happy Life of the Virginia 'Monitor.' " *Early American Literature*, 7 (1972), 130-47.

The Autobiography of Benjamin Franklin. Eds. Leonard W. Labaree and Others. New Haven: Yale Univ. Pr., 1964.

Boorstin, Daniel J. *The Americans: The Colonial Experience*. New York: Random, 1958.

Bowden, Mary Witherspoon. *Philip Freneau*. Boston: Twayne, 1976.

Bridenbaugh, Carl and Jessica. *Rebels and Gentlemen: Philadelphia in the Age of Franklin*. New York: Reynal & Hitchcock, 1942.

Brigham, Clarence S. *History and Bibliography of American Newspapers, 1690-1820*. 2 vols. Worcester: American Antiquarian Society, 1947.

Brown, Herbert Ross. *The Sentimental Novel in America, 1789-1850*. Durham: Duke Univ. Pr., 1940.

Brown, Huntington. *Prose Style: Five Primary Types*. Minneapolis: Univ. of Minnesota Pr., 1966.

Buckingham, Joseph T. *Specimens of Newspaper Literature*. 2 vols. Boston: Little, 1850.

Cairns, William B. *British Criticism of American Writings, 1783-1815*. Madison: Univ. of Wisconsin Pr., 1918.

Carlson, C. Lennart. "John Adams, Matthew Adams, Mather Byles, and the *New England Weekly Journal.*" *American Literature*, 12 (1940), 347-48.

Castles, William Henry, Jr. "The *Virginia Gazette,* 1736-1766: Its Editors, Editorial Policies, and Literary Content." Diss., Univ. of Tennessee, 1962.

Charvat, William. *The Origins of American Critical Thought, 1810-1835.* Philadelphia: Univ. of Pennsylvania Pr., 1936.

Christadler, Martin. *Der amerikanische Essay, 1720-1820.* Heidelberg: Carl Winter, 1968.

Clark, Harry Hayden. "The Literary Influences on Philip Freneau." *Studies in Philology,* 22 (1925), 1-33.

———. "What Made Freneau the Father of American Prose?" *Transactions of the Wisconsin Academy of Sciences, Arts and Letters,* 25 (1930), 39-50.

Cohen, Hennig. *The South Carolina Gazette, 1732-1775.* Columbia: Univ. of South Carolina Pr., 1953.

Coleman, Ernest Claude. "The Influence of the Addisonian Essay in America Before 1810." Diss., Univ. of Illinois, 1936.

Colonial American Poetry. Ed. Kenneth Silverman. New York: Hafner, 1968.

Conant, Martha Pike. *The Oriental Tale in England in the Eighteenth Century.* 1908; rpt. New York: Octagon, 1966.

Cook, Elizabeth Christine. *Literary Influences in Colonial Newspapers, 1704-1750.* 1912; rpt. Port Washington, N.Y.: Kennikat, 1966.

Cowie, Alexander. *John Trumbull, Connecticut Wit.* Chapel Hill: Univ. of North Carolina Pr., 1936.

———. "John Trumbull as a Critic of Poetry." *New England Quarterly,* 11 (1938), 773-93.

Critical Essays of the Eighteenth Century. Ed. W.H. Durham. New Haven: Yale Univ. Pr., 1915.

Cyclopaedia of American Literature. Eds. Evert A. and George L. Duyckinck. 2 vols. New York: Scribner, 1855.

Davis, Richard Beale. *Francis Walker Gilmer: Life and Learning in Jefferson's Virginia.* Richmond: Dietz, 1939.

———. *Intellectual Life in Jefferson's Virginia, 1790-1830.* Chapel Hill: Univ. of North Carolina Pr., 1964.

Dean, Harold Lester. "The *New-England Courant,* 1721-1726: A

Chapter in the History of American Culture." Diss., Brown Univ., 1943.

De Armond, Anna J. *Andrew Bradford: Colonial Journalist.* Newark, Del., 1949.

Ellis, Harold Milton. *Joseph Dennie and His Circle: A Study in American Literature from 1792 to 1812.* Bulletin of the Univ. of Texas, No. 3. Austin, 1915.

The English Familiar Essay: Representative Texts. Eds. William Frank Bryan and Ronald S. Crane. Boston: Ginn, 1916.

Evans, Charles. *American Bibliography.* Chicago: Blakely, 1903-34. (12 vols. covering 1639-1799; vol. 13, 1799-1800, by Clifford K. Shipton, Worcester, Mass., 1955. Supplement by Roger P. Bristol, Charlottesville, Va., 1970.)

Field, Vena Bernadette. *Constantia: A Study of the Life and Works of Judith Sargent Murray, 1751-1820.* Univ. of Maine Studies, 2d series, No. 17. Orono, 1931.

Ford, W.C. "Franklin's New England Courant." *Proceedings of the Massachusetts Historical Society,* 57 (1924), 336-53.

Free, William J. *The Columbian Magazine and American Literary Nationalism.* The Hague: Mouton, 1968.

Gibson, George H. and Judith C. "The Influence of the *Tatler* and the *Spectator* on the 'Monitor.' " *Furman Studies,* 14 (1966), 12-23.

Gimmestad, Victor E. *John Trumbull.* New York: Twayne, 1974.

Graham, Walter. *The Beginnings of English Literary Periodicals.* New York: Oxford Univ. Pr., 1926.

Granger, Bruce. "The Addisonian Essay in the American Revolution." *Studies in the Literary Imagination,* 9 (1976), 43-52.

———. *Benjamin Franklin: An American Man of Letters.* Ithaca: Cornell Univ. Pr., 1964.

———. "John Trumbull and Religion." *American Literature,* 23 (1951), 57-79.

Griswold, Rufus W. *Curiosities of American Literature.* New York: World, 1876.

Hastings, George E. *The Life and Works of Francis Hopkinson.* Chicago: Univ. of Chicago Pr., 1926.

Hawke, David Freeman. *Paine.* New York: Harper, 1974.

Hedges, William L. *Washington Irving: An American Study, 1802-1832.* Baltimore: Johns Hopkins Univ. Pr., 1965.

Horner, George F. "Franklin's *Dogood Papers* Re-examined." *Studies in Philology*, 37 (1940), 501-23.

Howard, Leon. *The Connecticut Wits*. Chicago: Univ. of Chicago Pr., 1943.

Howell, Wilbur Samuel. *Eighteenth-Century British Logic and Rhetoric*. Princeton: Princeton Univ. Pr., 1971.

Hubbell, Jay B. *The South in American Literature, 1607-1900*. Durham: Duke Univ. Pr., 1954.

———. "William Wirt and the Familiar Essay." *William and Mary Quarterly*, 2d series, 23 (1943), 136-52.

Humphreys, Arthur Raleigh. *Steele, Addison and Their Periodicals*. London: Longman's, 1959.

Irving, Pierre M. *The Life and Letters of Washington Irving*. 4 vols. New York: Putnam, 1862-64.

Irving, Washington. *Journals and Notebooks, Volume I, 1803-1806*. Ed. Nathalia Wright. Madison: Univ. of Wisconsin Pr., 1969.

Irving, William Henry. *The Providence of Wit in the English Letter Writers*. Durham: Duke Univ. Pr., 1955.

Johnson, Samuel. *Essays from the* Rambler, Adventurer, *and* Idler. Ed. W.J. Bate. New Haven: Yale Univ. Pr., 1968.

Joost, Nicholas. " 'Plain-Dealer' and *Free-Thinker*: A Revaluation." *American Literature*, 23 (1951), 31-37.

Kennedy, John Pendleton. *Memoirs of the Life of William Wirt*. 2 vols. Philadelphia: Lea and Blanchard, 1849.

Lane, William C. "The Telltale, 1721." *Publications of the Colonial Society of Massachusetts*, 12 (1909), 220-27.

Law, Marie Hamilton. *The English Familiar Essay in the Early Nineteenth Century*. 1934; rpt. New York: Russell & Russell, 1965.

Leary, Lewis. "The Dream Visions of Philip Freneau." *Early American Literature*, 11 (1976), 156-73.

———. "Joseph Dennie on Benjamin Franklin." *Pennsylvania Magazine of History and Biography*, 72 (1948), 240-46.

———. *Soundings: Some Early American Writers*. Athens: Univ. of Georgia Pr., 1975.

———. *That Rascal Freneau: A Study in Literary Failure*. 1941; rpt. New York: Octagon, 1971.

Lemay, J.A. Leo. "Franklin's Suppressed 'Busy-Body.' " *Ameri-*

can Literature, 37 (1965), 307-11.

———. *Men of Letters in Colonial Maryland*. Knoxville: Univ. of Tennessee Pr., 1972.

The Letters of Joseph Dennie, 1768-1812. Ed. Laura Green Pedder. Univ. of Maine Studies, 2d series, No. 36. Orono, 1936.

Letters of Washington Irving to Henry Brevoort. Ed. George S. Hellman. New York: Putnam, 1918.

The Letters of James Kirke Paulding. Ed. Ralph M. Aderman. Madison: Univ. of Wisconsin Pr., 1962.

Marr, George S. *The Periodical Essayists of the Eighteenth Century*. London: J. Clarke, 1924.

Marsh, Philip M. "Freneau's 'Hezekiah Salem.' " *New England Quarterly*, 18 (1945), 256-59.

———. *Freneau's Published Prose: A Bibliography*. Metuchen, N.J.: Scarecrow, 1970.

McCutcheon, Roger P. "Another Burlesque of Addison's Ballad Criticism." *Studies in Philology*, 23 (1926), 452-56.

McDowell, Tremaine. "Sensibility in the Eighteenth-Century American Novel." *Studies in Philology*, 24 (1927), 383-402.

Meserole, Harrison T. "The American Familiar Essay, 1815-1835." Diss., Univ. of Maryland, 1960.

Miller, Perry. *The New England Mind: From Colony to Province*. Cambridge, Mass.: Harvard Univ. Pr., 1953.

Mott, Frank Luther. *American Journalism: A History, 1690-1960*. New York: Macmillan, 1962.

———. *A History of American Magazines, 1741-1850*. New York: Appleton, 1930.

Myers, Robert M. "The Old Dominion Looks to London: A Study of English Literary Influences upon *The Virginia Gazette* (1736-1766)." *Virginia Magazine of History and Biography*, 54 (1946), 195-217.

Osborne, Robert Stevens. "A Study of Washington Irving's Development as a Man of Letters to 1825." Diss., Univ. of North Carolina, 1947.

Pattee, Fred Lewis. *The First Century of American Literature, 1770-1870*. New York: Appleton, 1935.

Paulding, William I. *Literary Life of James K. Paulding*. New York: Scribner, 1867.

The Prose Writers of America. Ed. Rufus W. Griswold. Philadelphia: Carey and Hart, 1849.

Queenan, John. *"The Portfolio*: A Study of the History and Significance of an Early American Magazine." Diss., Univ. of Pennsylvania, 1954.

Randall, Randolph C. "Authors of the *Port Folio* Revealed by the Hall Files." *American Literature*, 11 (1940), 379-416.

Reeves, John K. "Jeremy Gridley, Editor." *New England Quarterly*, 17 (1944), 265-81.

Richardson, Lyon N. *A History of Early American Magazines, 1741-1789*. 1931; rpt. New York: Octagon, 1966.

Robert, Joseph C. "William Wirt, Virginian." *Virginia Magazine of History and Biography*, 80 (1972), 387-441.

Roth, Martin. *Comedy and America: The Lost World of Washington Irving*. Port Washington, N.Y.: Kennikat, 1976.

Scott, Eleanor. "Early Literary Clubs in New York City." *American Literature*, 5 (1933), 3-16.

Shipton, Clifford K. *New England Life in the 18th Century*. Cambridge, Mass.: Harvard Univ. Pr., 1963.

Simpson, Lewis P. "Federalism and the Crisis of Literary Order." *American Literature*, 32 (1960), 253-66.

Smith, Frank. "New Light on Thomas Paine's First Year in America." *American Literature*, 1 (1930), 347-71.

A Southern Reader. Ed. Willard Thorp. New York: Knopf, 1955.

The Spectator. Ed. Donald F. Bond. 5 vols. Oxford: Clarendon, 1965.

Stein, Roger B. "Royall Tyler and the Question of Our Speech." *New England Quarterly*, 38 (1965), 454-74.

Sterne, Laurence. *Tristram Shandy*. Ed. James A. Work. New York: Odyssey, 1940.

Stewart, Donald H. *The Opposition Press of the Federalist Period*. Albany: State University of New York, 1969.

Sylvester, Howard E. *"The American Museum*, A Study of Prevailing Ideas in Late Eighteenth-Century America." Diss., Univ. of Washington, 1954.

Taylor, William Robert. "William Wirt and the Legend of the Old South." *William and Mary Quarterly*, 3d series, 14 (1957), 477-93.

Tourtellot, Arthur Bernon. *Benjamin Franklin: The Shaping of*

Genius: The Boston Years. Garden City, N.Y.: Doubleday, 1977.

Wages, Jack D. "Elegy and Mock Elegy in Colonial Virginia." *Studies in the Literary Imagination,* 9 (1976), 77-93.

Washington Irving's Contributions to The Corrector. Ed. Martin Roth. Minneapolis: Univ. of Minnesota Pr., 1968.

Watson, John F. *Annals of Philadelphia and Pennsylvania in the Olden Times.* 2 vols. Philadelphia: Carey and Hart, 1845.

Watson, Melvin R. *Magazine Serials and the Essay Tradition, 1745-1820.* Baton Rouge: Louisiana State Univ. Pr., 1956.

———. "The *Spectator* Tradition and the Development of the Familiar Essay." *ELH,* 13 (1946), 189-215.

Williams, Stanley T. *The Life of Washington Irving.* 2 vols. New York: Oxford, 1935.

Williamson, George. *The Senecan Amble: Prose Form from Bacon to Collier.* Chicago: Univ. of Chicago Pr., 1951.

Wright, Thomas Goddard. *Literary Culture in Early New England, 1620-1730.* New Haven: Yale Univ. Pr., 1920.

Wroth, Lawrence C. *William Parks: Printer and Journalist of England and Colonial America.* Richmond: William Parks Club, 1926.

INDEX

271

American Essay Serials from Franklin to Irving was composed on the Variable Input Phototypesetter in 10-point Trump with 2-point spacing between the lines. Perpetua in roman and italic was selected for display. The book was designed by Jim Billingsley, composed by Williams, Chattanooga, Tennessee, printed by offset lithography at Thomson-Shore, Inc., Dexter, Michigan, and bound by John H. Dekker & Sons, Grand Rapids, Michigan. The paper on which the book is printed bears the watermark of S.D. Warren and is designed for an effective life of at least three hundred years.

THE UNIVERSITY OF TENNESSEE PRESS : KNOXVILLE